Inspired INC.

First published in 2019 by
Crowd Press, an imprint of Inspired Companies,
in partnership with whitefox publishing

https://www.inspiredcompanies.global

HB 978-1-912892-19-8
PB 978-1-912892-13-6
eBook 978-1-912892-14-3

Designed and typeset by Tom Cabot/ketchup
Cover design and all related Inspired Companies illustrations
by Charlotte Cline/Onemanband.studio

Printed and bound by CPI Group (UK) Ltd, Croydon, CR0 4YY

Inspired INC.

Become a company
the world will get behind

THE END OF AN UNINSPIRED ERA

Profit is Good. Profit-as-Purpose is Not

To compete today, companies must stand for ideas bigger than profit.

7

Power Shift: The Rise of the *New C.E.O.s*

Meet the new C.E.O.s: Consumers, Employees, and Outsiders. They now have the tools, motivation, and power to make or break your business faster than ever.

21

Uninspired Companies and their Headwinds

When the new C.E.O.s work together they're unstoppable. If they don't trust a business or don't like what it stands for, they will make life very difficult.

35

A FRAMEWORK TO BECOME AN INSPIRED COMPANY

Inspired Mission:
Make a Promise with
Many Winners

Inspired Companies are led by big ideas.
Here you'll find the formula for the most
important set of words in your company.

47

Inspired Action:
An Introduction

Turning words into action is everything
in today's battle of authenticity. Here
we present the Inspired Action building
blocks to help you deliver.

71

Obsessive
Alignment

Big action and small action, every day,
by everyone. Wire your business to
deliver consistently and the first major
milestone is reached: your employees
believe you.

83

Shake up the
System

Have the courage to break rules and defy
industry norms when they get in the way
of pursuing your big idea.

131

Bold Conviction

You now have the new C.E.O.s onside.
Companies that make it this far in their
journey develop the confidence to fight
even harder for the ideas they stand for.

191

Make-or-Breaks

There are moments in business that
disproportionately define you. Inspired
Companies know intuitively what to do.

233

Inspired Profit

When the crowd is onside, inspired,
believes, and trusts you – they can and
will reward you.

263

A New Legacy

Becoming a company the world will get
behind is more possible than ever.

283

Note to our readers

A society-wide trust crisis has collided with a social media revolution and flung us into a turbulent, chaotic, and confusing moment in corporate history. Many of the ways we succeeded in business in the past don't work anymore and we need answers. Fast.

In the following pages, you'll encounter a lot of companies. We celebrate many of them and point out the missteps of others. We do this to reveal, very practically, what it takes to become a company the world will get behind – the only kind of company positioned to succeed in a world where the market dynamics have changed dramatically. What we know for sure is this: no company is navigating this new terrain perfectly and every company cited in *Inspired INC.* has the chance to adapt and succeed. The journey will be longer and harder for some than others.

Last we checked though, the corporate sector loves a bit of competition.

So let the games begin.

Chapter 1

Profit is Good.
Profit-as-Purpose is Not.

Signs that companies just aren't getting it

In a four-week window not so long ago, we saw an airline forcibly drag a paying customer off an aircraft, a soft-drinks company suggest its product is the answer to racial tensions, and a superstar ride-hailing app dragged down by an internal culture rife with sexual harassment – all in full view of anyone with an internet connection.

How did these companies respond? United took a full 24 hours to make a statement, and another week to apologize. A few months later they settled a lawsuit that legal experts estimate to be in the millions. Pepsi pulled its controversial advertisement and apologized to their celebrity endorser for putting her in such an awkward position. The message to everyone else they offended wasn't quite so generous: "Clearly, we missed the mark and apologize." As for Uber, an employee uprising and investor revolt eventually took down the founding chief executive, while a board member continued making sexist remarks to staff at the same time as he was making the announcement about the leadership change.

What were all these executives thinking when these events unfolded? It's impossible to say without being there, but it sure looks like they thought they had a lot more time and public goodwill to manage the situation than they actually did. Or perhaps they were assuming that the approaches that worked well in the past will still work today.

These examples aren't limited to a few bad decisions at United Airlines, Pepsi, or Uber. They're also not limited to American companies. They are symptoms of a bigger issue:

Companies have been so focused on profit, that they've completely disconnected from the real world.

Well, our luck in the corporate sector has finally run out. Everyone knows everything now. Values conflicts are no longer tolerated, and profit without meaningful purpose will only lead to similar and more frequent mistakes. With so many well-educated and bright people leading businesses today, you might ask: what is going on?

We are in an era of uninspired companies

"A business that makes nothing but money is a poor business." – Henry Ford

In today's dollars, Henry Ford's net worth would be north of US$200 billion. It's a safe bet he wasn't saying profit is bad.

Henry Ford made things that mattered to people. When Ford Motor was founded in 1903, cars were little more than playthings of the ultra-rich. But Ford believed cars could connect people to opportunity in a nation spread across vast distances. He saw a world in which the average worker would own a car. Turning vision into reality meant revolutionizing the manufacturing process. It also meant rethinking work life. By 1914, Ford factory workers were paid twice as much as their counterparts at other companies. The result? They could afford the product they made, and by 1923, half of the world's autos were Ford Model Ts.[1]

That's pretty inspiring stuff and it changed all our lives. So why was Ford worried about businesses that make nothing but money?

Ford gives us one of the earliest examples of a leader whose vision to deliver big ideas was at odds with the short-term demands of shareholders. In 1919, he wanted to forgo dividends and invest a capital surplus in more plants, more employees, and higher wages. The Dodge brothers – two major Ford shareholders at the time – sued, arguing that the company had a responsibility to deliver maximum return to shareholders. The Dodge brothers won and the era of shareholder primacy was born.

Businesses have been separating from their other stakeholders – the people who buy, sell, make, and use their products and services – ever since.

The corporate sector's 100-year break-up with society

A century ago, serving various stakeholders was simple. If someone wasn't happy, the feedback loops were short: suppliers, manufacturers, sellers, and buyers all lived around the corner from each other. Businesses were closely tied to their stakeholders and the connection was personal.

But the world changed.

Over time, for many good reasons associated with development and progress, our relationship with individual companies was eventually reduced to the distant monitoring of their stock price. The factory system of the industrial revolution drove out craftsmen in favor of mass-produced products, separating makers and builders from buyers. Transportation and communications innovations from the highway system to the telephone provided even more ways for companies to limit their interactions with actual people.

Without physical proximity, a company's primary connection to a broader set of stakeholders became marketing – the ads, logos, packaging, and stories we deliver to anyone who'll pay attention. But all too often these have been vehicles for inauthentic messages that fail to achieve lasting connections. For many companies, the deepest connection they achieve is an evocative Super Bowl commercial or a dancing pony video people will remember for as long as it takes to post it on Facebook.

An era of shareholder primacy also shaped another defining characteristic of today's corporate sector: the expectation that companies deliver profits quarterly and grow infinitely.

Almost every chief executive in the world is under the constant strain of quarterly earnings growth. Its importance has created an operating environment where profit-at-all-costs is a defining job requirement. Even if a board recognizes the issues with short-termism and structures half of a leader's compensation to reward long-term outcomes, they'll still fire anyone whose numbers fall over three consecutive quarters.

Here's how Mark Wilson, most recently CEO of the U.K.'s largest composite insurer, Aviva, describes it[2]: "I trained for a marathon but only get to run a series of sprints. The markets have become short term to the nanosecond. Regulators oftentimes don't think more than three months out. As leaders, we have to think more long term. But as economies, countries, and companies we haven't learned – even after a major financial crisis."

Is all of this the fault of the financial markets? No. The evolution of capital systems has enabled companies to access the resources they need to enable innovation, global trade, economic development, job growth, and many other great things. We also don't take issue with profit. Profit is good. Without profitable businesses, societies fail.

The more glaring issue is that, over time, profit became the corporate sector's main reason for being – its *primary purpose.* And it is now so normal, we don't think to question it. Even when a company has a compelling mission, vision, or purpose statement that claims something bigger, everyday decisions often signal that profit maximization is the real goal – and when profit becomes purpose, things eventually fall apart.

Profit-as-purpose is a defining issue of our time and underpins the corporate sector's current systems, norms, behaviors, and reputation. While that may have worked in the past, it won't work anymore.

Why? Because after more than a century, the balance of power has shifted irrevocably to the fuller range of stakeholders that companies impact – employees, customers, ordinary citizens. These folks just don't have to tolerate profit-as-purpose business models anymore.

Society reemerges with unprecedented force

Plenty of people predicted the internet would change business as we knew it, but not many saw *this* coming: A power shift led by ordinary people with smartphones displacing shareholders from their throne and bursting corporate bubbles wide open.

Business leaders are now under unprecedented pressure from their stakeholders and it's not going away. It will only strengthen with the exponential growth, adoption, and application of new technologies and increasingly empowered citizens.

The truth is, we've been in an uninspired era for a long time now. We disconnected from our stakeholders and put profit maximization first.

Now we're paying the price.

We are now in an era where the corporate footprint is no longer proprietary information. Employees' experiences aren't a secret and neither are their opinions of you. Policymakers and regulators answer to digitally savvy and increasingly influential watchdogs, activists, and ordinary consumers – not just public affairs departments. Researchers have the tools to translate scientific findings about your products to a broader audience faster than ever. As for customers, they don't just talk about their experiences. They rate, record, and review them. The share button can be a company's best friend or its greatest enemy.

In short: after a century of physical, practical, and emotional separation, the internet has put us all back into the same neighborhood where everyone knows a lot more about everyone else. Business and its full spectrum of stakeholders are all newly reconnected (Figure 1).

Historically dismissed stakeholders have resurfaced, with speed and collective impact that unprepared businesses simply can't keep up with. Even people who don't consider themselves activists can, and are, engaging today. This once-fragmented group of stakeholders has

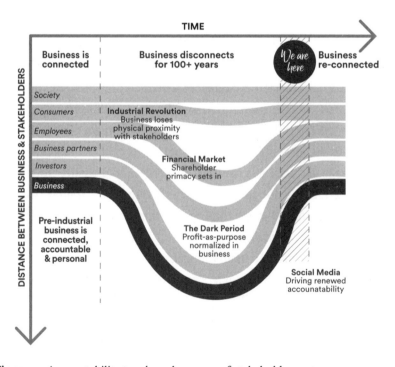

Figure 1: Accountability to a broader range of stakeholders returns.

become a powerful and collective *crowd* who can change things in an instant. Their influence has snowballed to a point where the balance of power has shifted in their favor.

The really bad news:
Business is not trusted ... *at all*

People are suspicious of most types of institutions, but thanks to a long era of profit-as-purpose, there is a special disaffection for business. Accounting fraud scandals from the likes of Enron and WorldCom, devastating oil spills and fatal mine collapses or explosions in Brazil, Turkey, and the U.S. are just a few of the monumental corporate disasters we've experienced in our lifetimes. Fraud, environmental damage, cultures of bigotry and harassment, stolen and misused information – the list goes on. These kinds of experiences have led people to expect companies to eventually fail them in some way.

In the U.K., for example, only 33 percent of people have a lot of trust in major corporations.[3] In the U.S., the figure is a dismal 10 percent.[4] Chief executives rank very low on the list of trusted sources of information, with only 44 percent of people globally believing what they have to say. That's only slightly ahead of board members, whose credibility levels have dropped to a low of 41 percent.[5]

If you think these trust issues only relate to people outside the walls of your company, think again. In 2018, 21 percent of U.S. employees and 29 percent of U.K. employees say they don't trust their employers. In France, it's a staggering 40 percent. Meanwhile, in Japan – the least trusting workforce in the world – that number is 43 percent.[6] Once a worker loses faith, commitment is quick to follow: A survey of 155 countries found only 15 percent of people feel engaged at work. Western Europe is below average, with only 10 percent of their workers feeling engaged.[7]

What does this mean?

It means that the game has profoundly changed.

The combination of a trust crisis and a digital and social media revolution very abruptly transferred power into the hands of those who don't trust us – and who now expect far more from us. When they pull together, they can make or break companies faster than ever.

Ignore the new circumstances, continue as if nothing's changed, and you'll only face more problems. The speed and impact of the social media revolution mean that we don't have time to legislate, PR, or CSR our way out of it. None of those things will work on their own anyway.

The alternative is to figure out how to *thrive* in this new environment and turn it into advantage. This requires a redefinition of the problem we're solving for and a reimagination of the business model that will solve it.

Now is the time for *Inspired Companies*

Business leaders are in a tough spot. Buck the shareholder primacy system too hard and career suicide is assured. Ignore the demands of the powerful new *crowd* of broader stakeholders that rejects that system, and you'll also lose. Balancing the demands of both, while designing our companies to prioritize the *crowd,* is the only way to succeed. Those who don't evolve will not just stand still, they'll move backward.

Most companies today are wired to extract value from the *crowd.* The more *Inspired Companies* are embracing the power shift, redefining themselves to pursue ideas bigger than profit, and experiencing how the power of having the *crowd* onside fuels their success. We are witnessing how these companies create trust, brand distinction, and competitive advantage in ways that leave others behind.

We spent our careers inside Nike experiencing this power shift, and what it feels like when stakeholders outside your own corporate bubble are onside and when they are not. But it wasn't enough to be leaders in one company to get the full picture, let alone to know what to do about it. So we gave up our high-paying corporate jobs to spend more time analyzing how the new market and power dynamics are playing out around the world. We studied the strategies that work and paid equal attention to ones that don't. We dissected 30 combined years at Nike, interviewed a diverse set of chief executives and leaders in private and public sectors, and stress-tested our findings with companies ranging from communications to gaming, cosmetics, and legal services. We analyzed spectacular mistakes and impressive successes of companies from the airline industry to banking and chocolate, as they all work to tackle the significant shift in power dynamics and turn it into advantage.

Throughout *Inspired INC.* we pull from a diverse set of examples to reveal the learnings and the answers: Tony's Chocolonely in Amsterdam; LEGO in Denmark; Nike, Starbucks, Wildfang, and Netflix in the U.S.; eRepublik Games in Spain; British Telecom, Unilever, and Aviva in the U.K., and Kao Corporation in Japan – just to name a few. Some companies you'll recognize and others you won't. That's okay – and it's also the point. Our goal was not to find and declare the most *Inspired Company* in the world (spoiler alert: one doesn't exist). Instead, it was to look at enough examples of success and failure across industries, countries, and cultures until universal principles and clear patterns emerged. Here is our most important finding:

> The future belongs to companies that stand for big ideas with many winners. They organize themselves around those ideas and deliver them in a way that recruits the world to work with them, not against them.

We call these companies *Inspired Companies.*

A framework for *Inspired Companies*:
Mission. Action. Profit.

At the highest level, there are three things *Inspired Companies* do better than others: They stand for a big idea, they pursue it with fierce authenticity, and they make good money.

It's hard to argue with any of those statements. They're great ideas that we can all get behind. Oh, and don't get caught in a debate about whether you call these statements a mission, purpose, or vision. You only need one and it needs to be big.

Inspired Mission

The pursuit of inspired ideas is the foundation of an *Inspired Company*. Framing that pursuit as the ultimate expression of *why your company exists* is the crucial first step. These must be big ideas with *many winners*:

Enriching life through communication (Huawei)

Organize the world's information and make it universally accessible and useful (Google)

Accelerate the advent of sustainable energy (Tesla)

Create a better everyday life for the many people (IKEA)

Make sustainable living commonplace (Unilever)*

It's hard to argue with any of those statements. They're great ideas that we can all get behind. Oh, and don't get caught in a debate about whether you call these statements a mission, purpose, or vision. You only need one and it needs to be big.

---

* Mission statements are italicized throughout the book so that you can spot them easily.

Inspired Action

Anyone can put lofty words on paper. The real work comes in aligning an organization, its everyday actions and decisions, operations and incentives, brand, communications, and behavior in pursuit of your *Inspired Mission*.

The newly emerging *crowd* has a heavy level of skepticism and low levels of trust to overcome, so consistent and deliberate *Inspired Action* is a prerequisite to earn their attention, trust, and support. Inviting them into your business and enabling them to participate directly in new and exciting ways will propel your business forward faster. Old rules and arbitrary industry norms will have to be questioned and overturned. Silos and hierarchies will need to be broken down if you want to be positioned to succeed and be taken seriously.

Inspired Profit

This is about making good money, in both senses of the word. It's both the payoff from having the *crowd* onside and the way you keep them: Happier, more productive employees do their best work *and* cost less; loyal customers build and promote your brand with their powerful global networks; business partners give you priority and find new ways to unlock mutual value; civil society, media, and regulators are onside when trouble hits, and investors stay with you over the long term. The *crowd* defends you when you need them, gives you answers, ideas, and solutions when you ask, and refers you to their friends when they trust and believe you.

This translates to more revenue, better margins, lower transaction costs, and more resources than your uninspired competitors have to reinvest.

The power shift is underway and the first movers are making traction fast. The payoff is real and it's more realizable than ever. Data to support the benefits and return on investment is strong and only getting stronger. If you wait for more data, *your* business will not be in the data and it's all the more likely that your competitors' data will be.

Which means they will be in front, fueled by the *crowd*. And you'll be behind, forgotten by the *crowd*.

Inspired Companies are not perfect. That's entirely unrealistic. However, a true commitment to the pillars of **M**ission, **A**ction, and **P**rofit is what will attract, build, and keep an ever-powerful *crowd* onside.

This book is for anyone who wants to participate in the upside

We've delivered this framework, core building blocks, and series of strategies to support those who want to authentically connect into the power of the *crowd* now and into the future. No matter who you are, this book will help you decide:

Who to buy from.

Who to work for.

Who to work with.

Who to invest in.

How to lead an organization that has the world onside.

The framework is practical and actionable. By design, the approach breaks down hierarchies and unites organizations, so it won't matter if you're in brand marketing, sales, operations, corporate affairs, HR, or the C-suite. The concepts we explore and strategies we suggest are functionally agnostic and can help anyone move the ball forward in some way.

The principles explored can be adopted by any organization – for-profit or otherwise. We focus on the corporate sector because that's where we come from and where the market is demanding the fastest change to occur.

The good news here is that pretty much any company of any

size can be an *Inspired Company*. The only exceptions? Companies whose business models rely on human rights abuses, environmental extraction and depletion or whose products, when used properly, make people sick or die.

Those businesses are on their own.

In the next two chapters, we spend time getting to know the *crowd*: who they are, what they want, how they use their newfound power, and what happens when you ignore them. Getting to know them is the first step to figuring out how to get them onside. In the remaining chapters, we dive deeper to provide guidance on how to move forward – from establishing an *Inspired Mission* to moving into *Inspired Action* and realizing the benefits of *Inspired Profit*.

A vision for an inspired future

We see a future not so far away where *Inspired Companies* reset the corporate playing field and reputation. They'll reshape our expectations and experiences of companies, and move us forward to a place where shared value is bankable value.

Part of our optimism comes from companies – like Tesla, Ben & Jerry's, Huawei, Starbucks, and Nike – that either don't stumble quite as spectacularly as their peers or that recover fairly quickly when they do. Maybe they were founded on big ideas or maybe they've made enough serious mistakes in the past that they were forced to evolve earlier. Either way or both, these companies have more good days than bad ones, they are celebrated by the *crowd* when they take a stand, and we expect them to inspire us. Not just with marketing, but with everyday decisions.

This is a new environment and there is a ton of work to be done to navigate it. Whatever a company's size or industry, adapting to the power shift is possible. It's also imperative. Companies that are succeeding are driving forward-thinking missions with benefits for everyone and many supporters. They act on their missions with a fierce sense of purpose, a clear set of values, and impressive consistency. When established corporate norms and financing models get in the way, they create ways to work around them. Profitable growth – and there's plenty of it – comes from embracing and harnessing the trust and power of the *crowd*.

With more people influencing the success or failure of brands than ever before, *Inspired Companies* will be positioned to turn an abrupt power shift into 21st-century competitive advantage. They will achieve what so few have in the past half-century: they will become companies the world is willing to get behind.

For almost a century we have underestimated the power of inspiration, big ideas, and authenticity to move whole populations and markets forward. But now the time to harness this power has come.

Today is looking like a great day to be a company.

Chapter 2

Power Shift:
The Rise of the *New C.E.O.s*

The chief executive officer is no longer the only one calling the shots

For as long as we can remember, the world has turned to the chief executive officer as the ultimate determinant of business success or failure.

That is no longer true.

We are at a moment when historically low levels of trust in the corporate sector have met the internet's powerfully decentralized, *crowd*-driven social media platforms. The result is that someone else is now gaining increasing levels of power and dramatically influencing the performance of mainstream companies. While chief executives may not have a name for it, most leaders sense something new and uncomfortable is going on and that it's happening fast.

If the appointed CEO isn't the only one in charge anymore, who is?

In This Chapter

- The rise of the *new C.E.O.s*: the **C**onsumers, **E**mployees, and traditional **O**utsiders shaping the future of your company

- The specific ways the *new C.E.O.s* exert their influence, and why we've given them the most powerful title in the corporate sector

- Looking beyond millennials: their little brothers and sisters, parents, and grandparents are *all* impacting your business

- The choice facing every business leader today: share power with the *crowd* of *new C.E.O.s* and bring them onside – or ignore them and further erode their dwindling trust and fuel their collective will to work against you

In Chapter 1, we talked about that large and noisy *crowd* of historically ignored stakeholders who are demanding more. They're looking for inspiration and authenticity, and they are dramatically impacting business outcomes. They existed outside the corporate bubble for decades and have now found powerful ways in. They are players creating an entirely new game with a set of rules that don't line up with the way business has been done for decades. Their influence is so profound that we call them the *new C.E.O.s*:

Consumers, **E**mployees, and **O**utsiders.

Consumers, **C**lients, **C**ustomers – whoever buys from you. (To keep it simple, we tend to use **C**onsumers throughout to reference an all-encompassing buying force.)

Employees – past, present, and future – full- and part-time, contractors, temps, candidates. (We shorthand this broader definition to **E**mployees or workers throughout.)

Outsiders – a diverse set of players we've traditionally kept at a comfortable distance: civil society actors; regulators; federal, state, and local government; supply chain partners; media; the broader investment community; academia.

Assigning the most powerful title in the corporate sector to regular **C**onsumers, **E**mployees, and **O**utsiders is not something we take lightly, but we do it for a reason. We believe in the corporate sector and the caliber, training, experience, and intentions of many of its leaders. If you are one of those leaders, we need your attention: This *crowd* now has the power to make or break your business faster than ever. Here's how:

Consumers will be painful brand activists *or* powerful brand ambassadors.

Employees will deliver their best work and be an invaluable army of brand ambassadors *or* underperform, undermine, and maybe even sabotage your entire company.

Outsiders – there's a lot more they can do today with a lot more speed and impact:

- Business partners will put you first *or* last.

- NGOs will be watchdogs *or* defenders.

- Civil society will point fingers *or* lend a hand.

- Investors will grill you on short-term numbers *or* be long-term partners.

- Regulators will put up walls *or* pull them down.

- The media will rip you apart *or* tell your story.

The dynamic of having stakeholders for or against a business is not new. What is new is the speed and potency of their impact. It's like nothing we have ever had to face in the corporate sector – and our companies are simply not wired to handle it.

It's far more than managing a bit of bad PR now and then. This *crowd* of *new C.E.O.s* is shifting the very axis of the corporate sector. The power shift marks a permanent change in the operating landscape for business. Getting to know the *crowd* and forging meaningful relationships with them is the backbone of success for companies today. Companies that sideline them in a quest for short-term profits will experience headwinds that punish the bottom line in ways we have not experienced in the past.

On the other hand, companies that get it right and chief executives who recognize that their power is now shared will gain benefits and tailwinds that flow directly to the bottom line: expanded revenue sources, higher margin sales referrals, higher employee productivity, less unplanned employee turnover and issues management, increased resilience, and higher levels of brand distinction. Having the *crowd* onside today is the only way to outperform everyone else.

So who are these *new C.E.O.s* and what do they really want? How are they exerting their influence?

First things first: they're not all millennials

We talk about the *new C.E.O.s* as a singular entity. In reality, they're no more a homogenous group than "homeowners" or "voters" are. Every one of the *new C.E.O.s* has the potential to simultaneously be an activist, citizen journalist, investor, advocate, customer, employee, and several other things all at the same time. The other thing to know is they aren't all millennials. Yes, we talk a lot about the power of this digitally savvy generation. That's because they are the largest and fastest-growing segment of the workforce and consumer demographic in many parts of the world. But millennials aren't the only generation driving new expectations. Centennials are right behind them, emerging rapidly, while their parents and grandparents continue to find ways to exert their influence.

Here's how each generation's experience is playing out in this new world:

Millennials* are suspicious and self-aware. They live in a conversation-based world. Social networks have existed for most of their lives and made sharing their way of life. Innovation is a daily occurrence and they expect everything on-demand – in large part because they know it's possible. They are also mired in debt and have little reason to trust established institutions. They grew up impacted by their parents' layoffs, foreclosures, and bankruptcies. They don't expect to stay in the same job for life. As for their loyalty as customers, it turns out that uninstalling an app isn't really that difficult.

Centennials† are high-speed pragmatists. Their influence has been overshadowed by millennials, but that will soon change. They already make up 27 percent of the global population and total 2 billion people.[8] Some 58 percent of them live in Asia.[9] In the U.S., 25 percent of the population is centennial,[10] 90 percent of whom have a digital footprint.[11] This group didn't just grow up digital; they grew up high-speed. They've never known a world without Facebook or Twitter – both of which are platforms their parents use. Real-time sharing is their way of life. Digital interactions have as much meaning as real-world interactions. This is a group that reportedly has an eight-second attention span.[12] Oh, and they intend to make a difference. They volunteer their time and see social entrepreneurship as an ideal career choice.[13] Companies without a more meaningful purpose than profit maximization will not be receiving their applications.

Gen X and boomers: the other half of the working-age population. Youth isn't the only thing making this crowd of *new C.E.O.s* more powerful. Experience and opportunity are factors as well. Older generations do not bestow their trust easily (they've seen more than one financial crisis) and they know the promise of pensions

---

* Born between 1980 and 1996.

† Centennials were born in or after 1997, making the oldest ones 22 in 2019.

and stable retirements is a fairy tale. You know what else? They're not Luddites. They have smartphones and use social media – even the oldest of the group. Six in ten baby boomers (ages 50 to 64) use Facebook, and their numbers are growing stronger.[14] They're reporting on their experiences as much as anyone and they've got a few more years in the workforce to draw on too.

That's your *crowd*. It turns out it's everyone. Your marketing team has likely spent a fortune understanding them. What may not have translated yet is how to get them on board to fuel your success. Doing that properly will require your business to function very differently. You'll probably have to move away from marketing strategies that talk *at* them, and start enabling your whole organization to work *with* them.

What makes a millennial celebrate you on Instagram? What inspires their parents to validate you on Facebook? Understanding how Consumers, Employees, and Outsiders create and use their power is essential to knowing what to do.

Consumers have taken control and it's going to stay that way

Despite all the energy and effort you might put into crafting your message, there's a good chance Consumers aren't listening to you. It turns out they don't have to. They'd rather hear directly from your employees and from other customers to figure out whether they will buy from you. They know watchdog groups will broadcast anything they might need to know about your activities and they can do their homework in a single Google search. Their trust and loyalty have to be earned. Consider this:

> 92 percent of people read online reviews before making purchasing decisions[15] – making sales referrals more valuable than ever.

> 75 percent of consumers will back out of an intended transaction

because of a bad experience[16] – making customer complaints more expensive than ever.

67 percent of consumers use Twitter and Facebook to get customer service[17] – meaning their interactions are public and your customer service departments cannot contain what they once could.

More than half (52 percent) of consumers will share a negative experience with friends, family, and on social media, while 56 percent will share a good experience[18] – making customer experience more important than ever and ensuring there's nowhere left to hide.

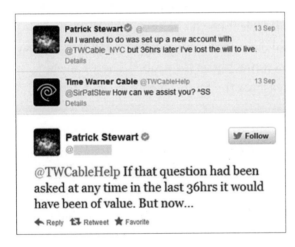

The bottom line is that **C**onsumers will no longer be ignored. They're going to shout about their experiences – good and bad. And the public is now more likely to listen to them than they are to listen to you.

Employees have always been a number. Now they are a voice

Pretty much anyone would agree that a happy employee is a more productive employee. And we all know that top talent at any level is increasingly hard to find. Even so, half of employees in the U.S. say they don't believe their employer is being honest with them.[19] Globally, the same number say their job has *no connection to their company's mission, and has no meaning or significance.*[20]

That tells us talent is one seriously underleveraged asset. But today, employees' influence goes well beyond being the makers and sellers of a company's product or service.

Employees are now also the people inside a company most trusted to speak about the companies they work for.[21]

Not the chief executives or the spokesperson from PR. Those folks aren't trusted at all. This should be great news. It means that companies already have an army of trusted spokespeople seen as an authoritative source of information.

And while the law may care how you classify "employees" – full-time, part-time, contract, temp – Twitter doesn't. Pretty much every one of them will talk about your business in very public ways in real time. That includes candidates – two-thirds of whom say they'll talk about a negative experience of applying for a job.[22] There's even a calculator today that measures the financial cost of candidate resentment.[23]

The rapid growth of Glassdoor has made the shift to **E**mployees as de facto spokespeople very real for employers. Founded in 2007, the website features anonymous reviews of companies, chief executives, and upper management by current and former employees, interns, contractors . . . you get the picture. Want to know the pros and cons of working somewhere? How about what interview questions to expect? Care to see what advice current and former employees have for the big boss? Now you know where to go. Reviews are posted for all to see and the anonymous platform means users are protected from retribution.

We were surprised to find that several chief executives and business leaders we've engaged with over the past few years had never heard of Glassdoor and had no idea they were being publicly reviewed and rated. If you haven't already, we suggest you take a quick look.

Companies like Glassdoor have flipped the employee–employer power dynamic on its head. No longer is management protected from their own performance evaluations. In fact, Glassdoor has become so influential that it now determines media lists for the best and worst places to work. For example, Bloomberg's 2017 list of the "50 Best Places to Work" didn't come from the traditional self-nominations and extensive vetting complete with interviews and site visits. Nope, today's list is based entirely on employee reviews submitted anonymously on Glassdoor.[24]

There's also a new generation of labor organizers working to amplify the collective voice of workers. The Workers Lab, founded in 2015, described as "a tech incubator with a union heart,"[25] gives a hint at what labor organizing of the future might look like. In its portfolio is Coworker.org, a site that enables employees of any company to start and run campaigns to advocate for changes within their companies. Within two years, Coworker.org has won policy changes in 10 companies, including paid parental leave at the footwear company Keen and in-app tipping for Uber drivers. The Uber win is particularly meaningful given that Uber had already settled a US$100 million lawsuit that allowed drivers to accept cash tips, although long refused to allow it in-app. Now it's done, thanks to the power of the *crowd.* It seems even lawyers can't help you avoid the *crowd* today.

All of this will dramatically affect your reputation, talent pool, and bottom line in increasingly dramatic ways. If Glassdoor or a similar platform hasn't hit your geography, or employees haven't rated your company yet, it's just a matter of time. When it happens, chances are that your HR and PR policies will not be equipped to handle it.

The good news is that the first step to operating successfully in this new reality is simple: listen and respond. Here's an example of how the buy one/give one shoe company, TOMS, did just that.

"Many employees start off passionate about the mission and the "good" you are doing, but TOMS has a long way to go."

★★☆☆☆ ▼ Former Employee - Anonymous Employee in Los Angeles, CA (US)

■ Doesn't Recommend   ■ Negative Outlook   ■ Approves of CEO

I worked at TOMS full-time (More than a year)

Pros
Flexible work hours (if your boss permits)
Bring your dog to work
Free coffee
Opportunities for travel and off-site events
Some great people that will be your friends for life

Cons
NO accountability - many senior and junior level employees have been able to get away with unacceptable behavior (stealing, lying, disrespect to their jr. level employees) because C level turns a blind eye or feels unequipped to handle disciplinary actions.
Freelance/contract staff are not valued or rewarded for their hard work, although they keep the company functioning and in operation.
Many people have been discouraged by lack of & change in leadership. The two biggest thorns in the side of the company are last-minute changes to enormous campaigns and projects, and un-vetted & unequipped director- and VP-level leaders.
TOMS has lost an uncountable number of talented people because of the stifling environment created by the above, along with unrealistic budgets, and an uneven distribution of power and resources. Many manager and coordinator level workers are not properly managed or monitored for efficiency, and abuse company resources and time due to the lack of attention placed from the mid-level down.
Show Less

Advice to Management
Empower your C-level leaders to make actual decisions and support them in the process. Instill accountability in your senior level employees with hard deadlines and consequences if projects are not completed. Jim Alling is a great CEO and leader, he should embrace his position and continue to engage with and empower his employees.

TOMS Response
23 Jan 2017 – Manager, Culture and Experience

Thank you for your feedback. We're always working to improve. If you'd like to discuss your experience of C level employees turning a blind eye or any other points mentioned further offline, please reach out to Natasha.Ballard@TOMS.com. ▼ Less

TOMS evaluation on Glassdoor, post-2017. (Image from glassdoor.com)

We're not talking about complicated stuff here. Companies create advantage when they value what employees and job candidates have to say, and encourage and participate in the conversation. Those that don't will lose.

Messing this up, however, is just as easy as getting it right. It could be as simple as a candidate not getting an acknowledgment of their carefully crafted cover letter. (FYI, jobseekers *hate* that.) Or maybe the hiring manager canceled three times or the interviewer acted like he was doing the candidate a favor. Ever interviewed for a role internally with your company only to find out afterward that it was always going to be an external hire? These are the simple things that undermine the strength and credibility of your company's leadership and brand – today more than ever.

On the other hand, it's fairly straightforward to do things the *crowd* appreciates. LEGO interviews employees from around the world and posts videos on their careers website so candidates can get a picture of what it's like to work there. Questrade, a Canadian online investment company, is transparent about team structures so that prospective candidates know exactly who they'd be working for. They also host online Q&A sessions so people can get the real story on what it's like to work there.[26]

None of these things are hard. They'll require a good dose of intrapreneurship and creativity to execute, though, because they likely aren't part of your current HR process or comfort zone.

Outsiders can put up walls or open doors. You decide

Traditional corporate **O**utsiders are a large and influential group of stakeholders. They're the reporters, researchers, watchdogs, whistleblowers, and activists who call business out for doing wrong. Nike met plenty of these folks during the factory crisis of the 1990s. Banks are no strangers to their power, nor are retailers, tech firms, or manufacturers of almost anything. PR, communications, community relations, and public affairs teams spend a lot of time keeping these stakeholders at bay.

Also included among the **O**utsiders are the regulators. These folks roll out the red tape, invent new rules, and require new forms. Their increasing influence has made "Compliance Officer" the hottest job in America.[27] Some chief executives we've spoken to estimate they spend more than 40 percent of their time dealing with regulators. That's a heck of an opportunity cost absorbed by the most important leader of a company.

If it seems like traditional **O**utsiders are getting stronger and louder, it's because they are. They have the tools now to mobilize supporters and take a stand fast. Think about an advocacy organization like Greenpeace or the National Resources Defense Council. They used to take years, sometimes decades, to raise the money and awareness needed to bring about change. That's not a knock on them. It was just reality. A documentary to raise awareness, a mailing list of 100,000, media attention . . . those things took a serious investment of time, personnel and money.

Today, **O**utsiders operate on a completely different playing field and timeline. Movements are built overnight, marches are organized and executed in weeks, and boycotts of advertisers by an angry online *crowd* can have popular TV shows canceled within days. Independent influencers on social media can reach hundreds of thousands of followers in an instant, whether their point of view is informed or not. All this change also means regulators have real-time information about how their constituents feel about things.

It also makes their stick that much bigger to whack you with.

Australia's Commonwealth Bank (also known as CommBank) knows first-hand how today's outsiders can completely blow up the status quo. In early 2017, the company came under attack from environmental groups for financing almost AU$4 billion in coal and other fossil fuel-based projects. In 2016, CommBank reportedly made the largest investment of any of the major Australian banks in these projects despite their public commitments for action against climate change. Led by Greenpeace's massive network of grassroots activists, a campaign was launched to pressure the company to divest of coal projects. A social media firestorm ensued, "Coalbank" was coined, and all of us on the mailing list received very clear and regular direction about how to make life painful for CommBank. Protests were staged outside the bank's headquarters. Huge banners were suspended over Sydney's busy and iconic Pyrmont bridge directly in front of CommBank's headquarters.[28] Driven by social media, thousands of protests were held over two years outside the bank's local branches throughout Australia.

By August 2017, CommBank had ended its role as financial advisor to a major coal project and formally announced it had ruled out financing it. What would have been a small blurb in the paper a decade or so ago became an ongoing and daily concern for CommBank to manage. And then it got worse.

A money-laundering scandal came to light in the same month of 2017. On top of the reputation hits it was taking from climate change activists, CommBank faced criminal charges and a class-action lawsuit by shareholders for a reported 53,000 breaches of anti-money laundering laws.[29] No, that is not a typo. Within 10 months CommBank settled with the Federal Court for AU $700 million[30] – the largest civil penalty imposed on a private company in Australian history. The money laundering and environmental concerns are presumably unrelated – other than to say it's got to be pretty uninspired to be involved in both. The common thread here is the microscope the company finds itself under and the army of critics who are ready to bring them down. Friends of the bank are in short supply after a few decades of charging their customers too many fees.

In 2018, a Royal Banking Commission was established to investigate misconduct across the sector. The findings are *not flattering*. Such is the power of the *new C.E.O.s* when the once-untouchable banks of Australia can now be brought to their knees by everyday Australians.

After more than a century of being locked out of the daily decision-making and priorities of the corporate sector, the *crowd* has returned. Only this time, the tools and platforms these stakeholders have at their disposal allow their voices to be louder and more effective than ever. The *new C.E.O.s* demand transparency and assert their power through their formidable social networks. Here's what you need to know:

They expect to be listened to.

They expect to participate.

They don't work in silos.

They work as a *crowd*.

They'll either work for you or against you.

Let's take a look at what happens if you choose to ignore them.

Chapter 3

Uninspired Companies
and their Headwinds

It might sound extreme to talk about companies alienating the *crowd* but, as you've already started to see, this isn't just about extractive industries or the obvious bad guys like tobacco. Plenty of less obvious companies and industries are alienating the *crowd* every day. For every arbitrary fee, rigid policy, power tactic, or ignored concern, the *crowd* is pushed further and further away from your business.

Here's a practical example: The first draft of this chapter was written in a hotel room in a major metropolitan city, yet for some mysterious reason cell phone data connections from two different providers wouldn't work. Though it's illegal in the U.S. for hotels to block data connections to get customers to pay for Wi-Fi, the practice remains common. The result? Two very annoyed customers and a complaint to the Federal Communications Commission.

People have come to expect these kinds of shady tactics. An internet provider levies a fee to repair leased equipment, a satellite TV company charges customers to return equipment the company no longer uses, a phone company adds a tariff for bills paid over the counter . . . the list goes on and on. If you think about it for less than 10 seconds, most of us will admit that we've worked for (or even run) companies that profit in uninspired ways.

With the dramatic power shift already underway, how long can this last?

In This Chapter

- How fees, penalties, one-sided contracts, and other uninspired tricks extract profit from the *crowd* – and ultimately become the most expensive revenue you'll make

- Why our past methods to manage the impact of the *crowd* – departments devoted to PR, compliance, government affairs, and so on – no longer work

- What painful, *crowd*-generated headwinds look like and the effect on your bottom line

- How being a new collaborative-economy company will not protect you from painful headwinds. The *crowd* does not discriminate when it comes to uninspired companies.

Uninspired forms of profit can last for a while. At least until the crowd decides against it

It is entirely possible to chart a course that doesn't include the *new C.E.O.*s and still be profitable for a while. After all, that's what the vast majority of companies are doing today. Uninspired companies are set up at a very granular level to pursue profit maximization. They will still have opportunities to make money – opportunities that look like this:

Fees, fees, and more fees: Banks formerly made their money from investing their deposited assets. Eventually, they discovered the real cash is in people who lack the financial security to avoid overdrafting or falling below arbitrary minimum balances. That's how U.S. banks with over US$1 billion in assets made 8 percent of their 2015 revenue from overdraft fees, representing 65 percent of all account-related fees.[31]

Retail's long con – extended warranties: Many consumer goods retailers rely on our natural concern that what we buy with our hard-earned dollars might break and so they sell us warranties. The best companies stand by their products. The others sell us warranties with conditions like requiring a physical receipt two years after purchase (even though they have all our data) or demanding that customers return products in their original packaging. One study found these warranties have a 200 percent margin,[32] so it's been a no-brainer. Until now.

(DILBERT © 2012 Scott Adams. Used by permission of ANDREWS MCMEEL SYNDICATION. All rights reserved.)

Ancillary revenue: Give airlines credit for coming up with a fancy name. These are surcharges for checking luggage, printing a boarding pass, aisle seats, window seats, carry-on bags, phone booking fees, and, of course, the costs to check dead bodies and goldfish. Ancillary fees are so normal now, the only thing that keeps changing is how ridiculous they're getting. But airlines have a strong incentive, with 7.8 percent of global 2015 revenue now attributed to fees.[33] In Australia, until regulators cracked down in 2016 on excessive surcharges for flights booked on credit cards, Jetstar (a low-cost carrier) was charging AU$8.50 on an AU$85 fare.[34] A 1,187 percent mark-up on the actual cost of a credit card payment and an opportunity to deceptively advertise their flight as cheaper than its competitors. This is how a small, short-term win can lead to a massive loss of brand trust in the long term.

Selling addiction: The tobacco in cigarettes themselves isn't addictive; it's the nicotine that is. Cigarette companies figured out early on that the natural nicotine in a tobacco plant wasn't being released when burned, so they added fun things like ammonia to make sure smokers would keep coming back for more.[35] Then they famously invested in junk science to convince us that cigarettes are harmless – even though the *actual* science tells us that when the product is used as recommended by the manufacturers, it eventually kills half of its regular users.[36]

Putting people last: In the 1960s, the sugar industry borrowed Big Tobacco's playbook to downplay its product's connection to obesity. The National Football League did the same in the 2000s to convince the world that no long-term damage is caused by repeated concussions.

Squeezing the supply chain: Many companies have turned a blind eye to human rights and environmental abuses that generate cost savings. These are the supply chains squeezed so tightly for cost efficiencies that they eventually lead to disasters. Consider the low-cost, high-fashion retailer H&M. In 2013, the factory of a supplier to

H&M (and several other apparel companies) collapsed in Bangladesh, killing 1,134 workers. By 2016, a watchdog group found a majority of the company's "gold and platinum" suppliers still lacked even basic safety measures like fire exits.[37]

There are plenty of other instances where squeezing the supply chain has resulted in negative business outcomes without that level of tragedy. In a classic example, Toys "R" Us promised Christmas delivery for all online orders received by December 10. This sounds perfectly normal today, but in 1999 Toys "R" Us didn't realize just how many people had taken up online shopping. When they couldn't fill the orders – despite employees working as many as 49 consecutive days – they sent an "oops" email two days before Christmas. The reaction was not good. As one company VP put it, "I have never been exposed to fouler language."[38] The company was fined US$1.5 million by the Federal Trade Commission and had to give affected customers US$100 each.[39] The moral of the story: If the quest for profit angers parents during the holiday season, things probably aren't going to end well.

The problem with everything on this list (aside from general rottenness) is that it leads to a downward spiral (Figure 2). Monopolies, exclusivity agreements, one-sided customer contracts, hidden fees, and cutting corners – they've all been generated by a system that's designed to keep the *new C.E.O.*s out while still making money off of them. Each one triggers a series of headwinds as the *crowd* feels they deserve better. Eventually, it will seem like just about everyone is out to get you.

Because they are.

There's a good chance you've experienced headwinds. Even the smallest companies face criticism from a range of stakeholders whether in person or online. The corporate model has evolved to anticipate it. Just think of the massive investments in departments and leaders to manage or mitigate the impact of **C**onsumers, **E**mployees, and **O**utsiders. PR, HR, government affairs, compliance, and corporate communications are largely viewed as a cost of doing business. A high and increasing cost, but anticipated and budgeted for nonetheless.

Here's the thing: The *crowd* of *new C.E.O.s* is only growing stronger and the departments you've invested in over the years to handle them will very likely be too big, too expensive, or too policy-burdened to move fast enough to get out of the way.

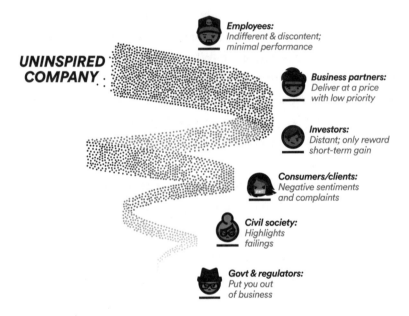

UNINSPIRED COMPANY

Employees:
Indifferent & discontent; minimal performance

Business partners:
Deliver at a price with low priority

Investors:
Distant; only reward short-term gain

Consumers/clients:
Negative sentiments and complaints

Civil society:
Highlights failings

Govt & regulators:
Put you out of business

Figure 2: Headwinds: The downward spiral of uninspired companies.

Uber knows a thing or two about headwinds

When Uber started out, the company delivered a mobile solution that connected drivers and passengers. Anyone who's ever tried to get a cab on a rainy Friday night would agree that the world has been desperate for a better solution for a long time now. And Uber delivered it – faster, easier, and cheaper. Uber's technology is a great thing.

The problem is that for too long the company has operated in a way that suggests they don't care how their business impacts real people and communities. In other words, they've paid very little attention to how the *crowd* of *new C.E.O.s* perceives their way of doing business. For Uber, the news is not good. Consumers are mad about surge pricing, unfair customer ratings, and charges of discrimination. According to some courts, drivers are treated an awful lot like employees, without the benefits, security, and employer tax contributions. Uber drivers get all of the downsides of having a boss, with none of the perks. As for the people Uber *does* call employees: they've enjoyed a culture of widespread sexual harassment, discrimination, and retaliation, as discovered in internal investigations in June 2017.[40]

As for outsiders, plenty of them *despise* Uber. Labor rights advocates are up in arms about the treatment of workers by a company that claims it is not subject to labor laws. Unions representing trained, licensed drivers who pay for the privilege of doing business argue that Uber is playing by different rules. The news media has uncovered instances of discrimination,[41] failure to monitor drivers' compliance with insurance requirements,[42] and resistance to fingerprinting,[43] to name a few. As for the regulators, Uber is the company "cities love to hate." [44] From Karnataka, India to Frankfurt, Germany cities have been suing, regulating, and pushing the company out, with London Transport refusing to renew Uber's license in 2017 on the basis that it was not "fit and proper."[45]

Of course, there's an explanation for all of this. As one investor said of Uber's former CEO Travis Kalinick, "It's hard to be a disrupter and not be an asshole."[46]

We respectfully disagree, by the way.

At its core, Uber's business model is designed to profit off regulatory loopholes – from employee classification and consumer protections to driver training, insurance, and licensing. This doesn't exactly create the right conditions for passionate support from the *crowd*. At one point in 2017, virtually every leadership position in the company was vacant. We're talking the CEO, CFO, president of ridesharing, and SVP of engineering and general counsel. There is also still an ongoing #deleteUber social movement in play.

Uber went from market darling to toxic because they aggressively (and arrogantly) pursued a growth-at-all-costs strategy. How long can that last without a dramatic overhaul?

We're not suggesting they are doomed. Yet leaks of financial data in early 2017 indicated that, despite growing revenues, the company was carrying significant losses and that costs vastly exceed revenues.[47] Company executives would probably tell you this is an inevitable part of a startup's lifecycle.

To us, at least some of it looks an awful lot like painful headwinds kicking into high gear.

The good news for Uber is that their new chief executive Dara Khosrowshahi seems to have the crucial missing ingredient to Uber's reputation overhaul: listening skills.

The high cost of being uninspired

The data is in on uninspired companies. While their annual reports may tout extractive profits, they can also mask the absolute fortune the profit-as-purpose model costs. For example:

Uninspired employers pay a talent tax: It's not that companies with bad reputations aren't able to attract talent. They can. It just costs a lot more - salaries run about 53 percent more for men and 60 percent more for women.[48] Of course, paying more for talent because of reputation issues may not even work in the future. Centennials will take the concept of social conscience to an entirely new level.[49]

Companies without purpose make less: A recent study found 42 percent of purpose-starved companies saw a decline in growth.[50] Another study found that disengaged teams sacrifice about 17.4 cents on the dollar in profit.[51] On the flip side, consider this from Unilever: 70 percent of the company's growth came from brands that are acting on purpose.* Growth rates are 46 percent higher and costs are lower than for the brands where they have not cracked purpose yet.[52]

Uninspired employees go elsewhere: Disengaged employees of small and medium-sized businesses are 21 percent more likely to leave their companies.[53] Another global study found employees are far more likely to quit a job when their manager is uninspiring. In fact, the increased likelihood of leaving is between 19 and 37 percent depending on the industry.[54]

Employees who stay are less productive: Even when uninspired companies manage to hang on to talent, they contribute less. People on disengaged teams have been found to be about 15 percent less productive. Part of the reason could be that they're calling in sick – absenteeism is about 29 percent higher.[55]

Uninspired companies have to buy their friends: U.S. corporations now spend US$2.6 billion per year lobbying. This is otherwise known as money spent to convince lawmakers not to regulate them out of business. Wouldn't it be easier to have the lawmakers (and their constituents) onside?

Uninspired companies lose relevance with the *new C.E.O.*s and have to pull all sorts of uninspired tricks to stay afloat. They spend a disproportionate amount of time looking for new ways to extract profit from consumers, the environment, business partners, and workers instead of creating additional value. They will increasingly encounter external stakeholders who are difficult to work with, and have declining customer bases and uncommitted employees. These are headwinds that have always existed but have never been this forceful.

---

*   Referred to at Unilever as their "sustainable living brands."

This outdated model forces companies to prioritize things like reactive crisis management, constant onboarding to manage turnover, scrutinizing and monitoring business partners, and scrambling to eliminate the hurdles government and society put in the way. The result is a cycle of falling returns that will ultimately lead to failure. These companies might be posting short-term profits, but they're digging a very deep hole. Just ask half of the pre-deregulation airlines and the folks who used to own your mobile number.

Plenty of leaders have tried to break the downward spiral of headwinds created when the *crowd* is not onside. John Antioco, Blockbuster's CEO, tried to save the company years before its demise. Blockbuster LLC was an American-based provider of home movie and video game rental services back in the days when we drove to a store to pick them up. Operationally it was organized into silos to enable its retail operations to grow and stay focused on pursuing its mission to be the #1 market leader. Late fees were core to the business model. While we haven't seen evidence that the company strived to be inspired, Antioco did try to reconfigure the customer experience into something considerably more appealing: namely, a focus on online delivery and the elimination of late fees. That all seemed like a pretty good idea until an extremely influential activist investor, top executives, and eventually the board thought these new plans were too costly for the market leader to incur.[56] The rest is history.

And so is Blockbuster.

Our point here is simple: These are not sustainable revenue-generating models, even if they're the go-to moves to stay afloat for a while. In a world where the power has shifted to the *crowd*, this kind of extractive growth stands on shaky ground. The moment customers are presented with a viable alternative, they will leave. The instant science proves you wrong, you're in trouble. Once regulators, and more importantly their constituents, notice you're skirting the regulations, the regulations will change and your business model may very well fall apart. The founders of gig economy apps and fantasy sports sites may well back us up on this.

Consumers, Employees, and Outsiders are gaining momentum at an exponential rate. When they work together as a *crowd* united by their frustrations, mistrust, and anger, their power is all but unstoppable. If you've had headaches in the past, you're about to experience a migraine.

It doesn't have to be this way.

Inspired Companies have the crowd onside

Broadly speaking, the *crowd* is onside when they buy from, advocate for, and defend your business because they believe in you. Consumers seek out and celebrate these businesses. Employees are passionate about working there. Outsiders make life easier, not harder.

Having the *crowd* onside is what separates *Inspired Companies* from the pack.

The remaining chapters of this book explore the three pillars key to setting your business on a path to becoming an *Inspired Company:*

You'll know you're on the right track when your workday starts to feel more like this:

> Your business has a mission with many winners. You lead and execute it with passion. You are unapologetic in your refusal to be railroaded by existing systems or corporate norms. You are committed to doing the right thing. All of your profits are derived from your mission, not from penalizing customers or other stakeholders. Traditional company

outsiders and multiple sectors of society become as invested in your success as you are. Financial markets react to you – not the other way around. That's a company the world can get behind. A company the world wants to see win.

The first step to having that kind of a day?

Define your company's mission in a way that opens the door.

Chapter 4

Inspired Mission: Make a Promise with Many Winners

Stand for something bigger

Most corporate mission statements today leave a lot to be desired.

The internet is littered with automated mission statement generators that will instantly organize the latest corporate buzzwords into meaningless statements. They generate stuff that sounds a lot like this:

- Our mission is to be the world's favorite destination for discovering great value and unique selection.

- We will produce superior financial returns for shareowners by providing high value-added logistics, transportation, and related business services through focused operating companies.

If you had to read those statements twice in an attempt to understand them, you're not alone. They just go to show the bar for mission statements is set way too low. And by the way, these aren't from a sarcastic online mission statement generator. They are the real mission statements for eBay and FedEx, respectively.

In This Chapter

- Take the first step towards becoming an *Inspired Company*: define a reason to exist that matters to the *crowd*

- How to spot mission statements that just won't work for the *new C.E.O.s*

- How to find your way to an *Inspired Mission* that binds you with the *crowd:* avoid the most common traps and find the words that mean the most

- The transformative effect of a tiny set of words and the opportunity that unfolds when companies get it right

---

A mission should be clear about why a company exists

We use the word mission here, but it doesn't matter if you call it a mission, vision, purpose, or anything else. What's most important is that you spend the time to define *why* your organization exists and make sure the answer works for that powerfully growing *crowd* of **C**onsumers, **E**mployees, and **O**utsiders. Having an *Inspired Mission* provides the foundation for getting them onside.

The concept of having a meaningful purpose statement isn't new. In fact, it's probably the least new idea in this book. What is new, is having an awareness of the role it can play to attract "the outside in." You know, the *crowd* of *new C.E.O.s* we've been talking about who will ultimately determine how well you do.

There's very little about the average mission statement today
that will result in greatness, let alone get the *crowd* onside. Very few
shoppers wake up thinking, "I hope my grocery store becomes #1
today." Employees don't get excited by convoluted descriptions of
shareholder returns or an unsubstantiated desire to delight customers.
A company mission that promises to treat suppliers fairly or avoid
destroying the environment? Shouldn't that be everyone's baseline?

Your mission should be the ceiling, not the floor.

Inspired Companies do much better with their most important
declaration to the world. They understand that a few carefully selected
words can give shape to a powerful mission statement that an entire
organization can get behind. *Inspired Companies* recognize the role of
their mission in attracting a larger *crowd* to help them succeed.

One way to know what an *Inspired Mission* looks like is to learn
how to spot uninspired missions. Luckily, they're not that hard to find.
Most mission statements today are comically uninspired.

(DILBERT © 1993 Scott Adams. Used by permission of ANDREWS MCMEEL
SYNDICATION. All rights reserved.)

There are plenty of reasons today's mission statements fall so short.
At the top of the list are the ones that play to profit-as-purpose and
speak primarily (or even solely) to shareholders. After that, companies
don't always have a clear idea of how to use a mission statement to
its full power, so they don't know what it should say. Some mission
statements are starving for meaningful self-reflection – something
groups of busy people aren't known for.

This doesn't have to be complicated. You just need to be able
to recognize a few common traps that are so prevalent they can be
spotted in most corporate mission statements today. Avoid these
pitfalls and you'll already be a step ahead:

Uninspired missions are chronically narcissistic.
They typically focus on winning where there is only *one winner* (e.g.,
"be the world's #1 provider of something"). These kinds of mission
statements are narrow and say nothing about why it matters. Purpose
and meaning are woefully missing. They beg the question: Besides
shareholders, who cares?

Ford Motor Company, for example, makes no apologies for its
efforts *to become the world's leading Consumer Company for automotive
products and services.* Given the company's unintentional role in
establishing case law to advance shareholder primacy a century ago,
that may not be surprising.[*] Still, it's an uninspired statement of
purpose that speaks to no one other than short-term shareholders and
leaders. It's not hard to see how a company can move from there to
being so myopic that it fails to see the bigger picture of a sustainably
profitable transportation sector.

Ford is certainly not alone. Many financial services institutions love
narcissistic missions. Things like, *to be the nation's leading retailer
of financial services for consumers and small businesses.* Of course,
that didn't work out so well for the now-defunct American bank
Washington Mutual. Disgraced telecom provider WorldCom didn't
do any better when they sought *to be the most profitable, single-source
provider of communications services to customers around the world.*

Becoming #1 is a great outcome, but a bad purpose. In the end, it
will lead to behaviors and strategies that repel the *crowd,* not attract it.

---

[*] Those wishing to learn more about Ford's role in shareholder primacy might be
interested in *Dodge v. Ford Motor Company,* 170 NW 668 (Mich 1919).

Uninspired missions focus on a business model, product, service, or single competency.

Barnes & Noble, a large retail bookstore chain in the U.S., begins their mission statement with "Our mission is *to operate the best specialty retail business in America, regardless of the product we sell.*" They go on to say a lot about how great books are and the communities their booksellers will operate in, but the core message is that they intend to be famous for retail – which is an operating model. It's not something that will rally the world or even a community. It is a single competency or business-model description, not a shared value proposition or an inspiring idea.

FedEx, mentioned earlier, goes the distance with its promise *to produce superior financial returns for its shareowners by providing high value-added logistics, transportation, and related business services through focused operating companies.* Now, there are a lot of things FedEx does really well, but writing mission statements is not one of them. It's jargon-laden and narrowly focused on the company's service offering. Chances are pretty good they can deliver a package faster than we can figure out what their mission statement means. There's a ton of opportunity here to reclaim a bigger idea for their business.

Promise to behave well? That's not a good enough mission.

A lot of companies of all sizes and industries make the mistake of using precious real estate in their mission statements to talk about how well they'll treat people and the environment. A few examples:

- Con Edison (a large U.S. utility company) aims *to provide energy services to our customers safely, reliably, efficiently, and in an environmentally sound manner; to provide a workplace that allows employees to realize their full potential; to provide a fair return to our investors; and to improve the quality of life in the communities we serve.*

- Albertson's, a regional grocery chain in the U.S., aims *to create a shopping experience that pleases our customers; a workplace that creates opportunities and a great working environment for our associates; and a business that achieves financial success.*

- Not to be outdone, Exxon Mobil Corporation is committed *to being the world's premier petroleum and petrochemical company. To that end, we must continuously achieve superior financial and operating results while simultaneously adhering to high ethical standards.*

These examples are a lot of talk about positive experiences, good behavior, and what should be baseline expectations of any company in the world.

Assuming these companies actually deliver, the *crowd* will appreciate these types of commitments. But a statement that commits you to a certain standard of behavior is different than a purpose or mission statement. Don't ditch your promises to behave well; just articulate them as something that you commit to *in addition to your mission.*

Uninspired missions try to say too much.
There are several things that every company needs to define for itself: what it stands for, its key goals, milestones, and ambitions, how it plans to achieve them, and how it promises to behave. Having these basics in place is critical for any high-performing organization. It only becomes a problem when a company uses the mission or purpose statement as the place to put them all. Here's a simple checklist of what belongs in a company but **not** in its mission statement:

- *Values, operating principles, distinctive characteristics*: how you're committed to behaving or your code of conduct.

- *Milestones and outcomes*: achievements that indicate progress and success (goals, targets, pacing).

- *Strategy*: how you're going to achieve your mission (business model choices, strategic priorities, investment priorities, retaining great talent, etc.).

- *Tagline* and *marketing messages*: from the shorthand you'd like to be known by, to a seasonal rallying cry. This one's a little tricky because the best missions are succinct and memorable – much like a tagline. But taglines *are* marketing statements. Nike knows "Just do it" is not a mission statement. A mission or purpose statement describes your reason for being.

To see what happens when one statement is expected to carry all of that baggage, have a look at Walt Disney Company's mission statement in 2017:

> *To be one of the world's leading producers and providers of entertainment and information, using its portfolio of brands to differentiate its content, services, and consumer products. The company's primary financial goals are to maximize earnings and cash flow, and to allocate capital toward growth initiatives that will drive long-term shareholder value.*

Walt Disney's previous mission statement was this: *To make people happy.*

To us, that's the sound of inspiration slipping away. For the generations who grew up on the joy that Walt Disney's obsession with happiness brought us, we hope it doesn't slip too far.

An *Inspired Mission* has just one job: to express the big idea behind *why a company exists*. It's a mighty big job, but it's just one job.

Is your mission uninspired?
Red flags to look for:

☐ Is it narcissistic or a narrowly focused internal goal? (e.g., To be the best, the biggest, #1, the industry leader, etc.)

☐ Does it focus on a business model or a single competency? (e.g., We will excel in lean manufacturing, specialty retail, or customer service.)

☐ Does it describe good behavior? (e.g., We want to treat employees well and uphold ethical standards.)

☐ Is it trying to do too much? (e.g., Here's our strategy plus our values plus what we want to achieve.)

If you answered yes to any of the above, you'll need a new mission statement.

We all make mistakes

The goal here isn't to pick on companies with uninspired missions. Instead, we want to highlight what's possible. Many companies lack an *Inspired Mission* and there's hope for almost all of them.

Maybe they're led by inspired people who sense it's time for change. Remember when we mentioned Ford earlier? Here's a company whose current executive chairman (Bill Ford) is a lifelong environmentalist who is responsible for many of the strides they've made in sustainable product innovation and managing the corporate footprint. See? Hope.

Maybe a company has suffered the same fate so many others have: It started out inspired, but lost its way as it grew. There's hope for these companies too. If a company has good intentions and great ideas – and many do – there is a path forward.

Take a look at Nike. It's a company that was founded on inspiration, but its mission went through periods of "drift" over the years. At one point in the 1990s, Nike's public objective was to become "The #1 Sports and Fitness Company in the World." Employees took that to mean "crush Adidas." It wasn't exactly a mission that would resonate beyond the walls of the company and shareholders. Though Nike achieved both goals, neither was a sustaining long-term idea. One could argue it led the company into a less successful period, away from its core and founding inspiration.

By the late 1990s, the need to re-examine Nike's mission statement to reset the company's compass was clear. It was a challenging time for Nike. Stock prices had been volatile* and there was still a lot of work to do to earn the trust of many of its stakeholders on supply chain issues. The company's largest market, the U.S., had also started to flatline, creating concerns that the company had reached market saturation levels. This challenging period became a defining moment in Nike's history, as it worked to return to its founding sources of inspiration.

A core group of long-time executives knew the Nike brand was better than this, and they eventually spearheaded the launch of a new mission statement that was outward-looking, ambitious, and inspiring. By the early 2000s, Nike had a new expression of its mission: *To bring inspiration and innovation to every athlete* in the world. (*If you have a body, you're an athlete.)*

This was a transformational moment, perhaps even a salvation moment, in the history of Nike's business, brand, and culture. For those of us there who experienced it, this change brought a refreshed sense of inspiration into the breadth of the company. It is a better representation of Nike that's more relevant to the wider world and honors the truth that everyone has an athlete inside of them, whether

---

* Nike's stock price more than doubled between 1996 and 1997, but was a third of its high-point value by early 2000.

you're into football or skateboarding, running or walking, as a professional or amateur. Nike was back to selling "Just do it" – an idea and spirit the world fell in love with.

In our experience, this new mission has had a profound impact on the culture and overall performance of the company. It has also positively impacted and attracted the support of a wide range of stakeholders – from consumers who self-organize and promote Nike+ Run clubs around the world, to government agencies looking to industry partnerships to tackle issues like physical inactivity. Nike fundamentally transformed its reason for being, going from a company that sought to be #1 to a company that was back to standing for a big idea. So while Nike's spirit of competitiveness might have gone a step too far with its old mission, they changed it and re-centered.

It's worth noting that no number of inspiring words will counter outright deceit and ill-intent. For example, Volkswagen's move to install software to cheat emissions testing (discovered in late 2015) will not be easily forgiven by an outraged *crowd* of *new C.E.O.s*. Volkswagen actually didn't have a mission statement at the time and as such nothing to guide them other than perhaps an *implied* purpose to maximize profits. To ever fully recover, Volkswagen will need to reinvent itself first by rediscovering and articulating a more inspiring reason to exist and then also perhaps by hitting the reset button on their organizational values.

Mission statements that move us

The re-anchoring into an *Inspired Mission* for Nike was a welcome one but, as you've seen, even Nike fell into the trap of taking on what was thought of as a "grown-up mission" to be #1. The good news is that the traps of uninspired mission statements are easy to avoid when you are aware of the most common ones. The even better news is that the characteristics of *Inspired Missions* are a lot more fun to play with. When you get your *Inspired Mission* right, you'll know that your company has something real to offer in a world hungry for authenticity. It will be an idea meaningful to a broad range of stakeholders – your potential *crowd* of *new C.E.O.s.* You're ready for a new mission statement, now what?

You might be tempted to take the path that Universal Health Services took and, in a very literal way, try to say something that speaks directly to each of your stakeholders individually:

> *To provide superior quality healthcare services that PATIENTS recommend to family and friends, PHYSICIANS prefer for their patients, PURCHASERS select for their clients, EMPLOYEES are proud of, and INVESTORS seek for long-term returns.*

The good news here is that they're thinking of their *new C.E.O.s* and making sure there's something for everyone. That's a start. But there's a much more powerful place for an *Inspired Company* to stand. A place where all stakeholders are pulling together for an idea that's bigger than all of them. A place where the *crowd* of *new C.E.O.s* is united. Here are a few organizations who have found that place:

Alibaba Group: *To make it easy to do business anywhere*

Twitter: *To give everyone the power to create and share ideas and information instantly, without barriers*

Flight Centre[*]: *Open up the world for those who want to see*

Positive Luxury[†]: *To inspire people to buy better and influence brands to do better*

---

[*] Flight Centre Travel Group is a retail travel group founded in Australia.
[†] A company founded in the U.K. in 2011 by entrepreneurs Diana Verde Nieto and Karen Hanton MBE.

IKEA: *Create a better everyday life for the many people*

Ernst & Young: *Build a better working world*

Virgin Atlantic Airlines: *To embrace the human spirit and let it fly*

Microsoft: *To empower every person and every organization on the planet to achieve more*

BarefootLaw: *To use innovation and technology to increase access to law and justice*

Facebook: *Give people the power to build community and bring the world closer together*

Pinsent Masons:* *Champion change, promote progress, and empower everyone, to make business work better for people*

Try to resist judging whether these companies are fully delivering on these missions. Stay focused on the words for now. If these companies actually achieved these missions, how different would the world be? And how would people feel about them?

These are examples of companies from around the world. Global, local, large and small, high tech and low tech – all with mission statements that mean something to more of us. Where can you find this for your company? There's no guarantee you'll find it in high-priced brand consultants, communications firms, and marketing agencies. Smart consultants can help by listening, asking questions, digging up and sifting through your company's heritage, and holding up a mirror to your ambitions and core identity. They can give you some good words and clear direction. But you're the ones who will need to do the work.

---

* Pinsent Masons is an international law firm specializing in sectors such as energy, infrastructure, financial services, real estate, and advanced manufacturing and technology.

Key features of *Inspired Mission* statements

When we unpack a mission statement that moves us, here's what we find:

- It's a big idea

- There are many winners

- It focuses on real people and real needs

- It has longevity

- It reflects your company's unique spirit

- It contains a keyword or small phrase that focuses your big idea

An *Inspired Mission* is guided by a big idea

An *Inspired Mission* is visionary and describes what the company will deliver to the people and communities it seeks to reach and impact. A local grocer might seek to nourish a neighborhood, a global food and beverage manufacturer might seek to nourish the whole world. Both are inspired ideas that are bigger than any one company.

Whatever the size of the company, the inspired idea you pursue should be bigger than the company itself. It is a statement that the world would love to see achieved. It goes deeper into why it's important for the company to exist in the first place. Leaders of *Inspired Companies* don't fall into the trap of pledging allegiance to their business model or describing *how* they should behave or do business when they articulate a mission statement. Instead, inspired leaders are committed to a larger vision and work to capture the essence of *why* they are in business in ways that go beyond those things.

Take a look at Tesla. When it was formed, the electric car manufacturer didn't articulate its goal to be the biggest or richest player in the automotive industry (they leave that singular ambition to a few other car companies). Instead, they sought *to accelerate the advent of sustainable transport by bringing compelling mass-market electric cars to market as soon as possible.*[57] That's a big idea and it attracted many supporters.

In 2016, Tesla made its big idea even bigger. They dropped the part about cars. *To accelerate the advent of sustainable transport* is an idea that many across society would love to see come to life. By letting go of the attachment to a particular solution (electric cars), Tesla deliberately expanded its opportunity to move beyond cars, to trucks, trains, high-speed transportation pods, and other transport we haven't even imagined yet.

By the time it changed its mission statement, Tesla had already translated its technology and know-how beyond cars and transport into other energy sectors like home energy. And they want the whole planet to come along. Their new mission is *To accelerate the world's transition to sustainable energy.*[58] A good majority of the world is on board with this idea. There's a big powerful *crowd* of consumers, employees, civil society, and governments all willing and able to contribute to making it happen.

Tesla's purpose is inspiring but it's important to understand that an *Inspired Mission* doesn't always have to aim to solve a big social problem. The Container Store says one of its main goals is to have "their customers dancing in their organized closet, pantry, home office, etc. because they are so delighted and thrilled with the complete solution we provided them." If you reframe that into a mission statement, it might look something like this: *To free our lives from clutter and chaos, and make room for more fun and happiness.* That's pretty inspired, if you ask us – and a welcome relief for those of us who can't organize ourselves out of bed in the morning.

An *Inspired Mission* has many winners.

The Tesla case shows us how an *Inspired Mission* attracts and unites *a crowd:* it offers a reason for being that benefits a diverse set of stakeholders – inside and outside traditional company walls. It starts by speaking to the concerns and dreams of employees, who are emerging to be among companies' most powerful stakeholders and arbiters of success. Then it goes a step further, promising a better future state on an issue, problem, or opportunity that the rest of the world cares about.

Google is another strong example and was founded on an inspiring vision of the future: *To organize the world's information and make it universally accessible and useful.* Given information's role in dividing the haves from the have-nots (not just for money, but for education, health, safety, and almost anything else), this is a seriously ambitious mission. It's a bigger idea than any single company can pull off by themselves and by definition will require unique partnerships, collaboration, and creativity across traditional sector lines. Achieve the best version of this mission statement and the world will be a better place. That's inspired.

If you take the concept of *many winners* to other industries, here's what big ideas start to look like: banks that catalyze prosperous communities; investment funds that accelerate entrepreneurship; sports companies that inspire and enable everyone to find their inner athlete; food and beverage companies that seek to nourish generations of children into strong, healthy adults.

Some of the language used here to describe ideas with *many winners* might feel more like what we would expect from the government and nonprofit sectors. Don't be put off by that. Hire a copywriter.

The core mission of an *Inspired Company* sets it apart from others because it has *many winners*. This makes the mission worth fighting for and the *new C.E.O.s* more likely to want to be part of it.

What's *our* mission, you might ask? Well, we created the concept of *Inspired Companies* as part of a commitment *to transition business to a force the world will get behind.* If you're reading this book or in a role that influences the future of a business, we sure hope you're signed on to helping us make that happen.

Inspired Missions **focus on real people and real needs.**
Why are these important? Because unlike business models or
products, people never become obsolete. Their needs and their role in
society might change, but until robots start reproducing, focusing on
the needs of real people will be a safe bet.

You don't have to be a behemoth to get this right. Amsterdam-
based Tony's Chocolonely makes chocolate bars. Really good
chocolate bars. Their tagline? "Crazy about chocolate, serious about
people." Today, they have a 19 percent market share. Not bad for a
company you've never heard of. Their goal? A 100 percent slave-free
chocolate industry. They're not interested in plugging a fair-trade
product into a system that's otherwise exploitative. They want to
change the *whole* industry. Their mission? *To make other people as
passionate about slave-free chocolate as we are, from supply through
to demand.* That means everything from treating the farmers who
harvest cocoa beans fairly, to becoming a leading brand through great
chocolate and using their success to influence larger wholesalers
and retailers, to supporting sustainability consortiums and Ph.D.
programs. It's hard to argue with any of those aspirations, and it's
easy to see the mission show up in everything they do.

You know what else? In researching their market share, we did a
search for "share" in their annual report. The word appeared 60 times.
Only once did it refer to market share.

Kellogg's, the food company known for breakfast cereal, says its
purpose is *Nourishing families so they can flourish and thrive.* That's an
enduring human need. Now, we're not saying this company has been
perfect. It has faced challenges on food labeling, adding too much
sugar, and for making misleading claims, but as with all the mission
statements discussed in this chapter, we're not yet making a judgment
as to whether their missions have been consistently delivered. We'll
do that later. For the time being, we love the intent behind Kellogg's
mission and can easily see the connection to the acquisitions of
Gardenburger and Kashi, the launch of a respected Institute for Food

and Nutrition Research, and the commitment to evidence-based decisions like removing artificial ingredients from foods. It's tough to quantify the exact benefit of that, but we do know the share price rose 43 percent between July 2012 and July 2017. We'd take that return on any of our investments.

An *Inspired Mission* has longevity.
Good mission statements are sustaining ideas. They pass a 100-year test, not an annual test. Yahoo!'s mission statement was notoriously changed 23 times in 21 years. Yahoo! was on to its 25th mission statement by the time it was sold to Verizon in 2016, but who really knows, we all stopped counting. An identity crisis that cuts that deep will undermine everything. Especially your final sale price.[59]

An *Inspired Mission* should be a genuine reflection of your company's spirit.
Virgin Group has an official purpose, and it's a lofty one at that: *Changing business for good.* Not bad, right? Nevertheless, Virgin Group's CEO, Richard Branson, has joked that his company's mission statement is "Screw it, let's do it." It's a flippant statement, but we're pretty sure he means it.

Virgin is home to a disparate group of companies (airlines, mobile phones, radio stations, financial services, etc.) and "Screw it, let's do it" is pretty consistent with their unifying principle: disrupt market monopolies. Virgin is applying that mindset to environmental sustainability across its companies, including a multi-billion-dollar commitment to solving the climate crisis, working with business partners to innovate (like testing the viability of biofuel-run commercial aircraft with Boeing), and funding disruptive entrepreneurs. All in all, it's also a hell of a stance to publicly take when you operate in two of the most consumptive forms of travel on earth (airlines and cruise lines). It looks like the folks at Virgin think they can change the way things are done. Again.

Inspired Missions have a single word or phrase that the company cannot (and should not) escape.

This is the word that grounds a company's mission in authentic pursuit of a concrete idea. It's an anchor for the industry you're in, or the one you are about to transform. We don't expect a manufacturer of ink pens to expand financial freedom, but they could inspire the writer in you.

When a mission is too big and broad to be anchored by a powerful word, a company can justify moving into pretty much anything. This may work okay for a large conglomerate led by Sir Richard Branson, but for most companies, it will not be a focused enough idea. For example, the mission statement for the online retailer Zappos is *To provide the best customer service possible.* We admire Zappos for a lot of things, but its mission could be anyone's mission in any industry.

If you have a great mission, there's probably one word (or maybe two) in it that you can't get away from. This is the word that will help you understand whether to go broad or deep with your strategic investments.

That said, the word isn't always obvious. You might think LEGO's one word is "play" or "kids." It's actually "builders": *To inspire and develop the builders of tomorrow.* LEGO's efforts center on fostering creativity and childhood development through productive play – everything is about "the brick."

Today, LEGO is one of the most trusted companies on the planet. At the turn of the millennium, they faced near-bankruptcy. Their vision statement back then was *To be the strongest brand among families with children by 2005.* It had been criticized as being too broad, lacking clear direction, and leading them into the wrong strategies.[60] Corporate narcissism as a mission might create a long list of opportunities to land grab, but it ultimately has a short runway. Thankfully the brick reigns supreme and the company is benefiting from having its North Star back.

Make no mistake: the word will have influence. Let's go back to Nike for a moment. We noted that in the 1990s Nike aimed *to be the #1 sporting goods company in the world*. In addition to it translating into "crush Adidas," for practical purposes, it also translated into becoming the #1 *footwear* company. Influenced by the largest product category in the business, the *power word* became footwear. That opened Nike up to expanding into things that ultimately didn't make sense to its true core – dress shoes, military boots, and shoes designed for price more than performance. Frankly, those moves didn't make much sense to many employees either. Very few of us joined Nike to make dress shoes.

With Nike's current and more *Inspired Mission* statement,* Nike's *power word* became "athlete." Over a long period of transition and re-centering on the new mission statement, Nike divested from almost all of its acquisitions† with the exception of Converse and Hurley. The sneaker that made Converse famous? The Chuck Taylor, All-Star. A basketball shoe named after Charles "Chuck" Taylor, an athlete and salesman for Converse who introduced performance innovation to the world's first basketball shoe. The Phantom board short introduced by Hurley in 2008 that transformed the market? 100 percent focused on performance improvement for surfers around the world. Keeping these two brands in Nike's portfolio was not a coincidence. Listening to the "voice of the *athlete*" and innovating for them is core to Nike's mission and not just a design brief.

As you are assessing your current mission statement or deliberating on a new one, ask yourself, what's the one or two words you can't get away from in your mission statement? For Google, the word might be "information." If they held on too tightly to "search engine" as keywords they might never have expanded into driverless cars, flu maps, or made acquisitions like YouTube, Android, and Keyhole (which evolved into Google Earth).

---

* Nike's mission statement is *To bring inspiration and innovation to every athlete* in the world. (*If you have a body, you are an athlete.)*

† For example, the sale of discount footwear brand Starter in 2007 and the sale of dress shoe company Cole Haan in 2013.

Almost any company can get this right. As an example, and because both of us enjoy running outside, we picked Gore-Tex. Gore-Tex changed the outdoor sports experience forever when they invented footwear and apparel materials to keep us dry when it's raining. Gore-Tex – or, as it turns out, W.L. Gore & Associates – was founded by a scientist who wanted to *create innovative, technology-driven solutions*. That's a perfect example of a mission that could belong to almost any company.

From the outside, the company seems to be doing a lot of things right – especially in the areas of environmental footprint, workplace culture, and more generally in product innovation. While their current mission statement is better than many others, it could still use some help.

We took some time to think about mission statements on their behalf. Here's what we came up with: *To weatherproof the world.* Whether it's weatherproofing shoes, houses, cars, or widgets doesn't matter. The commercial application of their technology at any given moment is not the enduring point. *Weatherproofing* is the big idea and the *power word* in this hypothetical mission statement that they could commit to. With a mission as big as weatherproofing the world, where they choose to focus efforts still needs to be sensible. Focus is a good friend of every successful business. Defining a mission requires careful consideration. It does not mean, however, that the definition should be limiting. Imagine, for example, the opportunity cost if Gore-Tex had defined themselves as a footwear materials supplier. Only our feet would be dry.

We've just spent lots of words talking about the importance of one word. In the end, it really comes down to this: Every discerning leader and profitable business will need to decide between investment opportunities. If you have a magic word or phrase in your mission statement, it can more often than not help you stay on track with a core and big idea. You'll be clearer on identifying the investment ideas that are true to who you are.

And by the way, this thinking can apply to organizations outside of the corporate sector as well. Take the Wikimedia Foundation, which is most famous for Wikipedia. Its mission? *Through various projects, chapters, and the support structure of the nonprofit Wikimedia Foundation, Wikimedia strives to bring about a world in which every single human being can freely share in the sum of all knowledge.*

Wikimedia's word is *knowledge*. They could have gotten very distracted because their platform is great at crowdsourcing information, but thankfully the power of their mission keeps them honest. Because of that, they are unlikely to move into certain areas. There won't be a wikiyelp, for example, because they're about *knowledge* not *opinions*. By the same token, because they stand for knowledge, there can be a Wiktionary and a whole world of opportunities to grow knowledge-centered programs, services, and innovations.

So when it comes to *knowledge*, there's no disputing that Wikimedia brings it. At the same time, this mission could be cut in half to deliver greater clarity and, by extension, more impact. When you have something really precious, sometimes the best thing to do is to stop talking. Here's a re-edit: *Wikimedia envisions a world where all humans freely share in the sum of all knowledge.* That's cool. We'd like that to happen. How can we help you?

In summary, here are the things to think about when crafting an *Inspired Mission* or purpose statement:

Key features of *Inspired Mission* statements

☐ *Is it an idea bigger than any one company? Focused on real people and real needs?*	Is your purpose to dominate the road, or is it to open up the world for everyone to experience? Are you fixated on pushing sportswear into the market or do you want to inspire the world to move? Are you selling insurance products to those least likely to need it or are you focused on building resilient families and communities?
☐ *Does your mission have many winners?*	Does it create an opportunity for shared purpose? Does it attract others in and create opportunities for diverse and nontraditional stakeholders to participate in achieving your idea?
☐ *Does your mission have longevity?*	Is it an enduring idea that will pass the 100-year test?
☐ *Is it a reflection of your company's spirit?*	Don't copy someone else. Own your identity and find the right words to reflect it in your mission.
☐ *Does your mission statement contain a power word or small phrase that concretely focuses your investment decisions?*	A word or small phrase that keeps business decisions grounded in a core enduring idea. Not a business model or single product or service.

If you answered these questions honestly and feel good about your responses, you may very well be on the path to becoming an *Inspired Company*.

A north star and compass point

One final note: *Inspired Missions* are *internal* statements of purpose and should not be confused with external marketing messages. The most important outcome is that employees easily answer the question "Why does the business we work for exist?" and are very proud of that answer. They can describe in great detail what draws them to the company and why they stay. So, while getting it right will be something to celebrate, it is not something to issue a press release on.

If you're not direct about who your company is and why it exists, others will make it up for you (at best) or simply forget about you altogether. The worst case for companies that fail to come up with something meaningful is that your implied mission will be profit. As we pointed out in Chapter 1, profit is good, but profit-as-purpose is bad.

Get your mission right, and it will set your company on a path to create new forms of competitive advantage. When you deliver on these precious few words in a way that the *new C.E.O.s* can see and trust, they will be much more likely to advocate for you, forgive you faster when you mess up, and give permission to expand your playing field. These are all forms of what we call *Inspired Profit,* and they are more valuable than ever as the *crowd* gains increasing levels of power and influence over your business.

We cover *Inspired Profit* in Chapter 10, but for now, consider this: Yahoo! can't make a driverless car, but Google's expertise and focus on organizing information means it can. You probably wouldn't buy a Timex computer, but an Apple watch is a different story. You'd welcome Tesla inside to power your home, but not Chrysler.

Articulating your mission in a way that transcends individual business models to ideas that get the *crowd* onside is the first step to future-proofing a business.

The next step is delivering: moving from an *Inspired Mission* into *Inspired Action.*

Chapter 5

Inspired Action:
An Introduction

Turning big words into action is everything

Becoming an *Inspired Company* isn't easy. It takes the right words, the right action, and the right outcomes to get the *crowd* onside. We're talking about going up against a century-old system that is so entrenched most will assume it's not possible.

That's the beauty of it. They'll never see you coming.

But here's the reality of it, too: becoming an *Inspired Company* means entering territory where philosophy ends and action begins. It's where we give meaning to the words of an *Inspired Mission*. Right now, no one seems to have a perfectly formed, proven roadmap for this uncharted landscape, where established companies can transform themselves into fully purpose-led organizations, or build them from the ground up. If leadership is the hat you wear, you probably already know there's not much out there that digs into how to get this done. Most organizations are trying to figure it out on their own, interviewing as many experts as they can in their search for ideas that are believable, proven, and practical.

Over the next five chapters, we map this territory and identify what the more *Inspired Companies* do when they are at their best. We've drawn from our own experience of living through a transformational period at Nike, when the company lost and then found its way with a newly *Inspired Mission* at its core. We talked to chief executives and studied companies across the world from different cultures, industries, and markets. We also pulled lessons from Nike's corporate philanthropy, where we had to make many friends outside of the traditional corporate bubble to succeed.

In This Chapter

- Putting inspired words into action is *the* critical step toward becoming an *Inspired Company* – and to date there has been very little guidance available to help leaders do it

- After a century or more of companies being wired to deliver uninspired, internal-facing mission statements, here we introduce you to an approach to wire your company for *Inspired Action*

- There are five building blocks of *Inspired Action*

  o The foundation for action starts by pairing your *Inspired Mission* with a distinctive set of values – the bedrock for how your organization promises to behave

  o What follows are four categories of *Inspired Action*. Each illustrates the many different ways you can succeed with the *crowd*. Together, they demonstrate the progressive journey to bring them onside

After several years of investigating disparate ideas, breakthroughs, and approaches, we started to see that apparent one-offs could be shaped into a coherent approach – a set of building blocks to guide companies aspiring for and committed to becoming a company the world will get behind. Leaders and advisors who have had early and ongoing exposure to these ideas are already applying them and making them their own. That's the fun bit. Once set on the right path, *Inspired Companies* will find an infinite number of ways to put big *Inspired Missions* into action.

Ultimately, what we hope to see is companies busting out of the impasse across the corporate sector. Today we see many organizations adopting "purpose statements," but not changing much else. They have big words without enough action to be believable. Even business leaders we know who support the notion of purpose-led business struggle to find ways to consistently deliver. They've grown up inside a corporate system set up to deliver profit maximization as the underlying goal. What they need now to transition are immediate answers to the question: "So what do we do now?"

The approach introduced in this chapter and the remainder of this book answers that question. There are five building blocks to turn big words into action (Figure 3). The first requires you to codify your company's *values* and distinctive behaviors and put them into practice. What follows are four further categories of action that draw on a diverse set of ideas and examples from around the world: *Obsessive Alignment; Shake up the System; Bold Conviction; Make-or-Breaks.*

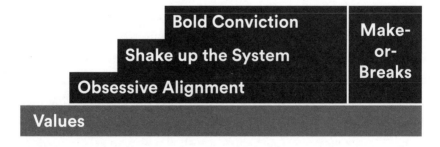

Figure 3: *Inspired Action* building blocks

Inspired Action Part 1:
Set expectations with a strong set of values

If you read Chapter 4, you know what an *Inspired Mission* is and isn't, and why every *Inspired Company* starts there. Assuming you've now got a big ambition with many winners, *how* you deliver is everything to your success or failure with the *crowd*.

The first part of moving to *Inspired Action* is to articulate your company's *values*, *code* of conduct and/or guiding *principles*. That is, how you expect anyone working in your business to behave.

While *Inspired Missions* have been sorely lacking in the corporate sector, most companies have a published set of values or set of behavioral expectations. Google any company and you'll probably find these somewhere on their website. What is far less visible from the outside is what meaningful mission they serve, and whether they're consistently put into practice. If we're all honest, what usually happens is a set of corporate values or guiding principles gets written and then put in a drawer.

To have any power at all, an organization's values must come to life every day. Are they led and celebrated by leadership at all levels? Easy to remember and reinforced with a variety of artifacts, icons, and rituals (events, symbolic behaviors, key operational policies, visible everyday decisions, and so on)? Are there consequences when the values are broken?

If your values aren't ever-present, they won't matter.

Netflix understands this. You can find Netflix's company values in a broader presentation about their culture, published openly by Netflix co-founder Reed Hastings in 2014.[61] This presentation has had more than 17 million views, so it's safe to say it has resonated with plenty of people. Even more insightful and important is what that Netflix presentation says about values: "The *actual* company values, as opposed to the *nice-sounding* values, are shown by who gets rewarded, promoted or let go."

In other words, it's not what you *say*; it's what you *do*. Employees will see the difference in a heartbeat, and in today's world, they won't keep it to themselves. If your company has clever writers among its staff who don't believe you, the outcome could look like this:

Values, Behaviors and Statement of Purpose

VALUES

As an independent communications marketing firm we value:

- THE RELENTLESS PURSUIT OF ~~EXCELLENCE~~ MONEY
- THE FREEDOM TO BE CONSTANTLY ~~CURIOUS~~ UNDER APPRECIATED
- THE COURAGE TO DO THE ~~RIGHT~~ LEAST EFFICIENT THING

This example is brought to us compliments of a global communications firm. When their newly published values didn't reflect the day-to-day experience of people on the front lines, those employees took the opportunity to rewrite them.[*]

This is not an isolated incident. It has been quite normal for people to work in an environment where company values are not put into practice. Or, in fact, for the company to do the opposite of what they espouse.

Mark Wilson, most recently the chief executive of the U.K. insurer Aviva, understands the enormous value created from defining and living a distinctive set of organizational values.

First, let's take a step back and think about insurance companies. If we're honest, most of us wouldn't list one in our top 10 most loved and admired brands. They are famous for complicated products, lengthy documentation, and cumbersome, stressful claim processes. Yet Mark found a way to contradict much of that and make Aviva both relevant and successful. He is well known for leading the turnaround of Aviva's culture and performance results and insists that resetting the company's purpose and values was, and will remain, core to success.

---

[*] The above image was shared with us by someone close to the "rewrite."

Aviva's purpose statement is to *Defy Uncertainty*. When he talks about it, he makes it feel very human. He simply says, "our job is to take the fear out of life so that we can all just get on with it." He paired a sharper sense of purpose with a set of new expectations for Aviva's 30,000 employees, now expressed formally in their corporate values.

OUR VALUES AND OUR PEOPLE Our values guide everything we do and the decisions we take:	
Care More	**Never Rest**
We start with the customer and prioritise delivering a great outcome for them. We do the right thing, making sure we and those around us are acting with positive intent. We don't shrink from the tough conversations. We're in it together.	We fail fast and learn fast, testing and learning at pace. We embrace digital. We are dissatisfied with the way things are done now. We challenge ourselves to learn about the cutting edge and harness it. We get it done at pace.
Kill Complexity	**Create Legacy**
We can list our priorities on one hand, picking a few things to do brilliantly. We make the call with the right information. We join forces and build it once.	We invest with courage, taking smart risks and making good decisions to ensure we allocate our resources where they can do most. We think like an owner, taking responsibility. We go for more than quick wins. We take the long view.

Aviva's corporate values (Aviva plc Annual Report and accounts 2017, page 12; www.aviva.com/investors/annual-report-2017)

A company that cares more, kills complexity, never rests until their customers are happy, and thinks long term. Now that's a company we'd like to see succeed. Aviva's values are powerful, simple, and fly in the face of what we might expect from an insurer. And that was the point. Mark fought hard when Aviva's board pushed back on having the word "kill" in a set of organizational values. He refused to negotiate. When he combined these distinctive values with the intention to let us all live our lives with less uncertainty, Mark put Aviva on a powerful course. Aviva has been killing it ever since with new product offerings and service delivery methods set to redefine the insurance landscape. Aviva is bypassing banks with the launch of Aviva digital wallet, for example. They are the first insurer to implement their own payments system that reduces the number of forms, fast tracks payments, and eliminates traditional bank fees. As for performance, as of 2018, Aviva's operating profits had been up for the fourth year in a row and all other key performance indicators reflected consistently strong results.

Pairing an *Inspired Mission* together with a distinctive set of values will set your company's compass for *Inspired Action* to follow.

Once you've articulated your values, you have to put them into practice like your credibility with employees and your company's future depends on it.

Because they do.

You've set your compass with an *Inspired Mission* and distinctive values – now what?

The worst case is that you launch your new direction internally with lots of color and buzz, and then you don't change much else. Your company's new purpose or mission sits at the top of the strategic plan but you continue to use profit and efficiency as the primary filters for decision-making. That's the path most companies are on today.

The second-worst case is only marginally better. You declare a new *Inspired Mission* statement and a supporting set of values, then "bolt on" new initiatives or only make incremental changes that are secondary to your organization's core. You might revamp CSR efforts, do more community work, and launch a new employee engagement initiative, but core business operations, old structures, and internal power-bases remain intact. "Purpose" becomes a sideshow, and the *crowd* is unimpressed.

The best case? You wire your company to be inspired.

Welcome to *Inspired Action.*

Inspired Action Part 2:
Give the words of your mission meaning

There's no silver bullet for turning your mission into action. There are, however, building blocks of action to get started with some clarity about what it's going to take. After you've set behavioral expectations (and remain committed to living them), *Inspired Action* rests on four categories of action:

- *Obsessively Align* to mission

- Find ways to *Shake up the System* and do things differently

- Emerge with *Bold Conviction*

- Manage your *Make-or-Break* moments

While not a strictly linear path, these actions build on one another as new practices and muscles are formed and flexed in pursuit of your big idea.

Here's a quick rundown of each category:

Obsessive Alignment

Your base for action starts here. It's a lot of internal heavy lifting and foundational wiring to the big ideas expressed in your mission statement. Skip this step and not much else will work in your pursuit of greater purpose and an inspired, high-performing culture. Deliver this step and the greatest initial reward will be that your employees believe you. Perhaps even trust you. In today's world trust has never been more important to success. Having an employee base that believes and trusts you is fundamental to success.

Inspired Companies obsessively align to mission. They do this by organizing around ideas instead of silos. If your mission is to be #1, eventually you'll have whole departments competing against and cannibalizing each other's business as they individually strive to be #1 in their own category. With an *Inspired Mission* and a shared set of values, you create the conditions for teams to work together. *Inspired Companies* figure out how to distribute leadership and align all functions, activities, and decisions to deliver the mission. This work is about big actions and small actions every day by everyone. The everyday action combines to build a strong culture that believes in what it does.

Building practical "bridges" to support the translation of a big, ambitious mission into day-to-day decision-making will be essential. As will ensuring that your company lifts up and measures what matters most to the *crowd* – big-picture KPIs. Aligning incentive structures and performance rewards is also fundamental to proving to your employees that leadership is serious. In *Obsessive Alignment* some under-resourced or historically undervalued competencies will suddenly need far more of your attention, and what you require from your most influential leaders will change. We cover the strategies supported by case examples to deliver *Obsessive Alignment* in Chapter 6.

Shake up the System

If you've been obsessive enough about everyday action and delivered on some major initiatives to align to your mission, employees now believe you. Want to show the whole world you're serious? Here's where you do it: *Inspired Companies Shake up the System.* They defy norms and engage the *crowd* by breaking rules once in a while. This takes guts. Arbitrary rules or industry behaviors that don't serve bigger ideas are out. Powerful strategies that change the way you work, innovate, and inspire are in.

This is where you give your customers an influential seat at the table. You trust your employees to show off your brand. (After all, it's their brand too.) You work with governments, regulators, industry bodies, and nonprofits in untraditional ways to innovate. You lead in entirely new, totally *crowd*-facing and engaged ways. Oh, and you show your shareholders who's driving the train: you and the *new C.E.O.s.* Chapter 7 highlights a number of strategies that deliver the type of action that signals to the world that you are serious and they can trust you, with examples of companies already doing it.

Bold Conviction

If you've done the foundational work of wiring your company to pursue big ideas and continuing to challenge the system when it gets in the way of your mission, your organization will emerge with powerful confidence and new levels of creativity. We call this having *Bold Conviction,* and we describe this phase in Chapter 8. This part of the journey is possible because your **E**mployees are committed and powerfully driven by the mission. **C**onsumers and **O**utsiders have also emerged in growing support of the ideas you are pursuing and the way you are pursuing them.

Companies that reach this stage have the confidence and conviction to fight for the ideas they believe in. They stand up for their *crowd* of C.E.O.s on issues that matter. They work assertively to do the right thing and lead with radical levels of transparency. They take advantage of opportunities others shrink from. If their *crowd* or their mission is at stake, they don't pull back. They accelerate.

Make-or-Breaks

Make-or-Break moments will test your commitment and disproportionately define you.

When the going gets tough, *Inspired Companies* know what to do and they over deliver. Leadership changes, scientific developments, crisis moments, regulatory pressures, and major growth milestones are just a few of the developments that give a company a chance to show what it's made of. *Inspired Companies* don't run from these moments. When a serious issue emerges, *Inspired Companies* have built the internal muscles to intuitively know what to do. They don't cave to the pressure of external forces that don't stack up with their values or mission. And while larger companies tend to face higher stakes and very public *Make-or-Break* moments, younger companies are not off the hook. Startups might have fewer *Make-or-Break* moments to begin with but they'll need to take precautionary steps to stay inspired or they'll soon experience the same headaches as the older, more established companies. Chapter 9 explores how *Inspired Companies* respond, pursue, recognize, and embrace these opportunities.

No company gets *Inspired Action* right 100 percent of the time.

Every company must make decisions for short-term survival. It's necessary, but it's also important to recognize them for what they are. If you don't, it becomes very easy to devolve. Enjoy a bit of success, and pressure to grow at all costs can soon follow.

The good news is this: You don't have to be perfect. Every company is evolving and every leader has off days, no matter how good they are. What sets the more *Inspired Companies* apart is their leaders' ability to constantly question the existing system and lead with conviction. Some companies and leaders do this a whole lot better than others. The *Inspired Action* building blocks are a way to understand how they're doing it.

For the practitioner in you, here's a snapshot of what's in the chapters ahead: how *Inspired Companies* navigate new territory and create distinction (Figure 4).

Inspired Action	Key Principle	Strategies	Key outcome
Obsessive Alignment **Chapter 6**	Wire your business for everyday *Inspired Action*.	• Distribute leadership at the start line • Organize around ideas not silos • Build bridges between mission, values and day-to-day decisions • Measure KPIs the *crowd* cares about • Build new muscles	Employees believe you.
Shake up the System **Chapter 7**	Show the world you're serious.	• Reimagine the top job • Bring the *new* C.E.O.s inside • Break rules • Play offense with shareholders	The outside world starts to believe you.
Bold Conviction **Chapter 8**	Separate from the pack.	• Fight when you have to • Disarm • Do something unexpected	The *crowd* is onside, will advocate for and defend your business.
Make-or-Breaks **Chapter 9**	Double down on your values and *Inspired Mission* in the moments that define you.	• Plan for the predictable • A better approach for common *Make-or-Break* moments • Show who you are when things really blow up	You'll push the *crowd* away or draw them closer in, depending on what you do and how quickly.

Figure 4: *Inspired Action* Practitioner Overview

Chapter 6

Inspired Action:
Obsessive Alignment

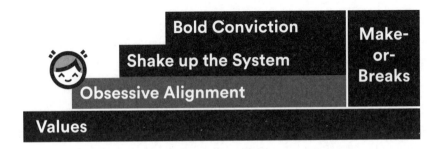

Wire your company to pursue big ideas

Everything an *Inspired Company* does comes back to the relentless pursuit of an *Inspired Mission*. It is wired to disproportionally prioritize day-to-day decisions through the lens of the big ideas it holds. Investments and divestments, hires and fires, innovation and transformation are all geared toward delivering the mission.

The key word here is "wired." If you want an *Inspired Mission* to mean anything at all, those words will need to translate into *Inspired Action*. And the first step is to build belief inside your own organization. It's fundamental to setting your company up in a way that the rest of the world might eventually work with you, not against you.

We call this work *Obsessive Alignment*.

This phase is largely an internal heavy lift. It's the nuts-and-bolts stuff that requires unyielding focus, consistency, and vision from leadership. *Inspired Companies* get creative about how to deliver their mission. They work to create alignment across the company by translating mission and values into big actions and small actions, ideas, and strategies that are memorable and repeatable. They measure, report, communicate, and celebrate progress with big-picture metrics in mind and a broader definition of success than profit. They hire people who are genuinely motivated and inspired by the ideas the company is pursuing, and they invest in and develop the competencies needed to work closely with the *crowd*. With refreshing confidence, *Inspired Companies* are transparent about their most significant challenges in ways that companies have historically tried to keep under wraps.

The biggest win from this phase of work? Employees understand expectations, are inspired by the company's mission, believe leadership is serious about pursuing it and start to put it into action without asking for permission. This is the first and most important part of building a powerful *crowd* to fuel your company's future. If your employees don't believe you, customers and outsiders won't either.

Compared to the other forms of *Inspired Action,* this work happens internally. It's not easy to see how it happens from the outside. If you're a startup working from a blank slate, this will likely be a bit easier than it would be for an established company. Large multinationals that have pursued narcissistic or internal-facing missions will need to embrace a pretty serious transformation process.

Whatever your company's size or complexity, there's no getting around the basics. If you skip the groundwork, expect to fail because the *crowd* of *new C.E.O.s* is now calling the shots. So, while it's true that *what* you do is important, *how* you do it is the key to building a company the world will get behind.

In This Chapter

- How to take the first and non-negotiable step of *Inspired Action:* wiring your company to align to your *Inspired Mission* and values

- Why *Inspired Companies* build from the core principle of *Mission first, business model second* – and what happens when companies do the opposite

- Strategies to support this nuts-and-bolt work including how to think about distributed leadership, organizational design, measuring success, the role of storytelling, and critical competencies to start hiring for

- The payoff of this internal heavy lifting: the essential part of your *crowd* – your employees – are aligned, inspired, and onside

Core principle: mission first, business model second

Obsessing your *Inspired Mission* is more important than obsessing your business model. You'd be amazed how many companies get this wrong, and how deliberate you'll need to be to get it right. *Both are critical to success* in the corporate sector, but putting mission first will prove more valuable in the long run. Why? Pursuing big ideas keeps you open to exploring the innovation, talent, and investment and divestment agendas necessary to stay relevant to the outside world.

Companies often fall into the trap of becoming overly invested in their business models to the point where they *become* the business model. Yahoo! is a great example of this. Yahoo! never really became anything more than a search engine. Google, on the other hand, is a search engine *and* creates accessible maps for just about anything, driverless cars, robot assistants . . . the list goes on. Google puts the idea of *organizing the world's information and making it universally accessible and useful* first, then figures out how to be good at whatever business model(s) they need to deliver it. It doesn't mean they *have to* do everything – it just means they stay open to it if the business case is there.

IBM is an example of a company that *became their business model* and lost sight of the bigger ideas they were founded on. IBM was one of the earliest pioneers of big data. They put magnetic strips on credit cards* and invented the floppy disc.[62] But now, they're famous for old computers instead of contactless payments and the cloud. Remember franchise record stores and newspaper publishers? It was the unrelenting pursuit of their business models at the expense of the ideas they were built from that ultimately put so many of them out of business.

Imagine if Sony had put all its chips on Betamax. For those who don't remember the 1980s, Betamax was a videotape format that rivaled VHS for about 15 minutes, although both were put out to pasture by DVDs, Blu-ray, and eventually streaming. Given the pace of technological development and acceleration of startups created to disrupt established systems, it's likely the future will bring more obituaries of companies that defined themselves by their business models instead of a big idea.

Let's revisit Blockbuster. For the longest time, this U.S. company sought to be the "leader in rentable home entertainment." At its most basic level, their story goes like this: The VCR was invented and Blockbuster built a worldwide network of retail stores to deliver movies and other content to local neighborhoods, customized to some extent by analysis of demographic data. Their growth model relied on building more stores in more neighborhoods, squeezing out mom-and-pop shops and making deals with movie studios to release

---

* IBM invented Magnetic Stripe Technology initially used for identification and transport cards. It went on to be applied to credit cards by connecting point-of-sale devices, data networks, and transaction processing computers and became a global standard. www-03.ibm.com/ibm/history/ibm100/us/en/icons/magnetic/

DVDs to them before selling direct to the public. Constant pressure to perform in the short term by opening new stores and by driving profits through late fees and candy sales reduced Blockbuster's ability to respond when they were being outplayed by new market entrants that were cheaper, more convenient, and not reliant on financial penalties.

For Blockbuster, the weight of being married to their business model blinded them to the reality that their bricks-and-mortar retail model was on the verge of becoming obsolete. Even Blockbuster's final annual report as a publicly traded company focuses first and foremost on the company's retail operations as its core and most valuable asset. Well, the asset turned out to be useless as Netflix redefined the home entertainment market. Blockbuster lacked a bigger sustaining purpose that could have allowed them to think differently and evolve faster. Talk about holding on until the bitter end.

Moving right along to bookstores, the now-defunct Borders[*] met a similar fate when it continued to open new stores and load up on CD inventory even while a different, high-growth part of their organization was outsourcing online sales to Amazon.

We realize we're not the first people to offer the earth-shattering revelation that the internet completely disrupted bricks-and-mortar retail. What's new here is the idea that these retailers could have done something about it.

Your business model is important. Obviously, you need to excel at running it. You also need to track the market position of product and service categories. The problem comes when maximizing the efficiencies and output of your business model becomes your company's primary purpose, obsession, or core identity. When that

---

[*]   Not to put too fine a point on mission statements that don't work, but this one belonged to Borders: *To be the best-loved provider of books, music, movies, and other entertainment and informational products and services. To be the world leader in selection, service, innovation, ambiance, community involvement, and shareholder value. We recognize people to be the cornerstone of the Borders experience by building internal and external relationships, one person at a time.* It has every red flag we pointed out in Chapter 4.

happens, functional leaders will interpret their jobs as delivering the model first and foremost, often with no questions asked. Employees will experience power as functional hierarchy and purpose as margin. Customer complaints will roll in. Civil society and regulators will look into your business very carefully and take a lot more of your time. The media will ask questions and make you a target. The cracks get bigger and bigger as you squeeze the business model tighter and tighter for margin and profitability gains. Worst of all, your organization will lack the agility, ability, and motivation to adapt when willing customers are presented with a better option.

Nike experienced this dynamic most acutely in the 1990s. Part of Nike's business model has been to work with contract factories located in markets where the cost of labor is cheaper. The commonly held belief during Nike's early decades was that responsibility stopped at selection of the factories. That was the business model, and it was considered a smart one – until activists, consumers, the media, and ultimately investors didn't. The contract-labor crisis is still considered the worst crisis in the company's history. If Nike had been unwilling to question its business model, this crisis could have marked the demise of the company.

After a lot of hard lessons were learned about what not to do when responding to business footprint issues, Nike turned an important corner. They began to invest heavily in understanding the underlying human rights and environmental issues, put consumer expectations of good corporate behavior first, and evolved operations and practices to a point where Nike's factory partnership model became a gold standard for the industry. In fact, this more strategic and thoughtful approach became a significant driver of product innovation and supply chain advancements and ultimately made Nike a stronger brand.

In some cases, whole industries are seeing the result of over-squeezed business models that can be traced back to the common mistake of prioritizing business model efficiencies before a meaningful mission. For example, the legal profession has arguably reached a plateau as far as its traditional business model is concerned. Below is a graphical representation of the business model run by almost every law firm in the world for the last several decades (Figure 5). It's known as Maister's profitability formula[63]:

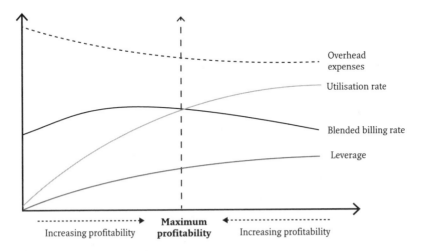

Figure 5: Maister's profitability formula
Leverage = ratio of solicitors to partners; Blended billing rate = blended hourly billing rate; Utilization rate = billable hours recorded

This model has been highly profitable as the best law firms got better at managing the individual levers and delivering them efficiently over time. Leaders of law firms don't want to take their eyes off of these levers – but they also don't want to become them. When your organizational identity consciously or unconsciously becomes your business model, daily decisions end up being held hostage to it.

The legal profession's obsession with this model has led to industry norms and assumptions like, "If it's not billable, it's not valuable." Lawyers taking time off for parental leave, pro bono work, time spent in management meetings, time spent problem-solving among peers – this is all time without value according to the model. Is it any wonder that the legal services profession has some of the highest rates of substance abuse and mental health issues?[64] Meanwhile, millennials with law degrees increasingly have one foot out the door within just a few years of service.[65] Many of them are now telling law firms what they can do with their business model.

The bottom line? *Deliver* your mission. *Evolve* your business model. Not the other way around.

Putting *mission first* into practice

How do *Inspired Companies* hold fast to this principle in the face of corporate systems that are all too happy to push business-model efficiencies and profit maximization as the first priorities? There are no silver bullets. Wiring your organization to deliver an *Inspired Mission* will require a focused look across a company's core infrastructure and operations, from its org charts to leadership of daily decisions, from what it measures to the competencies it builds. Those that get it right tend to do a few things particularly well:

- Distribute leadership at the start line

- Organize around ideas, not silos

- Build bridges between mission, values, and day-to-day decisions

- Define and measure KPIs the *crowd* cares about and that speak directly to the big idea in your mission

- Build new muscles (competencies)

These are not the most exciting areas to spend time on and they won't be seen from the outside in the short term. But do these things well, and you'll have a much better chance of enjoying business with the *crowd* onside.

Strategy 1: Distribute leadership at the start

The first thing to acknowledge when putting mission into action is
that there is no structure or process in the world that will single-
handedly create the conditions for success for you to become an
Inspired Company. The keys to success are in the hearts, minds, and
commitment of your people. If they are inspired by the big idea in your
mission and they trust the organizational values you've committed to,
congratulations, you've made it to the start line with a good chance of
winning if you follow through.

There are endless ways to think about how to encourage everyday
Inspired Action from your employees. To succeed, everyone in your
business will need to play their part. A basic yet entirely effective way
to get started is to ask your entire organization to consider a set of
simple questions:

What is your personal connection to the big idea in our
mission/purpose statement?

Where do you see it in action in the work that we already do
today?

What can you and your teams do differently going forward to
better deliver our mission?

How will you embed it into plans and priorities?

The company-wide result will be a stronger consciousness about why
your business exists and new ideas about what they can do to lead it.
This is not rocket science and is really that simple. By doing this as
leaders, you send a big signal to the wider organization that delivery of
your *Inspired Mission* happens every day by everyone.

Oh, and this is not something you do once and check it off the list.
These are the questions you challenge your organization with from
this day forward. Mobile apps to supplement your efforts with this

have come a long way. Check out Officevibe as one great example.

You'll also need to update your incentive structures and performance and reward systems to make sure they don't work against you, and be sure that your organization's commitment to mission and values is loud and clear in your onboarding and recruitment processes. These are the basics.

Strategy 2: Organize around ideas, not silos

Companies that intentionally or unintentionally pursue profit-as-purpose, or business-model efficiencies, are breeding grounds for unproductive territories and silos. Unhelpful barriers and behaviors emerge and embed to the point where we stop noticing them. The same is true of companies who lack a strong sense of identity. That is, where their purpose is neither inspired nor clear. When you have an uninspired mission, there is typically only one winner and the best ideas get stuck or lost.

When Nike's mission was to be "The #1 Sporting Goods Company in the World," it created some very real and unintended consequences. When you have a big goal like that, it inherently has to be broken down. To be #1 in every Nike product category and to deliver as efficiently as possible, the organization effectively divided itself into three mega-divisions: footwear, apparel, and equipment. For many of us who were working there, here's how that structure played out on our worst days: Product teams disconnected and operated independently from each other and support functions like marketing, sales, and retail were torn between which product group to support. The internal product war in pursuit of #1 created unproductive competition and tension.

This is not unique to Nike. It happens in almost every company in every industry as companies grow. This is particularly true when the ultimate goal only matters to the company and no one else. In our experience, the pursuit of Nike's #1 mission in the late 1990s also led to organizational structures, leadership appointments, and processes designed to perpetuate it. Silos and territories were strengthened to support maximum efficiency in business units. While this brought about some important financial gains, the disproportionate emphasis on efficiencies eventually and negatively hit the bottom line.

With the benefit of hindsight, for a period of time Nike had fallen into the trap of pushing individual products instead of selling ideas and inspiration. Practically speaking, this played out in so many ways it could be a book on its own. The easiest place for someone outside the company to see it was on the retail floor.

When the team who designed the running shorts hadn't connected with the team designing running shoes or gym bags, the retail folks were left with a lot of product that didn't go together. Each product group also had its own merchandising software (that also didn't talk to each other), which only made things worse. The situation was more pronounced for women's product than men's because men's product at the time was mostly navy, gray, and black. That wasn't true for women's, so we'd find ourselves dealing with a mix of colors that clashed on the retail floor.

Nike had become three companies: a footwear company, an apparel company, and an equipment company. Individual products were disconnected at retail without stories or experiences to unite them. This led to some serious growing pains for one of the most consumer-centric organizations in the world.

The Nike example shows us how even the most sophisticated companies can fall into traps as they grow, particularly if the growth is not deliberately engineered to align to meaningful and uniting ideas. And while being #1 may have been a common goal across the company, it was not a uniting idea. In the end, in our experience, it divided us.

Eventually, the impact of the #1 mission made it into Nike's voice. This was around the time the company launched the "you don't win silver, you lose gold" ad campaign. Others launched during the 1996 Olympics included "I didn't come here to trade pins" and "If you're not here to win, you're a tourist." Needless to say, the public didn't respond kindly when everything the Olympic Games stood for was being openly insulted. Edginess for edginess' sake doesn't work. It was not the same company that gave us "Just do it." This was an imposter.

If you've ever operated under an internally focused, "let's become the #1 in our industry" mission (and there's a good chance you have), you might have experienced the same type of silos that get in the way of doing your best work and, frankly, having any real fun.

As we covered in Chapter 4, this chapter in Nike's history came to a close with the launch of its new mission statement: *To bring inspiration and innovation to every athlete* in the world. (*If you have a body, you're an athlete.)* Nike's new mission re-centered the organization on what was really important. It tapped into ideas that the world had previously responded to in the essence of "Just do it." It reimagined and vastly expanded Nike's target audiences, and created a new mandate for teams to work together.

But the hardest part of this fairy tale was still to come: realigning a very large and complex organization to serve an entirely new and much bigger ambition. Ever had concrete fully set in and then wish you'd laid it somewhere else?

It's hard to undo, but not impossible.

Structure your organization in favor of your mission

After years of aligning to the "#1 sporting goods company" mission, Nike had a lot of internal realignment work to do. To achieve its more *Inspired Mission*, the company needed to find a better balance between efficient product engines and transferring power to consumers who love sports. Nike fought hard to achieve this over more than a decade, with several reorganizations. Today, a core dimension of the company is structured around sport categories (running, basketball, football, training, etc.). An equally important decision was made to bring the separate footwear, apparel, and equipment divisions together under one leader to better enable them to partner with the sport categories and serve consumers.

These combined moves were a big deal. Nike had now structured itself in favor of consumers. That put the kids who love basketball, football, running, fitness, or whatever at the center of the company's organizational framework. Once that happened, our only job was to inspire and innovate for every one of them.

Having been at the company before, during, and after the realignment, we can say that this sounds easier than it was (it took several tries to get it right). We can also say the impact over time was dramatic. Nike was back to selling integrated ideas, stories, and inspiration.

Of course, the focus on product didn't go away. It's just that the balance got better. Now kids and their sport of choice became what mattered most. As for the result of that from a business standpoint, they say a picture is worth a thousand words.

Figure 6: NIKE vs. the Dow Jones Industrial Average and S&P 500

Strategy 3: Build bridges between mission, values and day-to-day decisions

Leaders make decisions every day. Some are big; some are small.

As Kenichi Ohmae, a mentor to one of the authors and a long-time strategic advisor to some of Japan's and the world's largest corporations puts it, " . . . large companies and their internal departments will always be somewhat set up to fight each other."

But what if we could lighten the load of that bureaucratic tension that creates so much internal distraction? When you can make decisions through the lens of a big idea that people have bought into, it makes the decisions and their ultimate delivery so much easier. Creating an environment for this to happen is crucial to aligning your organization. It'll also be a lot more fun than the old way of doing things.

Patagonia goes as far as providing a framework and set of guideposts to support internal decision-making. In the book *Let My People Go Surfing*, Patagonia founder Yvon Chouinard lays out a mission to preserve the environment. Not a CSR commitment. An entire corporate mission commitment. Chouinard's theory is that existing corporate systems are at odds with Patagonia's mission, so a new kind of corporate values must be developed – most notably: "All decisions of the company are made in the context of the environmental crisis." Where Chouinard really enters groundbreaking territory is in outlining the guiding philosophies and their specific relationships to product design, production, distribution, brand, finances, human resources, management, and environmental impact. Chouinard intends for these principles to outlive him, ultimately standing the test of time – or, as he's said, at least 100 years.

By overtly providing these guidelines, Patagonia extends the authority to deliver on the mission to its people. Rather than focus exclusively on transactional measures of success within a function, the message is that every function should be delivering on this mission. So, find ways to be intentional about it, measure it, and lead it.

Nike has similar guidelines for the similar purpose of connecting a big audacious mission to daily behavior – but Nike's are expressed in fewer than 50 words, not a whole book. Brevity is intentional, making them easy to remember. Pretty much any Nike alum can cite the Maxims long after departing the company. Next time you meet one, ask.

For Nike employees, the Maxims articulate clear behavior expectations and serve as filters for decision-making. We recall them being integrated into every strategy document, used consistently in leadership communications, and visually prominent in office locations globally. Enormous effort was, and still is, put into an annual Maxims award ceremony (similar to the Oscars but with more comfortable shoes). There's an award given for each Maxim, highlighting an exemplary effort in the previous year from a list of finalists. Employees and teams are acknowledged and celebrated by their peers and management in an extraordinary way – and the whole company is exposed to a fresh set of examples of the Maxims and mission in action. Thanks to these deliberate efforts, Nike's Maxims are more than a plaque on a wall; they are a living, breathing aspect of everyday life at the company. The Maxims are revered at Nike as a contract for how the business is run. They even remind everyone in Maxim 11 to "remember the man" – the company's co-founder, Bill Bowerman, and his original obsession with "making athletes better." Openly celebrating behavior aligned with purpose is the best way to make sure you deliver it.

Nike's 11 Maxims
It is our nature to innovate.
Nike is a company.
Nike is a brand.
Simplify and go.
The consumer decides.
Be a sponge.
Evolve immediately.
Do the right thing.
Master the fundamentals.
We are on the offense – always.
Remember the man.*
[the late Bill Bowerman, Nike co-founder]

Setting clear expectations and creating a deliberate bridge between your mission or purpose and how it translates into daily behavior works for Nike and Patagonia. It's different from a general set of values published in isolation of your mission statement.

On the other side of the world, Kao Corporation's version of the Maxims is called The Kao Way. Kao is a large Japanese company dedicated to *creating products that enrich people's lives*. They have a diversified portfolio ranging from household cleaning products, to healthy beverages, to cosmetics and skin care. They do not consider themselves a "fashionable company" – fancy awards ceremonies are not for them. In Japanese they describe themselves as "guchoku" – otherwise known as "diligent, a bit boring, and straight." Kao's stock price has increased 260 percent over 10 years,[66] they have enjoyed steady increases in revenue and net profits, experience almost no unplanned staff turnover, and are one of the few companies in the world to be honored 12 times in 12 years by Ethisphere's "World's Most Ethical Companies."[67] Oh, and they most recently won the Grand Prize for Japan's Corporate Governance Company of the year award for focusing on mid- to long-term profitability.[68]

For a company that claims to be "a bit boring," they are certainly winning a lot.

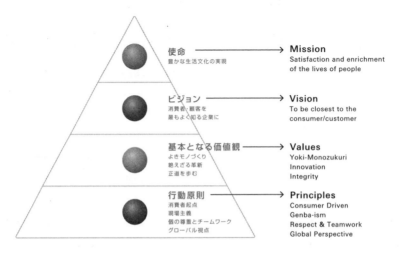

The Kao Way. (Image from KAO Corporation)

Chief executive Michitaka Sawada believes The Kao Way is a key driver of their success. Just over 10 years ago, Sawada decided to turn what was an intuitive way of working at Kao into an identifiable icon and practice that would be reinforced daily. It specifically links Kao's purpose, values, and principles for running the business.

Now imagine this icon appearing in the physical environment where Kao runs its operations – even as far afield as Germany, where the icon has been displayed on the side of large company water tanks, visible to the whole surrounding community.

KAO Corporation manufacturing facility in Germany. (Image from KAO Corporation)

It is not unusual for a Japanese company (or any company) to have this type of framework. It is unusual, however, for that framework to be consistently acknowledged and referred to in the course of everyday work, for the chief executive to routinely talk about it, and for it to show up in unexpected places. The result reinforces The Kao Way for everyone.

Building practical bridges to reach a huge new powerful mission statement and a defining set of values is essential to an *Inspired Company's* future achievements. In the preceding chapter, we reviewed how insurance industry chief executive Mark Wilson pushed hard to articulate a distinctive set of values for Aviva and a purpose that would make a difference. A year or two in, a number of important learnings emerged. The first was that the new mission and values resonated most with employees who worked closely with him or directly with customers. Beyond that, though, they weren't having enough impact. "Bridging the gap to reach [our] middle management layer is crucial to success," says Wilson. Among many chief executives, this phenomenon is referred to as the impenetrable internal permafrost.

Enter the agora.

Agora is the Greek word for gathering. In Athens, the agora was the central marketplace and center of the city's civic life. For Mark, the agora is seen as an "icon for change," and he invested to make the concept a feature of all Aviva offices around the world. It's a place to encourage discussion and debate and a way for employees to experience Aviva's purpose and values. Big or small, conservative or quirky, local offices design their own agorae and use them for team and company meetings. Hierarchy and silos are not welcome in agorae.

The unique design of the agora flips the traditional presenter-audience dynamic. It has the audience surrounding the speaker and sitting higher. A foam-ball microphone is tossed about during meetings to determine who speaks next, and audience members engage directly with each other. "It works a charm," says Wilson. "You can only speak if you have the ball. It takes hierarchy out of the equation, makes each voice important and the discussion more honest."

Agorae have been an iconic feature of Aviva's offices around the world. Mark made it a priority to do things like this as a practical way of breaking down silos and building bridges to align the organization.

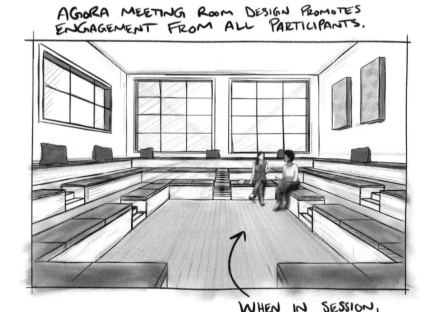

Artist's impression of Agora meeting room (Artist: Mitchell Rush)

There are many ways to create bridges to a company's purpose. To be effective, they need to be simple, iconic, and memorable. They'll also need to be repeated, embedded, celebrated, and reinforced to the point where they become a natural part of organizational culture and language. Sometimes, it can mean operationalizing the mission by finding ways to put power directly into the hands of the people who can deliver.

For the past 14 years, that's exactly what BT (formerly British Telecom) has done. They run a company-wide annual competition called The Challenge Cup. To be part of it, all an employee needs is a customer-facing issue they want to fix. They then need to form a diverse team of people from across the company – perhaps people they've never worked with or even met before. Over 12 years, the

Challenge Cup has become so popular and high profile that in effect, almost all entries end up supported and prioritized from somewhere within the company in some way. This means that internal hurdles are cleared away and typically disconnected departments find ways to make things happen together.

In 2017, the winning Challenge Cup team focused on reducing mobile network not-spots (aka dead zones) across the U.K. Anyone who's ever tried to make an uninterrupted call there will be delighted to hear about these efforts. The basic idea was to install 4G cells (base stations) on utility poles. This wasn't a new idea. People in the company had kicked it around for years, but the hurdles seemed insurmountable. For one, CapEx approval was next to impossible when it had to compete with investments like laying new fiber. Then, individual local village councils needed to approve the project, new equipment had to be designed to fit within existing utility pole boxes, crews needed to be deployed, feasibility tests had to address noise pollution … The point being, delivering on this idea was always going to be a massive undertaking that involved a lot of players inside and outside BT. Competing priorities had always won out in the past.

This is where the power of a competition fueled by a meaningful purpose comes in. BT's purpose is *to use the power of communications to make a better world.* The requirement to explain how team entries delivered on BT's purpose was always embedded in the subtext of the competition guidelines. But in 2017 the scorecard and entry categories featured "delivering our purpose" much more overtly. In doing so, it not only increased participation in the competition, it increased diversity of participation across BT's employee base by debunking the perception that the competition was only for technical and operations endeavors.

2017's winning team were driven by a powerful sense of purpose. In this case, the injustice that manifests when remote populations don't have access to the internet or other communications technologies. Over the next three years, the team will be supported to deliver access to 800 out-of-the-way villages across the U.K. They are now an official task force within the company, able to fast-track capital investment approval processes, product innovation requirements, and more resources to help resolve regulatory obstacles with local councils to get it done. The result will newly connect 400,000 U.K. citizens who were previously locked out of ways to compete, apply for jobs, learn new things, and connect with distant family members.

What's interesting about this example is that it shows how companies sometimes already have the muscles in place to succeed. Sometimes all they need to do is flex them. For more than a decade, BT has worked to refine and strengthen the Challenge Cup into a system that breaks the silos and hierarchies that too often plague large companies from delivering. They've built a muscle to get big things done in a way that serves their big inspiring purpose.

BT started with an internal competition. In 2017, nearly 7,000 employees from 37 countries participated. To us, that's no ordinary employee competition – that's a powerful bridge for *Obsessive Alignment.*

Strategy 4: Define and measure KPIs the crowd cares about

What you measure and reward in your company is one of the most powerful drivers of organizational alignment. Company performance metrics deeply influence behavior, prioritization, and decision-making. They have a miraculous ability to focus the individual and collective efforts of employees and leaders. That's why flipping the whole approach to performance metrics in favor of an *Inspired Mission* is critical to an *Inspired Company's* success.

In a world where *Moneyball* and *Freakonomics* are best sellers, data scientists are the hot new hires, and algorithm is a commonly used word, there is still a lot of room for improvement on what gets measured and rewarded in companies.

Inspired Companies evolve their metrics, reporting, and reward systems to account for what matters to the *crowd.* At the broadest

level, we see two promising strategies emerging here that we will
address in turn.

- First, the best companies *upgrade their baseline efforts*, metrics, and
  reporting to be better at and more transparent on the environmental, social,
  and governance (ESG) aspects of their business.

- Second, the best companies *identify and measure big-picture metrics*
  that link directly to their mission.

Doing both is essential to driving the right behaviors and creating a
strong enough base to pursue more aggressive *Inspired Action* down
the track. We have seen companies that are earnestly trying to reorient
themselves to an *Inspired Mission* and that miss this fundamental part of
the equation. Then they wonder why they aren't reaping the benefits of
being purpose-led. It's as simple as this: you won't be able to deliver a
meaningful purpose if you don't have the metrics to match.

4.1 A more inspired baseline for ESG

The *crowd* (and this includes investors) expects today's companies
to demonstrate a higher baseline level of accountability. The new
baseline requires increased effort and better information on your
environmental, social, and governance activities – general proof that
you aren't a bad actor. Large companies will get heat for being overly
secretive or opaque about their behavior, and they'll be buried once
flaws are discovered. By definition, it's not possible to be an *Inspired
Company* without meeting the new baseline.

Take Rip Curl, for example. The Australian surfing company
makes strong claims about their sustainability commitments. They
have great initiatives to clean the ocean and, compared to many
others, may be doing a good job. Unfortunately for Rip Curl, "good"
isn't always good enough these days. In 2016, the *Sydney Morning
Herald* reported that Rip Curl had sold millions of dollars' worth of
product labeled as "Made in China," but that was actually produced in

"slave-like conditions" in North Korea.[69] The same report published management's response on social media:

> We are very sorry that Rip Curl has breached the trust our customers put in us to make sure that the products they wear cause them no moral concern. That's our responsibility to you and we have let you down on this one. The Founders and Directors of Rip Curl take full responsibility for this screw up . . . We were made aware of this some months ago and took immediate steps to investigate and rectify the situation . . . Regardless of this, two styles totaling (sic) 4,000 units of Rip Curl ski wear did slip through and was shipped to customers.[70]

Most of that message was perfect. The part that wasn't created huge problems for the company. Here was the response from a media outlet[71] that is representative of what many had to say at the time:

> Sorry, did you just say, "slipped through?" 4,000 ski jackets, suits, and pants? That's one hell of a crack. Possibly more of a crevasse into which Rip Curl's trust, reputation, and image are all now plummeting.

The same article pulled in a range of responses from the *crowd*.

> You expect us to believe you didn't know where your garments were being made? Are you kidding? Do you just draw up some designs and send them off to "Asia" and hope for the best?
>
> Ignorance is no excuse. If a major company (or a small one for that matter) does not check where their stock is being sourced from, there is something wrong.

In this case, one of Rip Curl's suppliers had reportedly diverted orders to an unauthorized supplier in North Korea.[72] This is not uncommon in the apparel industry, but that doesn't make it okay. Your supply chain might be 95 percent clean, but the last 5 percent will painfully punish you when the *crowd* finds out about it.

We deliberately use this example to illustrate how high the bar is today. Pushing for a more *inspired ESG baseline* will help mitigate against the increased risks associated with supply chain weaknesses. Weaknesses that exist in any business, and risks that are more costly than ever to ignore.

The upside is equally if not more compelling, however. Companies that prioritize and embed ESG impact activities into core business operations enjoy higher valuations and earnings. Research published in October 2017 reveals just how significant the reinforcing link is: 11 percent higher valuation for companies in consumer products group, 12 percent in pharmaceuticals, and up to 19 percent in oil and gas compared to peer group companies that don't.[73] Turns out that best-in-class ESG strategies create competitive advantage.

Take Huawei, for example. The company had cell phone technology that wasn't compatible with U.K. or European energy-efficiency expectations. To make inroads in the European market, they would need smaller, greener, higher-performing technology.

To meet expectations they could have just matched to the specifications of other European competitor products and made it cheaper. But that's not been part of Huawei's track record. In the end, they didn't just create more energy-efficient base stations when they entered Europe. They created a distributed system that enabled radio access for everyone from Mt Everest to the Arctic Circle.[74] This ultimately ended up cheaper for European cellular carriers, exceeded expectations on environmental sustainability, and also proved to deliver better mobile performance. It also helped Huawei to chip away at Apple and Samsung's market share in countries outside of China.[75]

Here's another tip: to move your company's baseline ESG activity and reporting to a new level, don't get caught in the trap of immediately turning to global social and environmental indexes to determine what to measure. You may end up measuring everything but lose sight of the most important issues impacting your specific business. Instead, this is a key moment to turn to your *crowd* for answers – *then* find the indicators and indices that match their priorities.

In practical terms, periodically pull a diverse and representative base of **C**onsumers, **E**mployees, and **O**utsiders together to identify the most important issues to your business 5, 10, 20, and 30 years out. The issues should be 100 percent stakeholder driven. Then turn to the indexing and reporting experts and don't recreate the wheel. Leverage work already done to push your company's baseline commitments and reporting to a more sophisticated level, and at the same time decrease the risk of supply chain and governance issues, and push your social impact and innovation agenda further forward.

The Global Reporting Initiative, or GRI, has created a broad and consistent reporting framework to help businesses and governments worldwide understand and communicate their impact on critical sustainability issues such as climate change, human rights, governance, and social wellbeing.[76] It's an incredibly valuable resource to challenge your existing approach.

For increased impact and comparability, you can then selectively choose from a range of indices that specialize in the issues that disproportionately impact your specific business. B Lab (which certifies B Corps, for example) has created B Impact Assessment and B Analytics to help companies measure what matters most to their individual industry sector. Leaders of B Corps say one of the most valuable things about being a B Corp is the set of external measures that are benchmarked against other companies in their same industry. It upgrades their accountability to a different and broader set of KPIs, allows them to see what's already possible, and forces them to lead with greater context. Even if you don't want to register as a B Corp, look at leveraging the work that has already been done to upgrade and guide the way you identify, commit, measure, and report on ESG practices.*

By now, at least one thing should be obvious. *Inspired Companies* think bigger than baseline. While everyone else is trying to reduce their carbon footprint, more *Inspired Companies* are aiming to add back more than they take. Take a look at a U.S.-based company called Interface. They're not exactly the biggest carpet manufacturer in the world, but that didn't stop them from rejecting their industry's notoriously consumptive norms. In 1997, the company set Mission Zero *to eliminate any negative impact Interface has on the environment by 2020*. That means *zero* greenhouse gas emissions, waste, or net water use among other things. And while we said earlier that committing to environmental best practices doesn't make you an *Inspired Company*, Interface might be a rare exception. Carpet manufacturing processes involve heavy use of materials, while delivery, installation, removal, and disposal are resource-plundering activities. This is something people inside and outside the industry simply accept. In that context, Interface doesn't just set a good example. They've completely revolutionized how business in their industry is done.

By 2016, these kinds of goals were more common and Interface was well ahead of schedule. Not content to sit back and congratulate themselves on a job well done, Interface shocked the industry once again. The company announced the next evolution of Mission Zero: Climate Take Back. The new goal is about going from negative (reducing) to positive (restoring).

The concept of a net positive contribution to the world speaks to where society has now moved. People expect more from today's companies and they think companies should expect more of themselves. As one of Interface's partners puts it, "If we're reducing emissions by 50 percent, we're still 50 percent bad." What he means is

---

* B Corp is currently in 50 countries and covers 140 industries. For more information see www.bcorporation.net/what-are-b-corps/about-b-lab.

that it's not enough to be less bad in today's world. Because being less bad is not the same thing as being good.

Another company that understands how a high bar for ESG outcomes is a prerequisite for becoming inspired is BT. As a reminder, BT uses *the power of communications to make a better world*. That's their unique inspiration and they have doubled down on their goals and their reporting as part of that commitment. BT's leaders use a scorecard that organizes business objectives into areas like sustainable business practices, building a culture of tech literacy, and employee volunteerism. To make sure they're tracking toward an even bigger picture, BT has set ambitious 2020 targets that include working with their global base of customers to achieve a 3:1 net positive carbon abatement and helping 10 million people overcome social disadvantage by connecting them into the digital age. The targets are designed to align with the United Nations' Sustainable Development Goals (SDGs). The picture doesn't get much bigger than that. And it's not just the Chief Sustainability Officer's pay that gets hit if they miss their targets: 20 percent of compensation for BT's chief executive, and each of the divisional CEO's, is linked to the delivery of the targets.

What BT's doing is obviously a great thing for society, but it's no coincidence that these areas will also serve to make the company more competitive. Tech literacy – a big part of their community-giving emphasis – empowers young people to participate more fully in digital communications and the opportunities that can come from that, while expanding the market for BT's services. As for employee engagement, think about who these employees are. You're talking about in-demand technical talent, skilled trade workers, and customer service reps with specialized expertise. In many cases, these are employees with options. Lots of them. BT employees volunteer thousands of hours each year to deliver tech literacy training to teachers across the U.K., who in turn teach children to be better prepared to safely navigate the digital era and transition into a future of work that increasingly requires digital communications and technology expertise.

Put simply, BT is thinking long term. They're making sure the environment they operate in continues to be sustainable, that society has the skills they need to benefit from their products and services, and that the employees who drive the company forward actually want to be there. These social and environmental responsibility investments are building blocks for BT's future success, and as such they measure progress and tie performance accountability back to them aggressively.

BT's efforts don't stop within their own walls; they actively engage the *crowd* in their efforts. That includes the company's business partners. For example, Sagemcom worked with BT to design an energy-efficient router called the BT Home Hub 5 that, through various new design features, reduces power consumption by 30 percent and saves over 13,000 tons of carbon emissions a year. One very practical feature is that the router is designed to fit through standard mail slots, reducing return trips by delivery drivers and delighting customers who no longer need to wait unnecessarily to get their high-speed internet service up and running.

Accelerated by their ambitious 2020 social impact targets, BT has taken these types of partnerships to entirely new levels by introducing sustainability clauses into their supplier contracts. BT's supplier contract with Huawei, for example, includes a requirement for the Chinese company to review the carbon performance of its supply chain and make emissions savings over the five-year contract term.[77] BT didn't have to fight with Huawei to make this happen. The two companies are committed to making improvements all the way through the value chain, and both recognize mutual value when they see it.

Just like most companies, BT, Interface, or Huawei don't get everything right. But their efforts and achievements in this area unequivocally move the baseline for excellence in ESG to levels difficult to catch up to if you're in their competitive set. And just as the Rip Curl example painfully highlights, it's the not-so-perfect 5 percent, not the perfect 95 percent today that will awaken the *crowd* to work for or against you.

4.2 Measure the big picture

You can see where this is going. *Inspired Companies* find ways to meet or exceed the new baseline expectations for ESG. What sets them even further apart, however, is when they take the next step. Here's what we mean by that:

Nike won't survive if the world around them is becoming more and more physically inactive. Neither will ESPN. Coca-Cola won't continue to dominate grocery store shelves if diabetes and obesity continue to spiral out of control. Banks rely on real families and communities to have some level of financial prosperity for loan products to be viable. These are material human issues that will get in the way of sustained growth for each of these industries if not addressed. They are bigger than any single company or organization. And they are issues the broader *crowd* really cares about.

In practical terms, companies don't do this very well today. (Or if they do, they're making quite a secret of it.) However, there are a few bright spots that play out in two ways, broadly speaking:

1. The use of big-picture data as a lightning rod to mobilize broader action inside or outside the company;

2. Integrating big-picture KPIs into formal company reporting.

Some companies like Tony's Chocolonely and Tesla (as you'll see below) are clear enough in their convictions that they can jump right into the second point. For the rest of us, the first point is a good place to start.

Use data as a lightning rod to mobilize action

If Nike is going *to bring inspiration and innovation to **every athlete** in the world*, where the word "athlete" means "everyone," Nike needs to know a lot about the state of physical activity around the world. To gain that knowledge, in 2010 an internal group called "Access to Sport" was founded. It subsequently invested heavily to synthesize the existing global research base and commission new research.

The research uncovered that today's generation of children is *the least active in history*. We know exactly how serious the data was because one of us founded and led this work. For a company that obsesses over sport every hour of every day, the seriousness of the data took us all off guard. We dug deeper, partnering with many more organizations in government, academia, and at the grassroots level to learn as much as we could. The full research base was collated and published under the banner of a global alliance we created called Designed to Move.* It revealed the magnitude of the global physical inactivity epidemic and outlined how the dramatic decline in children's physical activity levels negatively impacts almost every aspect of their life – from academic performance and behavior to how much they'll earn in the future and how long they'll live.

Getting kids moving so that they become healthy, active adults is a place where Nike's expertise and future outlook directly intersects with what's good for the whole world. Physical inactivity is a direct threat to Nike's mission. Solving for it became a big idea that the rest of the company, and potentially the world, could rally around. The data and action framework in Designed to Move made Nike's mission personal for employees and anyone else who cares about kids.

---

* "Designed to Move" was co-authored by Nike, the American College of Sports Medicine, and the International Council of Sports Science and Physical Activity. It was peer-reviewed by over 25 internationally representative expert organizations, synthesized over 500 pieces of research, and has subsequently been endorsed and adopted by several hundred organizations.

Acting on it as a company became a no-brainer.

As Designed to Move became more broadly known across the company, employees and leaders were inspired to do something. Sports marketing started thinking about how athletes' voices could be used more deliberately and in unison to encourage children to be more active. Nike's athletes responded in force: Paula Radcliffe, Alyson Felix, LeBron James, Sarah Reinertsen, Kobe Bryant, and many others have since done a brilliant job inspiring the world not only to play sports, but to move more in general.

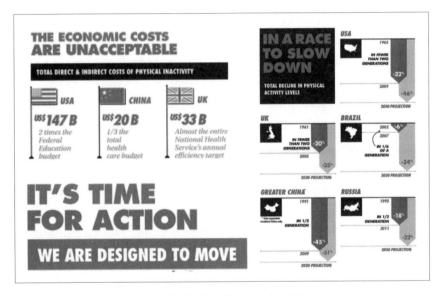

Extracts from the Framework for Action, Designed to Move.

Nike athletes weren't the only ones inspired to take action. They were just the beginning. Across Nike, teams rallied. For example, when the research revealed how children's sports experiences before the age of 10 would shape their behavior for life, Pat Zeedick (then VP of Nike's global kids' business) knew that there was more she could do. At that time, visual branding for the kids' business focused on the core sports of basketball, football, and running. This lined up nicely with Nike's new sports category business focus but it didn't show the variety of activities that the research proved kids needed to thrive. So Pat changed it. The creative direction of the kids' business evolved to include everything from dance and parkour to skateboarding, martial arts, *and also* the core categories of basketball, football, and running. It didn't matter whether Nike made specific equipment for all of those activities. What mattered was that Nike was still able to use the huge influence and power of its brand to send a message that whatever sport or activity you love, just do it. "It was the right move for the world and for the business," says Zeedick.

Internal momentum continued to build, sparked by the urgency and implications of the data. Nike's facilities team came up with a plan to look at all of Nike's workspaces and buildings to encourage all employees to move more (not just the ones already on the soccer field every day). The daycare center increased their efforts to ensure that kids and teachers were moving as much as possible during the day and that the activities were assessed to better ensure great experiences for all kids, not just some of them. Nike retail stores rolled out programs and evolved existing ones to work with schools and community groups in their local areas to deliver great sport and physical activity programs to kids who wouldn't otherwise have had the chance to participate. Country offices from Brazil to China to the U.K. and Mexico partnered with local organizations to train coaches and create more positive experiences for kids to be active.

The physical inactivity numbers weren't formal KPIs or line items in Nike's annual report. They were a call to action that inspired teams across Nike's global business to do something about it and subsequently became a priority in many functional plans.

The next level is for companies like Nike to figure out how this type of data translates into KPIs and integrates into formal reporting practices, complete with opportunities and risks to the future of the business and industry. Tesla and Tony's Chocolonely are already demonstrating how to do that.

Directly connect into big-picture KPIs

Let's start with Tesla, the energy company that in the beginning we all thought was a car company. With their updated mission *to accelerate the advent of sustainable energy*, it's clear that energy-efficient cars are just one of the products that can help Tesla achieve its mission. Battery-powered home energy is another. In 2015, Tesla announced the Powerwall, a battery system that can power homes and businesses.

Obviously, the company looks at market potential and reduced production costs when determining the commercial viability of a new product. However, in its Q1 2015 investor letter, Tesla executives hinted at a hugely inspired metric for Powerwall: "When combined with low-cost renewable energy, Tesla Energy batteries provide an achievable pathway to a 100 percent zero carbon energy system."[78]

Key to achieving that ambitious goal is Tesla's Gigafactory investment (the Nevada-based factory where Tesla batteries are made). Though operational, Gigafactory was only 30 percent complete by the last quarter of 2018.[79] Tesla intends to build more Gigafactories and, while it's not an expressed KPI (yet), Tesla's chief Elon Musk has given a sense of the big picture: "We actually did the calculations to figure out what it would take to transition the whole world to sustainable energy. You'd need 100 Gigafactories."[80]

Tony's Chocolonely is another company showing us just what big, audacious KPIs look like. Tony's is into making slave-free chocolate. But the thing is, they don't just want to make slave-free chocolate themselves. They want to make the whole industry slave-free – a pretty big deal since most of the major chocolate producers admit to supply chains tainted by child and slave labor.

Of course, Tony's has goals and metrics related to their financial health – revenue growth, net profit, market share, brand preference, and the like. Like many companies, they also look at their environmental footprint, aiming for full carbon offset, as well as offset across their supply chain, and initiatives to replant harvested product. But let's look at this slave-free business. "Tony's vision is 100 percent slave-free chocolate." In their 2016 annual report,[81] they specifically outline three key strategies to bring the whole industry in line with this vision: create awareness, lead by example, inspire imitation.

Tony's has figured out how to blend their financial measurements and results, along with the bigger-picture metrics associated with ending slavery in the chocolate trade. They invested heavily in understanding the supply chain – from sourcing and transporting cocoa to producing and distributing chocolate. They know where the majority of cocoa is sourced from, the issues faced by cocoa farmers and their families, and the concentration of buyers around the world. Remember that we are not talking about Cadbury's here. We're talking about an Amsterdam-based startup, founded in 2005, showing everyone how it's done.

As a matter of course, Tony's measures the number of cocoa farmers making a livable income and cases of illegal child labor and slavery across the industry. To enable imitation, they look carefully at governance and accountability across their supply chain, report transparently on issues, publish specific goals like those to increase the number of farmers trained to produce their product, and publish openly their entire sourcing and manufacturing process for anyone to copy. They also don't overstate their own results: they say their chocolate is "practically" slave-free. This accounts for the reality that they can't monitor all of their farmers all of the time. What's important is when they find a problem, they immediately look for a solution. A child working on a farm may indicate inexcusable trafficking; it may also be the result of a family struggling deeply with poverty. Claiming Tony's chocolate is 100 percent slave-free *now* would not allow others to see the full complexity of the issue – or bring their full creativity and innovation to solutions.

One of the coolest things is how Tony's figured out what to measure. Would you believe they actually asked the people their strategy impacted? So, these folks:

team Tony's | the cocoa farmers and their cooperatives | consumers | customers | suppliers

(Image from Tony's Chocolonely 2016 Annual FAIR Report)

Tony's customers, cocoa farmers, consumers, customers, and suppliers: looks like the *crowd* of *new C.E.O.s* to us.

Tony's figured out they had a ton of alignment with the *crowd* when it comes to what matters most. It turns out the cocoa farmers' wellbeing is at the top of everyone's list, while climate change and the relationship between chocolate and health are pretty important to their stakeholders. The big lesson here is you can learn some cool stuff when you bother to ask your *crowd*.

The standard KPIs that companies have tracked for decades don't communicate the broader picture of good or bad performance, and they don't reflect the real work of an *Inspired Company*. *Inspired Companies* need a more evolved set of KPIs that do a better job of confirming a company's authentic commitment to an *Inspired Mission*. If the new metrics are big enough, it also paints a clearer picture of the larger playing field they will have access to move into.

In pursuit of becoming an *Inspired Company*, you'll need to identify the best ways to measure progress in a way that works for your *crowd*. Doing it well will require new partnerships. Financial services that measure larger-scale community prosperity will need to partner with local governments, councils, and universities. Sports apparel manufacturers will need to collaborate with health departments to measure physical inactivity rates. Delivering on shared metrics will strengthen the tie between an *Inspired Company* and the *crowd*, reinforce the shared pursuit of big ideas, and build trust through deeper levels of shared accountability.

New reporting standards are coming. Fast.

As *Inspired Companies* become the rule rather than the exception, success metrics that matter to a broader set of stakeholders will increasingly be acknowledged as essential to success. Standard reporting requirements will have to adjust.

We don't think this is far off. In fact, we have witnessed an acceleration of thought leadership groups, global alliances, research papers, and frameworks published with increasing levels of sophistication on the topic.

One such initiative is the Embankment Project for Inclusive Capitalism.[82] Formed in early 2017 and led by Ernst and Young, the initiative brought together over 30 of the world's leading companies and investors, representing almost US$30 trillion of assets under management. Its vision is to make long-term investment the norm. A central deliverable of the initiative is standardized metrics that measure how companies deliver value for all stakeholders. This framework contains categories beyond financial value, to include measures for societal value, human value, and consumer value. It assesses these categories through their overall implications for investors – as well as customers, suppliers, employees, and governments.

New standards for reporting and measurement are coming. We predict they are right around the corner. Companies that move first to measure in these more evolved ways will mark the difference between companies that *say* big things and the companies that *do* big things; the companies that bring others along and the companies that push them away.

Strategy 5: Build new muscles

If you've been to any conferences in the past few years where they talk about running a purposeful business, you probably heard a lot of ambitious and visionary rhetoric. That's good. *Inspired Companies* won't get anywhere without ambition and vision. It's the rare meeting, however, where someone is brave enough to say, "This is really hard." And it is. Particularly for established companies, reorienting your company to be outward-facing and to draw in the *crowd* will take some new muscles, unrelenting commitment, and a whole lot of patience.

Everything we've talked about here – distributing leadership from the start line, aligning your entire company to mission, structuring the company around ideas, and advancing bigger picture KPIs in partnership with others – raises a few questions. What new competencies and intelligence do we need? And who the hell is qualified to make this happen?

The words that make up a mission are easy to come by. Operationalizing those words and infusing them into every aspect of corporate action is nothing short of revolutionary. It also takes courageous leadership. None of it happens by accident. Planning for an *Inspired Company* is both art and science, head and heart.

Oh, and one other thing: The advice in this section isn't sequential. Trial and error will be a big part of your new obsession with alignment. Let people learn from their failures. Yes, that means making it okay to fail in the first place.

5.1 New levels of intelligence: get to know your crowd

You won't make much headway if you don't fully understand who it is that you're trying to get onside. We often talk about the *crowd* or *new C.E.O.*s in collective terms. But as pointed out in Chapter 2, in practice they are no more a homogenous group than "women" or "voters." For your business to gain the support, trust, and loyalty of the *crowd*, you'll need to understand who they are now and who they could be in the future.

Many companies have become quite good at understanding the nuances of their customers (just look at Amazon's product recommendations system or Google's ad targeting). Traditional consumer segmentation work has moved to an entirely new level. If you look at Enso's work on Brand World Value,[83] you'll see hyper-segmentation of consumers to better understand how they value brands. Sure, the study looks at millennials and moms like everyone else, but they also look at people who are active on social media, tech skeptics vs. tech enthusiasts, political/social activists, etc. This kind of deep segmentation is central to understanding the value people derive from your *Inspired Mission* or purpose, and how they are likely to connect with it and communicate about it. We explore this further in Chapter 10 *Inspired Profit* but, at a headline level, Enso is modernizing traditional consumer segmentation approaches so that it's no longer just a study of demographics and shopping preferences, but rather an analysis of what consumers care about and how your company's purpose and values impact the probability of brand affiliation. The Enso brand index is only in its infancy, but we think they're onto something very powerful.

Most companies rarely, if ever, go to this level of effort or granularity when they think about other influential parts of the *crowd* like the media, regulators, investors, or even their own employees. This matters. When you're pursuing a big idea, the list of people who can influence it today is expansive and fluid. We suggest investing however you can to get to know more of them.

So how do you build this particular muscle? It's not new to the corporate sector, although it goes by different names: ethnographic research, human-centered design, user-centered design, insights-driven design, good old "qualitative data." The gist of it is the same. It's Nike shadowing five high school cross-country runners for a day, gleaning insights that help drive core strategy across the whole U.S. women's running business. It's P&G trying to keep up with a busy mom with three kids and discovering that cold washing powder would make a huge difference in her day and ever-increasing energy bills. It takes diving into real lives, building actual relationships, and having the confidence that – if you pick the right people to hang out with and learn from – their needs and desires will lead you to broadly applicable insights that might just lead to your next big business breakthrough.

For many companies, this type of qualitative work is a huge leap of faith – especially in the era of big data, when we can collect information about the *crowd* at an unprecedented rate and in unprecedented volumes. Looking at a big mountain of data from a distance might feel reassuring – after all, there's safety in numbers. However, there is a big difference between collecting data and *translating* it into meaningful insights that lead to the next big business, product, or service innovation.

The good news is that companies can have it both ways today. While the internet enabled the problem of too much data and not enough intelligence, it does pose an opportunity to tap into the collective consciousness of your *crowd*, if used in a discerning way. The next time a research company says to you, "Are you looking for quant or qual?" say: "Both, please." While big data allows us to do and learn about things at a scale we have never achieved before, sometimes the most powerful insights will be drawn from far fewer but much deeper interactions with your *crowd*.

The payoff of getting to know your *crowd* is that you'll learn how to earn their trust. That competency will become mission-critical, as you'll see in the next chapter. This is the muscle that will ensure you'll do more than simply observe your *crowd*. You'll end up being able to invite them right into your business.

5.2 Prioritize competencies that drive alignment

Aligning an organization to pursue inspired ideas will very likely require dedicated support and reinforcement across business units and functions. And the larger a company is, the more important the strength of these competencies become. To fully turn the *crowd's* power in your company's favor, your organization will need leaders that can do two things really well:

1) Rally cross-functional teams around ideas

2) Build relationships that are multi-sector and multi-stakeholder

These are not the leading competencies most companies have recruited for in the past.

We are looking for leaders, planners, coaches, storytellers, and connectors. Translate that into the boxes we're used to putting people in and you'll find yourself re-examining your C-Suite, prioritizing strategic communications and strategic planning, and seeking those in your organization with multi-stakeholder, multi-sector experience.

Let's start at the top.

Don't be afraid to shake up the C-suite

We've already talked about how organizations can structure themselves to have a better chance of delivering inspired ideas. That philosophy needs to be owned throughout the organization, right up to the top leaders. Today's typical C-suite doesn't necessarily measure up. In his review of the historical evolution of executive leadership, Deloitte CMO Eamonn Kelly argues that over the past century, the pendulum has swung from *generalist* leaders who looked across the business to a bias toward *functional* leaders who tend to separate a company rather than unite it.[84]

Here's a quick overview of how Kelly describes this evolution: A century ago, a small group of generalist leaders was in command of organizational leadership and management accountability. By the 1980s, businesses found that general managers weren't equipped to handle the technical and functional expertise required by an increasingly global, competitive, and automated environment. Functional experts suddenly had a place to call home and made it to the C-suite. Over the next few decades, the size of the average executive team doubled. Suddenly we had a "chief of" just about everything – marketing, retail, product, operations, HR, finance, etc. In Kelly's opinion, this pendulum has swung too far.

By definition, *Inspired Companies* will need a C-suite that better balances generalists with functional experts to carry big ideas forward. Without deliberate processes, efforts, and leadership to mitigate it, the divisive tendency of functional experts will kick in. *Inspired Companies* will need more leaders who understand how to infuse ideas across organizations and with the outside world. We mean leaders with the ability to make more authentic connections, rally others around stories, and drive alignment through strategic plans that achieve purpose and business-model efficiencies in parallel.

Relationship builders: multi-stakeholder, multi-sector

Let's go beyond the C-Suite to the whole company. It turns out that one of the most important competencies for an *Inspired Company* goes completely unnoticed in most companies today. Delivering big ideas and growing a *crowd* of supporters requires playing well with others. Specifically, it means finding a shared vision, goals, and objectives outside the traditional corporate bubble. This is not a practiced skill set among most people in corporate environments.

Today, business leaders typically approach a meeting outside the corporate sector with one of two mindsets: "Get out as quickly as possible with minimal damage" (meetings with regulators) or "We'll tell you what's best, make a donation, and you can then get on with it" (meetings with civil society). Neither of these is a recipe for collaboration.

Fortunately, this is a skill set that can be taught. We both learned it at the Nike Foundation. When we started that work, we knew we'd need partners – other foundations, researchers, development banks, etc. In the early days of our new jobs at the Foundation, we'd show up to external partnership meetings with a slick presentation and a brilliant plan. Meanwhile, people who'd worked in poverty alleviation for decades looked at us like we were nuts. Those meetings went about as well as you think they did.

So where is all this new talent hiding? We get it. We're all in the midst of a pretty serious war for talent, and we just told you to go out and invest in the best of the best in areas you've never hired for before. Fortunately, these skill sets might be hiding in plain sight.

CSR and government affairs departments, corporate and private foundations, and other niche offices are the first places to look. While the people in these areas often work on local, national, or global development issues, they are underleveraged talent pools for a majority of companies today. These are the people who can gracefully navigate multiple sectors, diverse agendas, facilitate productive dialogue, and deliver meaningful and shared outcomes. That probably sounds a little on the touchy-feely side, but it's going to matter when achieving your *Inspired Mission* depends on the support of the media, regulators, activists, consumers, and any other outsiders you can think of.

For smaller companies, look at your sales teams and general managers on the ground. If anyone's in the trenches fostering relationships, it's them. Talent in sales, manufacturing, or retail is usually very attuned to working with people outside company walls. Another approach is to consider what happens when the sh#t hits the fan. Who do you call? That may well be your person and profile to build from.

Strategic communications: invest in your story

Evangelizing your company's narrative isn't the only job of your strategic communications team – but, for an *Inspired Company*, it's arguably the most important. *Inspired Companies* prioritize the development of their narrative and the right tools to spread it, inside the company and out. No matter how big or small a business is, aligning to an inspired idea should be marked as a historic moment. It's a huge milestone in the evolution and growth trajectory of the company.

Walt Disney is often quoted as having said, "Disneyland will never be completed. It will continue to grow as long as there is imagination left in the world." He's also credited with such gems as "If you can dream it, you can do it," and that he never loved a woman as much as he loved Mickey Mouse. Those are the sentiments that inspire and convince people that Disneyland is more than a place that counts visitors through a turnstile.

You know what else Walt Disney said? "Of all the things I've done, the most vital is coordinating those who work with me and aiming their efforts at a certain goal."[85] It may have been the 1950s, but Disney seemed to understand the importance of aligning his organization around the bigger idea.

In an *Inspired Company*, everyone has permission to lead the big idea. Big ideas require a groundswell of leadership. Just about anyone at Nike will tell you we spent a lot of time and money talking to ourselves – telling our story to people on the inside. Selling ideas internally and connecting it to a bigger picture was critical to success in Nike's culture. If you didn't have a compelling story aligned with mission and brand priorities, you wouldn't last 90 days.

As a leader, you can check all of the right boxes for technical acumen, but inspired leadership is what ultimately turns inspired ideas into reality. Good leaders at all levels of an organization set the tone, define the North Star and constantly remind everyone of where they're headed. They understand that making emotional connections accelerates buy-in and organic uptake of ideas. Inspired leaders talk about things the average person on the street would care about and make it okay to be irrationally, audaciously, and ridiculously committed to an inspired idea.

Large international companies will need to invest in creating a base of leaders and employees to evangelize the big idea in your purpose through storytelling in ways that translate across borders and cultures. This will probably mean increasing the capacity and effectiveness of internal communications teams and investing in training and up-skilling communications throughout the organization. It could also well involve serious investments in new academic research (to make the substantive case) and creative resources (to make a human and emotional case). In building your narrative, bring others in to make sure it works seamlessly internally and externally.

Powerful storytelling has always been effective, but these days it's non-negotiable. Your employees want to be part of pursuing meaningful ideas. If you don't provide an opportunity for them to do that, someone else will.

Strategic planning: turn the narrative into plans

Yeah, we know you're rolling your eyes. We've all seen strategic plans delivered by an overpaid consultant who doesn't understand the business. That is not what we're talking about here. If strategic communications drives the emotional case, good strategic planning will emphasize the rational and the practical. Taken together, it's a powerful combination.

An *Inspired Company* will need to invest in strategic planning as a competency because they're going to need to skillfully balance the needs of pursuing big ideas with running an efficient and profitable business – and they'll need to support this balance across the company. We put this work in front of executives at companies who believe (and we agree) that they're closer to the more inspired side of the spectrum. They all agreed that practical ways to support balancing delivery of results while doing everything to pursue purposeful missions were needed.

In many companies, strategic planning roles are often directly connected to finance. These folks are really financial planners. Other times strategic planners become the sacred unit of the chief executive's office and deployed for special projects. Both those roles are important, but neither of them is what we are suggesting here.

The skillset that balances the pursuit of big ideas with the reality of running efficient and focused businesses is something that over time ideally becomes a permanent skill of any general manager, ultimately showing up in everyday action. Pat Zeedick said, "This is important at every level of the company. Under pressure, when people are under tight timelines, panic (and exhaustion) can set in and a tendency to focus on short-term metrics, tactics, and results prevails." Creating the space for inspired, purpose-led thinking is difficult, but having it be someone's job on the team to help us all do that is a good place to start. Additionally, once invested in as a new muscle, strategic planning is a competency that can emerge as an agile force when the company is under the greatest pressure to derail from its mission.

You can probably tell at this point that we are passionate about this one.

To sum up, high-quality strategic planning should be a priority competency, particularly in more complex matrix-style companies. Their role in *Inspired Companies* is to find ways to partner with leaders across a business and marry powerful communications narratives with practical execution plans that balance results with the pursuit of big ideas. Such planners can help drive a shortlist of ideas and challenge people to prioritize and focus before, during, and after transformation. This is what good strategic planners do.

Get all of this right and the real fun starts

We know we've covered a lot of ground here. Unless you're running a startup and working from a blank slate, wiring an entire company to look outward and align with a big *Inspired Mission* will never be easy. If it were, everyone would do it. But these are the pieces that make up the foundation of an *Inspired Company*. Once you get them in place, your employees will know you're serious. And they're ready to let the rest of the *crowd* know it – a recent global study found that 21 percent of employees already proactively communicate their allegiance to their company, while an additional 33 percent are highly likely to, based on their social media habits and level of engagement.[86] That's over half of employees. When a company gets behind an *Inspired Mission* and wires itself to deliver it, we think that number will be much higher.

With this critical start, you'll know your *crowd* a whole lot better and the base you create will lead you to an entirely new level of *Inspired Action*. You'll have a stronger lens to facilitate faster and better decision-making across an organization that translates your *Inspired Mission* into *Inspired Action*.

Chapter 6 Summary

Building an *Inspired Company* means wiring your organization to pursue big ideas. There are a lot of ways to do this:

- Distribute leadership at the start line
- Organize around ideas, not business-model silos
- Build deliberate bridges between mission, values, and day-to-day decisions
- Define and measure KPIs the *crowd* cares about:
  - A new baseline for ESG metrics
  - Measure the big picture
- Build new muscles
  - Get to know your *crowd*: Aim for new levels of intelligence
  - Invest in competencies that drive alignment:
    - Shake up the C-Suite
    - Multi-stakeholder relationship building
    - Strategic communications
    - Strategic planning

The ultimate prize for doing the work of *Obsessive Alignment* is that it builds belief across your employee base. Once you have them onside and empowered to lead with purpose, you have a chance with the rest of the *crowd*.

Chapter 7

Inspired Action:
Shake up the System

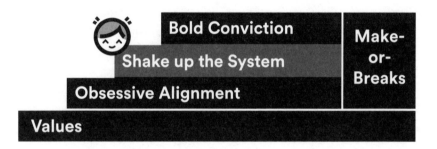

Lead with Courage

Say your company is already pursuing an *Inspired Mission.* You've worked hard to wire your organization using all of the levers you have available – your organizational structure and leadership appointments, success metrics, internal communications, planning processes, and unlocking the passion and everyday action of your people. It's a big lift. A necessary and ongoing lift. But you're not breaking through yet.

Here's why: Companies today sit inside a larger corporate system designed to fight for short-term gain and temper big ideas. For better or worse, we have come to expect companies will eventually comply with this system. To fight it, you'll need to enlist the power of the broader *crowd,* show them you can be trusted, and prove you're prepared to shake things up.

In This Chapter

- The next step of *Inspired Action* is to lead with courage. Show the world you're serious by demonstrating your commitment to the *crowd* and *Inspired Mission* in brave new ways

- See how breaking rules and defying industry norms might be necessary when they get in the way of your mission and challenge the way chief executives have traditionally shown up for work

- Learn how to burst corporate bubbles and let the outside in. See how some companies leverage the passion and expertise of the *crowd* to drive innovation, brand communications, and anything else we would usually shut them out of

- Explore how *shaking up the system* will bring more of the *crowd* onside and give them reasons to become your brand ambassador, champion and defender

This next phase is not about declaring success on the work of *Obsessive Alignment* and moving on. It's about layering big, authentic, and visible moves on top of that work to show the world beyond your employees that you're serious.

Here we cover some of the ways the more *Inspired Companies* are *shaking up the system*:

- Reimagine the top job

- Bring the *new C.E.O.s* inside

- Break rules

- Play offense with shareholders

In this phase, and if they already haven't, chief executives will need to move out of their ivory towers and connect directly and daily with the *crowd.* Corporate bubbles will need to burst wide open to let the *crowd* closer to the inside – offering them a real seat at the table to cast their influence across the business – from innovation to policy creation. The most unhelpful norms in your industry will need to be overthrown, and a balance will need to be struck with your shareholder community so that they don't continue to drown everyone else out.

Once you start to visibly go against longstanding norms in favor of your mission, you can expect it to strengthen your internal culture, further solicit the support and passion of your employees, and better attract the broader *crowd's* curiosity and attention. Question the system enough and the *crowd* will start to believe you. They'll get excited about what you're up to. Eventually, they'll want to be a part of it.

Let's start with the person or people who make it possible for everyone else in a company to buck the system: the chief executive, the senior leadership, the leaders who set the tone for everyone and everything around them.

Strategy 1: Reimagine the top job

Today, the chief executive's job has become even more complicated and high pressure. They are operating in a world short on trust and full of skeptics who question their intent. Investors want results, of course, and they want to understand how every decision will affect the stock price. Expectations are high from all sides and seem to be at odds more often than not. To make matters worse, only 44 percent of people worldwide in 2018 said they think chief executives are credible. That's actually a bit of an improvement over previous data, but still far from what any of us think is ideal.[87]

Here's the challenge: The skill set used to guide an organization to maximum profit while having the mechanisms in place to largely control external messaging is quite different than the skills required of today's chief executive. We've talked about the fact that a corporate footprint wasn't a thing 40 years ago. Neither were large-scale instantaneous social activations. Employees were always a number and sometimes a name. But they were never a voice. Customers could be managed through customer service departments and their woes largely contained as isolated one-off complaints. Today's business leaders now need to understand and anticipate their roles in a world filled with everyday people with newfound power. They'll need to be in touch with the *crowd* (literally and figuratively) and inspire both conversation and action.

To gain the trust of the *crowd*, leaders will need to be visible, accessible, and at the forefront of evangelizing the company's mission and values. What follows are a few of the ways some chief executives are doing just that.

1.1 Lead with purpose. Always

Leaders of *Inspired Companies* are driven by a larger purpose – not by the false notion that their primary job is to drive profit. For them, it's not just lip service. It's the motivation for everything they do. The world is clear on where they stand.

Take Elon Musk. He has been unwavering in his message. Whether it's opening up access to outer space (SpaceX) or advancing sustainable energy (Tesla), it's not difficult to figure out what Musk is fighting for. Peter Diamandis, innovation pioneer and founder of the XPRIZE, believes Musk's clear and obvious purpose contributes to Tesla's reputation as an innovator. In an informal poll, Diamandis asked his Twitter followers which company they thought was most innovative: Google, Amazon, Facebook, or Tesla. Tesla blew the competition away. Among the reasons Diamandis identified are a transformative purpose – and a passionate, outspoken founder.[88] We all know Musk is not perfect. Smoking marijuana during a live webcast in California (albeit where the drug is legal) was not his best move. Neither was his August 2018 tweet that said he was "considering taking Tesla private … " sending markets into chaos and landing him a US$20 million fine and a three-year ban on serving as Tesla's chairman.[89] But we are not looking for perfection in our examples. We are looking for guidance from leaders on their best days.

Arianna Huffington is another leader who forges her own path while always being clear about what she stands for. She founded Huffington Post (now called HuffPost), which gave the *crowd* a voice. Whether through user-generated content or the site's ubiquitous comments, Huffington Post was an early player in citizen journalism. That shifted over time as the platform grew and needed to balance quantity with quality, but the fundamental premise remained the same. Diverse voices provide relatively uncensored points of view on just about every imaginable topic. What this did was facilitate a global conversation, and Huffington has been at the center of it for well over a decade. She's an author, a prolific speaker, and a regular contributor to her own platform. Even after she sold the platform (to AOL in 2011 for US$300 million), she maintained editorial control for another five years – a period that included the launch of the Purpose + Profit section of the site.

Arianna Huffington is a leader the world has gotten to know. Her companies were founded on the idea of giving people a place to speak out. And even though she's no longer at HuffPost, the company just launched a new mission to tell the stories of people who have been "left out of the conversation." It would seem that Huffington has inspired the next generation of leaders at the company she founded.

At TOMS, the mission statement is *To make life more comfortable – for everyone*. How's that for an idea we could all use? Plenty of people know the TOMS story. Blake Mycoskie, the company's founder, went to Argentina and saw kids in need of shoes. A short time later, he launched his buy-one-give-one business model. Fewer people know *why* they know this story. It's because TOMS puts far more effort into storytelling than paid marketing. (The ratio is something close to Everything: Nothing.)

Mycoskie has been just about everywhere telling the TOMS story. Whether it's at trunk shows, business symposiums, or social change conferences, Mycoskie can be found there.

The impact of this is measurable, at least according to the Brand World Value index. Introduced in Chapter 6, this tool quantifies the extent to which consumers "perceive a brand to have a purpose bigger than making money, the degree to which that purpose aligns with their own values, and the extent to which they would be willing to actively support the brand's purpose."[90] For those under 35 years old – the ever-important, ever-growing, increasingly wealthy millennial demographic – TOMS ranks 22nd. To put that in perspective, Nike ranks 26th, despite spending a whole lot more on marketing.

There's no more important time to reinforce the mission or the purpose of a company than when people perceive a threat to it. When Microsoft acquired LinkedIn in 2016, CEO Jeff Weiner sent an open letter to his employees to remind them of the company's vision and why it remained as important as ever. Now LinkedIn's mission is a bit dry: *Connect the world's professionals to make them more productive and successful.* On the other hand, their vision – *to create economic opportunity for every member of the global workforce* – is insanely inspiring and what we would consider a statement closer to a purpose statement or *Inspired Mission.* Regardless, it's that sentiment that seemed to compel Weiner to write this:[91]

> Every day I come to work, I'm primarily guided by two things: First, realizing our mission and vision . . . Whether it's worker displacement, the skills gap, youth unemployment, or socio-economic stratification, the impact on society will be staggering. I've said it on multiple occasions and believe it even more so every day: creating economic opportunity will be the defining issue of our time. That's why I'm here and why I can't imagine doing any other job. Simply put, what we do matters, and matters more than ever.
>
> The second thing I focus on every day is making our culture and values come to life. Ten years ago, had you asked me about culture and values I would have rolled my eyes and recited a line from Dilbert. But when I started as CEO I began to appreciate just how important they

were. Culture and values provide the foundation upon which everything else is built. They are arguably our most important competitive advantage, and something that has grown to define us. It's one thing to change the world. It's another to do it in our own unique way: Members first. Relationships matter. Be open, honest, and constructive. Demand excellence. Take intelligent risks. Act like an owner.

That's who we are. That's LinkedIn.

LinkedIn's reputation and the ability of its leaders to work effectively with the *crowd* may actually have been central to Microsoft's acquisition strategy. When it was announced in 2017 that Reid Hoffman, LinkedIn's founder, would be joining Microsoft's board, *Wired* argued that it was all part of the plan to reorient Microsoft.[92] "There are few people in Silicon Valley as connected to its heart as Hoffman," the author wrote. Microsoft, on the other hand, is notoriously disconnected from the Silicon Valley *crowd* and the innovation and talent the Valley is known for. Adding LinkedIn, along with Weiner and Hoffman as leaders, just might turn out to be the most game-changing thing Microsoft has done in decades.

All of these leaders understand and believe wholeheartedly in the ideas their companies stand for. They also know that they need more than faith to *Shake up the System*. More than ever before, leaders need to get out of their corner offices and connect with the real world.

A lot.

1.2 Be accessible. Let the world get to know you

Leaders of *Inspired Companies* recognize that the ivory tower no longer exists. They know the *crowd* is looking for them to engage directly. But that's just the more inspired leaders. Many other leaders don't seem to have gotten the memo yet.

As recently as 2015, a majority of Fortune 500 chief executives (61 percent, to be exact) had no social media presence whatsoever.[93] None.

Not Twitter, not Facebook, not even LinkedIn. Trust is at historic lows, but that's not a call to retreat or stay silent. Chief executives must work hard to gain the trust of the *crowd*. Part of that means being accessible to them. Open and transparent communications that reflect your company's mission and values are critical to establishing authentic connections with the *crowd* of *new C.E.O.s*. Keep in mind, we aren't talking about a quarterly communication. We're talking about a constant connection and a way of doing business in real time.

This doesn't mean that jumping on Twitter or Instagram is a silver bullet. Far from it. The important thing is that leaders engage in ways that are authentic to the companies they lead and to who they are as people. If that's a tweet, great. It's also fine if it's a handwritten letter, podcast, or announcement from the international space station (we're looking at you, Branson and Musk). What matters most is that you're real.

Richard Foley is Senior Partner at Pinsent Masons, a very successful international law firm. Pinsent Masons has been acknowledged with awards for almost everything: 2018 Law Firm of the Year,[*] top 10 FT (*Financial Times*) Innovative Law Firms Asia Pacific 2018 and Europe 2017, *Legal Week* Innovation Awards 2017 for diversity and inclusion, and a whole slew of other industry-specific and business support service awards over the years in several different countries.

You'd be forgiven for assuming that, like most other "successful" law firms, they would operate in a stuffy, elitist, and hierarchy-driven environment. But Pinsent Masons is not like most other law firms. During Richard's tenure in the top job, he made the unthinkable decision to remove all offices from Pinsent Masons' workplaces. Including his own. On any given day you'll see him casually perched on a chair at a shared working table in full view of peers and staff. He reserves private rooms like everyone else to make confidential calls or participate in group meetings and leaves those rooms promptly when time's up. He eats at the staff cafeteria, any one of the 3,300 Pinsent

---

[*] The Lawyer Awards celebrate excellence across the industry globally.

Masons people can send him an email directly, and he works hard to reply personally and remember your name.

Pinsent Masons has invested heavily to create a stunning shared working environment where ivory towers are not welcome. Their corporate values are as simple as ABC: *approachable, bold,* and *connected.* Living them starts at the top.

Good leaders find ways to be accessible and are intentional about it. Salesforce chief executive Marc Benioff is everywhere. And it's a good thing too because he knows how to inspire people. Benioff's leadership is also a good example of how important it is to understand and connect with your company's unique *C.E.O.s.* A lot of Benioff's focus is on tech crowds – the developers who co-innovate and create apps using Salesforce's open-source platform. (That's not a novel idea today, but it was straight-up revolutionary when Salesforce originally opened up its code.) He speaks at tech conferences and writes blogs for developers – things the rest of us will never read. Meanwhile, Dreamforce – originally Salesforce's gathering for tech folks – is now the place to be for anyone doing anything inspiring. This is a company whose standard branding literally says, "Hello, we're Salesforce. We're here to help your customers love you."[94] Seems Benioff has figured out how to translate the tech world into the real world. That sure is something we could use a lot more of.

For some companies, the *crowd* of *new C.E.O.s* won't include everyone. Instead, the people who will champion and advance your work might be specialists of sorts. Take a look at Drupal. Whether or not you think you use Drupal, you probably use Drupal. It's an open-source platform that serves as the backend framework for 2.3 percent of all global websites[95] including the likes of Arsenal, Timex, Verizon, Lady Gaga, and the U.K., Brazilian, and Australian governments. As you might expect, Drupal's community of stakeholders includes a lot of developers and web designers – and founder and chief executive, Dries Buytaert, is really good at connecting with them. He does "Ask Me Anything" Q&As on Reddit where he covers everything from the fly-on-the-wall development process and biggest mistakes to the hair product he uses. He writes a regular blog that very openly covers the organization's plans for the future, along with personal musings like a vacation to see the Northern Lights. He's not shy about interviews and he's a regular on the developers' conference circuit. In all of it, he's looking for others to contribute ideas, criticism, questions, you name it.

What makes Buytaert so accessible is not just that he's constantly connecting with an audience. It's that he's constantly connecting with *his* audience. There are no talking points or key messages. He's not trying to be a celebrity. He's just connecting with people who can improve Drupal in the places that the people who can improve Drupal hang out.

For an *Inspired Company's* chief executive, accessibility to the *crowd* isn't planned. It's a way of life. When you get away from contrived moments and genuinely seek out interactions with your *crowd*, you'll be able to engage organically.

During his time as BT's Chief Executive, Gavin Patterson did what many other leaders don't. He only had one email address: Gavin.e.patterson@bt.com. Yep. That's the one. In interviews with the BBC, he very frequently asked viewers to write it down so that they could email him directly. Now, like many other leaders, Gavin was never looking for more things to fill his calendar. For five years as chief executive, he led a business of over 100,000 employees in 180 countries, with all of the U.K. relying on him to ensure their internet service was not interrupted. Notwithstanding his incredibly compressed schedule, he insisted on having unfiltered access to the opinions of the *crowd.*

"It's incredibly helpful," says Patterson. "It gives me direct visibility to the difference we make to people's lives when we fail. You see things the big system has missed . . . there are little hints. You see patterns." Patterson went on to describe a situation where he passed a complaint about service interruption from an individual customer onto the executive in charge of BT's network. Despite being told that it had been resolved, Gavin's inbox continued to suggest that it hadn't.

So with customer emails in hand, he went back to BT's network executives two more times. The extra investigation revealed a larger problem caused by a faulty component in the network exchange – a component commonly used and sure to be impacting other exchanges across their national network. Needless to say, there were probably several thousand people with notably less frustration about their internet service after that component was universally changed out.

This is the impact of leaders who deliberately commit to staying connected with real people.

Let's go back to the sports industry and take a look at REI's CEO, Jerry Stritzke. REI is a U.S.-based outdoor sports retailer. During an open online dialogue about a wildly successful retail campaign, Stritzke unexpectedly fielded off-topic questions from employees who were more concerned about low pay and overemphasis on membership sales. Instead of shutting the conversations down to focus on the campaign, Stritzke stayed online for two hours and followed up with an interview in *The New York Times* a few days later in which he said, "I believe in stepping up, listening to all sides, and taking action. Transparent leadership is the only way to go in a transparent age."

Another leader not shy to engage directly is Sir Richard Branson. He is so good at social media, he actually writes blogs telling other chief executives how to use it.[96] On any given day, you'll see inspiring stories about Virgin employees, reflections on his career, data on climate change, funny anecdotes, and political opinions. In other words, there's no one sitting in corporate communications writing social posts on his behalf. Whether or not you agree with everything Branson has to say is not important. Whether he gets it right all the time isn't either. The important thing is that you don't have to search high and low to see what he, and by extension his companies, stand for.

You know who's not the most exciting social media influencer on earth? Unilever's former CEO Paul Polman – arguably the highest profile purposeful business leader of the last decade. Yes, he has an active Twitter account, but it's a little on the wonky side. Polman's an old-school communicator. He does panel discussions, television interviews, and newspaper interviews. And guess what? There's nothing wrong with that. It's who Polman is. He's out in the world all the time talking about business as a force for good and, frankly, he's talking to the people who might care what the chief executive of an extremely successful multinational conglomerate has to say. (Unilever's brands – like Dove, Hellmann's, Ben & Jerry's, and Omo – are set up to speak for themselves.) As Unilever's chief executive, Polman traveled in business circles, showing us what responsible capitalism looks like, proving that companies can thrive on sustainable practices and that the old rules don't always need to be followed.

These are all leaders who value the *crowd's* input. They operate on equal footing with them and engage directly. When a Tesla driver stopped to charge his battery in California, he found himself waiting behind fully charged cars while their drivers had apparently gone to the store. The driver voiced his frustration on Twitter and Elon Musk responded within minutes. "Will take action," Musk's tweet said. Now the average person might think "Yeah, right." But this is Elon Musk we're talking about. Within *six days* the company had implemented "idling fees" across its entire network to discourage drivers from using the charging stations as parking lots.[97] That's a whole new level of accessibility and customer influence that didn't exist back when chief executives sat in ivory towers. The key takeaway? Leadership today looks very different than it once did.

In return for their accessibility and commitment to purpose, these inspired leaders get input, insights, trust, and relationships that can't be bought. They have reimagined their roles and embraced the power shift that has put the *crowd* in charge. They've learned how to listen and they've shown they can act decisively with courage. In other words, they're *Shaking Up the System* to pursue big ideas – and, even more importantly, they set an example for the rest of their organizations.

Strategy 2: Bring the *new C.E.O.s* inside. Run a participatory business model

When chief executives step out of their towers to embrace the *crowd*, they set the tone for everyone else to follow. This transition is critical. Connectivity with the *crowd* of *C.E.O.s* must become muscle memory for your entire organization. Achieving that will probably feel a bit uncomfortable at first.

Most companies, especially large ones, exist in a bubble. Information is closely held and communications are tightly controlled. Sometimes the bubble is useful, like to protect the timing of a major product launch announcement. Most times it's not, especially when the bubble disconnects your company from the real world. Corporate bubbles keep insiders in and outsiders out. If you think your company might be an exception, think again. Insulation has been *completely normal* in the corporate sector. Most leaders believe it enables them to manage reputation, company narrative, and daily operations. That may have been true in the past, but it isn't anymore.

Inspired Companies know that to succeed with the powerful *crowd*, the bubble must burst. We don't mean for that to sound flippant. It's a big change and should be done thoughtfully. The idea of "bringing the outside in" is about understanding when and where bringing parts of the *crowd* into the workings of your business can make you better. Many startups today have figured out the power of disrupting the status quo and they bring the outside in from the outset. Dries Buytaert and Drupal demonstrate that in spectacular fashion. But most mainstream companies won't get this right because they aren't built to get it right, and they see it as a threat. It requires a huge mental model shift. And the stakes are high, especially for public companies. But if you do get this right, and make it work, you can unlock significant value that others are too afraid to capture. This is how you accelerate innovation and create shared "ownership" of your mission and brand. Directly engaging the *crowd* of *new C.E.O.s* gives them a stake in the results, builds trust, and advances loyalty.

There's no single way to do this. Instead, there are endless ways for the *crowd* to be strategically involved in your business, and it doesn't always need to be as daunting as redesigning your entire business model or supply chain. If you think about all the things a company does on a daily basis – sales, recruiting, PR, operations planning, campaign design, events management, and so on – there are many entry points for the *crowd* to help you. Perhaps even lead you.

In our experience, bringing the *crowd* of *new C.E.O.s* inside is usually the most uncomfortable of all the *Inspired Action* strategies when it's first suggested. Maybe that's because as leaders we love control and have been rewarded for having the answer ourselves too often. It's time to fully embrace that you can no longer control what you could before. Instead, you'll need to find ways to turn this new reality into competitive advantage. To demystify this here's a quick look at how some companies already do this:

- Every year, Ben & Jerry's receives over 13,000 suggestions for new ice cream flavors.[98] Their commitment to review every suggestion creates many hit flavors, including Cherry Garcia – an all-time best seller.

- Nike joined forces with NASA, USAID, and the U.S. State Department to launch a global competition to accelerate its sustainable materials innovation and create new materials for running shoes and sports apparel.

- Strava, a social media and performance-data specialist that started in 2009, has managed to map the best workout routes around the world. They receive around 3 million activity "segments" a week, with uploads ranging from the Prime Minister of Bhutan's favorite cycling routes to the forest runs trekked by professional runners.[99] Their database is so valuable that city and state governments around the world now use it to influence infrastructure plans.

Lost in these tidy bullets is this fact: All of these efforts make business outcomes better. Unfortunately, in most companies, bringing the *crowd* inside ends up being relegated to discrete, one-off activities pigeonholed as "good CSR practice," part of the "social media plan," or "focus groups."

We see things differently, and so do the more *Inspired Companies*. All of these activities are examples of bringing our all-powerful *crowd* closer to the inner workings of your business. It's about empowering and enabling them to support your business directly in ways they have been shut out of before. It's not intended for just one group in your organization or a single function.

In the following pages, we share examples of the *crowd* influencing decisions across all areas of a company, including:

- Core innovation in product, service, and customer experience design

- Visual brand identities

- Communications

- Brand campaigns

- Internal policy development

Making this a practice and not a series of discrete one-offs is the ultimate signal that you are truly bursting the corporate bubble and enabling a more participatory business model. One that many can engage in, be part of, and support – on your behalf and to everyone's advantage.

2.1 Crowd-led innovation

When Nike first started talking internally about NIKEiD, the company's consumer-customized footwear, some Nike insiders were not exactly comfortable with the idea. (Many were a little closer to the "hair on fire" end of the spectrum.) Today, the in-store studios, mobile app, and online customization options are everywhere, but when the idea was first hatched in 1999, it got a mixed reception. NIKEiD wasn't proposing that consumers design their own T-shirts. It was proposing that they design their own shoes. It was putting the heart and the core of the brand in consumers' hands.

On the one hand, no one could deny that footwear customization would be a game-changer. Getting there first and claiming the innovation spoils was a flat-out footrace: The technology that connected interactive websites to manufacturing and delivery processes was available to any footwear manufacturer who cared enough about its consumers to figure it out. And Nike cared about its consumers.

On the other hand: letting individual consumers design *Nike shoes?* Allowing them to choose their own colors, shoelaces and other design elements, and then apply the swoosh for all the world to see? What if they're ugly? Will there be an approval process? How much control can we give up? Talk about coming up against some knife-edge questions. As you would expect, Nike has a huge internal design team that obsesses over every detail. The thought of relinquishing some of that control provoked serious levels of anxiety. This was the first athletic footwear customization tool out there and there were no guideposts for how it should be done.

So what happened? Nike opened the door and burst at least part of the highly coveted Nike design bubble. NIKEiD was born and the process of learning how to do this together with consumers was initiated. It started out slow, offering a limited color palette and customization options. The shoes cost more, and you had to wait about six weeks to get them. Nike's consumers loved it. They posted their designs online and shared their experience with friends and anyone else watching this unprecedented move play out. Consumers were excited, empowered, and trusted. Nike had moved from a heavy dose of trepidation to celebrating their consumer's creativity. In a few short years, NIKEiD evolved into increasingly greater opportunities for consumers to participate directly with the brand and co-create products they cared about.

The move to bring consumers closer to one of Nike's most valuable assets had bumps along the way; Nike's design team fears were realized to some extent – people did make some ugly shoes. But the upside far outweighed the downside, and mutual admiration and trust were built in the process.

We are not telling you this because we think customization is the next big thing. We're suggesting you take a look at your most prized and protected assets and think about how you can open them up to the *crowd*.

When it comes to bursting the corporate bubble, you know you're doing it right if it makes at least someone nervous. Facing fears and building a company that trusts its most loyal **C**onsumers, **E**mployees, and **O**utsiders leads to opportunities to exceed expectations: yours and theirs. Being out of your comfort zone might mean you're onto something.

These days, whole companies are founded on the idea of customer-driven product design

When the *crowd* is the design team, there is no corporate bubble to burst. For example, when a six-year-old drew the dress she wanted, her mother found a way to turn the drawing into a dress. She launched a startup called Picture This Clothing. Its entire product line is the clothing kids design for themselves. If you've ever had a six-year-old or been close to one, you know there's always an outfit they won't stop wearing. For Picture This Clothing customers, it can now be the one they design for themselves. 'It's not just custom clothing,' says CEO Jaimee Newberry. 'It is an experience from end-to-end designed to reinforce individuality, creativity, and taking an idea from concept to completion.' That's what we call embracing the *crowd*.

Examples like Picture This demonstrate how the role of individual consumers has changed. When Nike first introduced NIKEiD, it was unheard of to let consumers design your product. Now they can design everything from apparel to cars to survival shelters. This kind of approach signals to consumers that they are trusted to influence how your brand is expressed in the world.

A Picture This masterpiece (Image courtesy of Picture This Clothing)

Picture This and Nike also cast a light on the difference between David and Goliath. Big, established companies have to do a lot of work to rewire themselves to trust outsiders with their brands. Startups are actually founding their businesses on it. By authentically engaging consumers at the outset, these new companies might actually emerge as the Goliaths of the future.

We introduced you to Drupal earlier – the open-sourced web content management system that powers many of the most popular, high-traffic websites in the world from the White House to NASCAR. Drupal is a groundbreaking example of where its products and services are built by the *crowd*, for the *crowd*. It's free to use because it's developed and powered by the Drupal Community – 1,000,000[100] developers, designers, and other such users around the world. Everything from their library of website templates to the community's code of conduct is created by the community. They debate openly across the global community to innovate, create, and solve problems as an agile network.

Drupal has found a way to create an unlimited innovation budget. They crowdsource code in the same way Wikipedia crowdsources facts and articles. Their approach to open-source innovation means that anyone can innovate, at any time, to improve the experience of Drupal's software platforms and services.

"Drupal is very Darwinian," says founder Dries Buytaert. "Five different modules for image galleries are available on our website. A traditional company would not build five to compete against each other. They would allocate a budget and assign a certain number of engineers to build one. But in an open-source innovation environment you don't have to apply for a budget to gain approval to build something you think will work. There are hundreds of thousands of developers in the community. Our job is just to encourage them to contribute."

Empowering and enabling Drupal's customers to co-create solutions and play a direct hand in shaping and driving Drupal's innovation agenda is what makes Drupal successful. Buytaert went on to tell us that several members of the community have Drupal tattoos. "That's how inspired they are – they will ink their bodies for the rest of their life." Take a look at Hilmar Hallbjörnsson, or Drupal Viking as he prefers to be known.

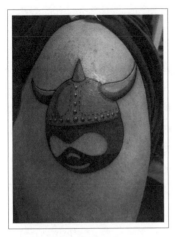

Drupal Viking and his tattoo. (Image from Hilmar Hallbjörnsson)

"Drupal is my life," Drupal Viking writes in his blog. "Ever since I first laid hands on it in September of 2011. I almost cried. Never EVER do I have to write another Login form or figure out how the best way to upload images to the site I'm building with (insert framework or whatever hack you're doing) again! Now I can focus on building awesome sites, with one of the best building tools on the market."[101]

Showing visible allegiance to Drupal's platform and being an outspoken advocate has become somewhat of a sport. Art director at software development and design company, Exove, created a range of instant Drupal tattoos and distributed them at a major Drupalcon event in 2012. Knowing the Drupal *crowd* well, Exove took it a step further: "... if your love is deep enough we can help you to make it permanent. Do inquire within."[102]

Instant Drupal tattoos designed & handed out by software development & design company Exove to participants of the DrupalCon community event.

This is about unleashing and rewarding your *crowd's* creativity
We talked earlier about how LEGO seeks *to inspire and develop the builders of tomorrow*. Many of us have first-hand knowledge of how good a job they do at this – whether it's through our own experience, our kids', or just seeing the staggering achievements of the company's most zealous fans. The folks at LEGO continue to see huge opportunity from harnessing the excitement and engagement of their *crowd* in product innovation.

LEGO created a social platform called LEGO Ideas that allows users to submit ideas for new LEGO product lines. People use existing LEGO sets to create theme-based builds that cover everything from a 1950s drive-in to the Mars Rover to the Mexico City skyline. Fellow users can comment, ask questions, and vote for their favorites. Once an idea gets 10,000 votes, it goes through the company's review process and eventually goes into production.

Some of the most sophisticated works of art are produced by adults, but LEGO's core audience and their big idea are centered on kids, so they have special "Kids Vote" rounds of voting to choose finalists.

This is a way to engage not just LEGO artists, but fans of all ages who want to have a voice and aren't necessarily up for replicating the underwater City of Alexandria. And LEGO puts its money where its mouth is, giving a share of profits to those whose ideas make it to market.

Nike, Picture This Clothing, Drupal, and LEGO all have examples of where they lean on the *crowd* to help innovate their products and services. Yet enabling the *new C.E.O.s* to participate directly in your business can come in many forms, as we'll see next.

Let the *crowd* design the customer experience

Recognizing that its audience is diverse and not always easy to reach, NASCAR created a Fan Council to collect insights from its most passionate followers. But this isn't just about focus groups or having a mailing list to send surveys to. NASCAR brought together 12,000 of its most committed fans to co-innovate the race experience.[103]

A members-only engagement platform lets fans give feedback and connect with each other on the sport's hottest topics. They also get regular news feeds and customized communications like celebration notes whenever their favorite driver wins a race. That's all well and good, but it's also something sophisticated CRM software can automate these days. What can't be automated is the direct interaction with fans. If a Fan Council member leaves a voicemail, NASCAR calls them back. When a 2009 race ended in controversy, feedback from the Fan Council led to changes in the long-standing race rules. Fan Council feedback was similarly influential in establishing how drivers would line up to restart after a pause (say, if there's been an accident). Now drivers start double-file (side by side), which is considered a much more exciting experience. These fans are seeing the direct impact of their contributions on race day.

When NASCAR sends out a survey to its Fan Council, 55 percent of members respond. Anyone who's well-versed in market research knows that's a pretty unheard-of response rate. On top of that, the Council delivers customer insights at a cost that would be the envy of any market research planner. For participants, there's no incentive here other than the opportunity to influence the sport they love. And that's the thing. Fans feel privileged and proud to be part of the Fan Council. It's considered an honor. Actually, it's considered such a big deal that it's not unusual for local newspapers to report on it when local fans are named to the Council.[104]

These are fans NASCAR would already count among the most loyal. What NASCAR did with the Fan Council gave them a reason to be even more loyal, more vocal, and more committed. Now they aren't just NASCAR fans, they're *super-fans* with an emotional stake in the organization.

Wildfang is another great case study in pushing boundaries to engage directly with their consumers. Wildfang is a rule-busting fashion retailer "for women who like to raise a little hell." And they've been consumer-obsessed from the start. Co-founders Emma Mcilroy and Julia Parsley were both Nike colleagues and frustrated shoppers who couldn't find anyone selling what they wanted to wear: menswear-inspired clothing designed for women. They knew they weren't the only ones. In fact, they knew there was a whole tribe out there, looking for not just fashion but community and validation. Wildfang captured all of this in their brand manifesto pictured here. Please take a moment to read it.

With this kind of commitment to their *crowd*, Wildfang directly engages as many potential consumers as they can find. This goes way beyond focus groups. According to Mcilroy, Wildfang consumers were single-handedly responsible for the company's sizing strategy. In fact, fit, body type, and diversity are essential to delivering on the company's mission and product design priorities. The company also works hard to make sure core consumers are well represented in brand communications and among store staff. Store location

WILDFANG

IS NOT A BRAND. WE ARE A BAND. MORE SPECIFICALLY, WE ARE A BAND OF THIEVES MODERN-DAY, FEMALE ROBIN HOODS RAIDING MEN'S CLOSETS AND MANIACALLY DISPENSING BLAZERS, CARDIGANS, WINGTIPS AND BOWLERS AS WE ROAM FROM TOWN TO TOWN IN THESE STOLEN STYLES OF OURS. LIKE YOU, WE ARE TOMBOYS BUT LIKE YOU WE ARE ALSO FRIENDS AND SISTERS, HEROINES AND HELLIONS, RASCALS, ROCKERS, SHAPESHIFTERS AND TRENDSETTERS. WE'RE HERE TO LIBERATE MENSWEAR ONE BOWTIE AT A TIME AND WE'RE DOING IT OURSELVES BECAUSE WE WANT IT DONE RIGHT. SO, WELCOME IT JUST SO HAPPENS YOU'VE HAPPENED UPON THE FRONT DOOR OF THIS REVOLUTION AND THE PASSWORD IS QUITE SIMPLY THAT LOOK IN YOUR EYES. YOU KNOW THE ONE, THE ONE THAT SAYS "PLEASE TELL ME I'M NOT LATE FOR THE PARTY?!" TO WHICH WE'D REPLY: HELL, NO. YOU'RE RIGHT ON TIME.

Wildfang's brand manifesto (Image from Wildfang)

decisions are also completely consumer-driven, as they should be.

When a company allows its product strategy, brand representation, and location decisions to be greatly influenced by the customer, you've got to wonder how tough it is to pull off. It turns out it's all about prioritizing. As Mcilroy puts it, "Sometimes you don't need a majority point-of-view. Sometimes it's one person that articulates what the other 99 can't say. We have offline [engagement through retail stores] where we connect with our consumers all day every day. The insight that will drive your decisions could come from one person. That's why I am so obsessed with qualitative insights."

2.2 Crowd-led branding

By now it should be clear that to "bring the outside in" and create a more participatory business model, you'll need to loosen up your grip on control. And yes, we know being in control is one of the central tenets of the corporate operating model. Rest assured, this is not about taking your hands off the wheel and letting the kids drive the bus. There are some things you should always maintain ultimate control over: your mission, your message, values, and where you stand as a company. No one should mess with the things that are central to a company's reason for being.

Inspired Companies are comfortable with the idea of the *crowd* having serious influence over the evolution of their brand expression. They understand it's not a threat, it's an opportunity. *Inspired Companies* are set up in ways that the *crowd* can come to the table with influence, ideas, passion, and creativity. When you see some of the things they come up with, you'd be crazy not to leverage it.

Going back to NIKEiD for a minute, some consumers were so inspired by their experience that they created art beyond the shoes. The footwear image pictured here is a custom design by a Nike consumer named Charles Hyde. After experimenting with NIKEiD, he created this image and posted it online.

A consumer's unsolicited interpretation of NIKEiD (Image from Charles Hyde.)

No one at Nike world headquarters anticipated how the most inspired NIKEiD customers might tell the rest of the world about their experience. It's a level of advocacy that was underestimated but more valuable than any in-house marketing campaign could ever have achieved. And that's the point. No one is better positioned to authentically and enthusiastically express your brand than the people who are inspired by it.

A graffiti artist defines a presidential campaign

The 2008 Obama campaign provides another good example of what happens when you loosen your grip on control. Keep in mind that this is

an arena where the stakes are about as high as stakes get and messages are maniacally controlled. But when a graffiti artist named Shepard Fairey created a poster of President Obama with the word "Hope," the campaign gave its blessing in the best way they knew how. They used it. Amplified it as a cornerstone image of the campaign, in fact. Eventually, the poster became an iconic symbol and one of the campaign's most famous images. Designed by an inspired voter, not the campaign team:

Shepard Fairey's poster of President Obama (Illustration courtesy of Shepard Fairey/ Obeygiant.com)

"I very quickly pulled together an illustration that I thought made Obama look like a leader with vision and conviction and was a patriotic image. I made it just like I made my normal posters. The poster symbolizes something really important. It's grassroots activism and a return to the people believing in democracy. Not just the people with the most power trying to manipulate democracy for their own ends." (Shepard Fairey)[105]

Fairey's poster was a completely new take on election posters, which arguably helped the campaign connect with audiences it wouldn't have otherwise reached. It worked because Fairey captured the essence of Obama and his ideals through art in a way that resonated with the masses. The takeaway? The most inspired people in your *crowd* can be a bridge between an organization and audiences that have yet to be reached.

A company is defined by the communities it creates, rather than by its logo

There's a pretty good chance you already know what CrossFit is, but you probably can't picture their logo. There's a reason for that.

CrossFit was designed to be an alternative – a really difficult, high-intensity alternative – to big-box gym chains. The company's "affiliates" are schools, fire stations, and local CrossFitters in their own local gyms. The bosses at CrossFit don't really care if the gym is actually a garage. They don't care if branded T-shirts are sold or what's featured in local advertising. They do not prescribe copy, colors, or typefaces. The only thing they seem to expect is that you spell CrossFit correctly. Every brand management norm on the planet seems to have been broken. And as you can see here, the result is pretty great.

A selection of CrossFit logos, from across the U.S. and Australia.

As it turns out, this logo collection is a perfect brand expression of the CrossFit community – a community held together by the spirit of competition. With an online platform where individuals and gyms can compare their performances, it's more like a massive, crowdsourced sports league than a company. Having your own CrossFit posse (with your own logo) intensifies the experience: White Mountain CrossFit goes up against Black Wolf CrossFit. And the whole community turns up for the annual CrossFit Games, broadcast on CBS and carried live by Facebook in 2017. Ordinary people get incredibly fit in a garage somewhere, and then become heroes on TV. No wonder some think CrossFit has achieved cult status.

In short: the company doesn't worry about controlling the creative execution because they don't confuse their *brand* with their *logo*. What they care about is the experience people have and the CrossFit community that's been built.

2.3 Crowd-led communications

This is an area where the system has been shaken up for every company in the world, thanks to the internet. Whether you like it or not, you'll need to get comfortable with the *crowd* speaking for you and your company. You don't have a choice on this one. The days of censoring blog posts are over. You trust your employees and customers or you don't. You believe in your business or you don't. And if you do, then go ahead, give them the tools to talk. There's a big upside waiting for you.

We get why it's scary. The concept of a company embracing uncensored feedback is revolutionary compared to just a few short years ago, but it really shouldn't be. People will criticize your product and business in very public ways whether you encourage it or not. The only difference – and it's a big one – is that you shouldn't be counting on third-party platforms (retailers, Yelp, Glassdoor, and so on) to gather insights about your products, your performance, and especially your *crowd*. You should be doing it directly.

Share what your customers say about you

This kind of transparency takes real confidence in your connection with the *crowd* – or at least your ability to address what they say. For Nike, this meant allowing consumer reviews on Nike websites, completely uncensored (save the obvious decency qualifiers). That's commonplace today, but it wasn't when Nike first invited them to comment on its products many years ago. If you're doing your job well enough, happy customers will do the job of coming to your defense when a portion of online comments are harsher than you might have hoped. And of course, Nike isn't the only company willing to bite the bullet. Here are a few others:

- A property management software firm called AppFolio publishes customers' uncensored feedback and survey responses on its website. The company says excellent support is central to its value proposition, so publishing the information is a signal that the company stands by its words. This approach is fairly standard these days for retail and consumer companies. What's unusual here is AppFolio is a B2B company. Their customers are property managers and developers, so every review has a lot riding on it.

- Tech companies from mobile providers to YouTube and Microsoft have online user support communities that allow people to ask and answer questions in a peer-to-peer environment. This enables faster service (at minimal cost to the companies) and creates shared ownership over each company's services.

- When U.S.-based movie theatre chain Alamo Drafthouse received a profanity-laden voicemail from a customer they'd kicked out for texting during a movie, the company did the unthinkable: They created an advertisement that played the message in its entirety and ended with, 'Thanks for not coming back to the Alamo, texter!' While most of us have grown accustomed to seeing reviews – good and bad – on a company's website, it's not often we see a company go out of their way to broadcast scathing comments for the world to see. In this case, Alamo also managed to let people know they mean business when it comes to texting during movies – and for anyone who's ever seen a fellow moviegoer's screen light up a theatre mid-movie, their stance is much appreciated. By the way, the video has more than 2.7 million views as of this writing, so it appears the risk paid off.

As covered in Chapter 2, there's another set of voices that are trusted almost as much as your customers. And it's even easier to give them the mic, because they're right down the hall.

Give employees a chance to exceed your expectations
Employees are the heart and soul of any company, but many companies don't recognize them as the powerful force they truly are. Figuring out how to bring them further on "the inside" in ways they may not have participated before can be your ace in the hole. As a reminder, when we talk about **E**mployees, we're also talking about contractors, consultants, partners, and even sponsored athletes, movie stars, or other brand ambassadors. We're referring to anyone who produces or works on behalf of your company.

When employees are inspired by the mission, they will self-organize and do amazing things. Zappos provides a platform on their website for employees to post completely unscripted videos about life at Zappos – everything from an Irish employee's first impressions of Las Vegas, where Zappos' headquarters are located, to employee bands and pranks.[106] They vary drastically in production quality and, as you might expect, some are a bit drier than others. Nevertheless, they make clear that freedom of speech and authentic representation of the corporate culture are things Zappos cares about.

Wildfang is another company that lets employees take control of communications. When a member of staff approached Mcilroy about being part of the social media effort, she jumped at the offer. The employee offered to dedicate 10 percent of her spare time and asked to be briefed on the rules. She wanted to know what point of view Wildfang wanted to express on social media. Mcilroy replied with, "What issues do you care about? What fires you up?" Slightly confused at first, the eager employee said, "anything to do with women of color, hip hop ... "

Mcilroy then declared, "Great – you should tweet about that." When the employee asked if Wildfang usually comments on those issues, Mcilroy said, "Well, it doesn't matter what we usually do – you care about it, you know a lot about it, you'll be authentic – you tweet about it for Wildfang."

That, in a nutshell, *is* Wildfang's social media policy. On any given day, you'll see retweets of political stories (including "Texas Teens Hold Quinceañera Protest at the Capitol"), quirky science ("T-Rex Couldn't Run!"), dress codes in the U.S. Congress, movies about female superheroes, and any number of GIFs, images, and stories in support of dogs. Oh, and they occasionally post about their product line and sales. In our first search, we had to go back nine days to find a product reference. This is one of those *Inspired Actions* that's a bit easier for startups. While it's unlikely a Fortune 100 could manage going nine days without a product mention, they can learn from the overall effort to use social media to express *who* you are rather than *what* you sell. In Wildfang's case, by giving employees control of the social media accounts, they were able to authentically represent who they are and build relationships with like-minded consumers.

As Mcilroy says of her decision, "Now you see a lot of really rad comments about the issues many of our consumers care about on Wildfang platforms. Now we have an ability to run and jump. We didn't before until we empowered her to do it."

Mitel, a Canadian communications company, has enlisted all 3,000 of its employees as social media ambassadors, encouraging them to post at will. If this sounds easy, it wasn't. Mitel was an established (read: old) brand. The company was growing fast and they knew they needed to transform their image. A brand audit helped them to see what customer expectations were. It also showed employees were invested in the company. But a social audit revealed that only 35 employees were talking about the brand on social media. That's 35 out of 3,000. When they launched the new brand identity, they included an effort to engage all employees in social media.

None of this was rocket science. Martyn Etherington, Mitel's CMO, read a book in an airport called *The Social Employee.* The book had an impact. "I figured if companies and brands such as Dell could do this, surely a little old 41-year-old company with 3,000 employees could do this."

This is about trusting your employees to represent the brand and be proud of who they work for. They don't need to be babysat or handed talking points. In fact, they're likely to do better on their own. Mitel thought so too, which is why they threw out the rulebook and designed a program that assumed people would be responsible. While the company provided training on social sharing and brand advocacy, the only policy was to "Use your best judgment at all times."[107]

Did it work? Well, a company with almost no brand awareness after 40-plus years in business was named a Top 5 Social Brand within one year.[108]

So yeah, we'd say it worked.

2.4 Crowd-led campaigns

Anyone who has ever read, heard, or watched an advertisement knows all about brand voice, whether you're enough of a marketing geek to call it that or not: it's the singular voice of the organization. It might be irreverent or earnest or lofty or boring, but it's one voice. That's part of the corporate marketing rulebook, right? Not for *Inspired Companies.* For any company that wants to talk about big ideas, one voice often isn't enough. The *crowd* won't buy it.

KPMG is an example of a company that understood the power of sourcing multiple voices to bring a big idea to life. Most people know KPMG is a professional services organization specializing in areas like accounting, tax, and consulting. From the outside, anyone will tell you that's not the sexiest line of work. But the inside is a different story altogether, particularly in recent years as the company worked to articulate its new purpose statement: *Inspire confidence. Create change.* As part of that effort, a well-known HBR article[109] chronicles how KPMG took a systematic approach to reminding KPMG employees how their predecessors changed the world. From establishing the

Federal Reserve to certifying South Africa's first democratic election results (in which Nelson Mandela was elected president), KPMG used storytelling to reinforce the company's role in "Shaping History."

Once employees were inspired, KPMG invited them to share their own stories with an internal initiative called the 10,000 Stories Challenge. Employees and partners were asked to submit stories about how they change the world in the course of their everyday work. They hoped to get 10,000 stories within six months. Instead, they got 42,000. It turns out people were itching to share the meaning behind their work and they wanted just as badly to understand the difference their colleagues were making.

What's interesting about KPMG is that they didn't expect people to wrap their stories up in a bow. Employees sent in words to describe their best experiences at work. Creatives were hired to bring them to life in a way that allowed them all to sit together as 42,000 stories from one team – a team that was shaping history together.

The success of KMPG's *crowd*-led internal campaign shouldn't be a surprise. It turns out plenty of research shows how writing about your personal experiences actually makes you happier. You become more empowered and have a better sense of self.[110] Who wouldn't want that in an employee?

Our only question for KPMG (and any other organization with a new purpose or *Inspired Mission* statement) is whether the connection between purpose and the daily work of employees sustained, deepened, and strengthened over time. Only people on the inside of a company will be able to answer that.

Which raises a larger point: short-term campaigns that come and go, change seasonally or with new leadership don't do much to keep the *crowd* onside – inside or outside your company walls. Sustaining ideas – reinforced, evolved, and creatively re-expressed over long periods – are what enable your big idea to stick and stay with the *crowd.* Short-lived campaigns today just become fading data points for a *crowd* of *new C.E.O.s* who will move on quickly if they're not reminded why it's so inspiring to stay.

Campaigns created with outsiders become campaigns more of us can get behind

We've looked at bringing **C**onsumers and **E**mployees "inside" and finding ways to enable and invite them to participate directly in your business. What about the **O**utsiders in your *crowd*? Unilever's purpose statement is *to make sustainable living commonplace*. Despite having a staggering 2.5 billion touchpoints with customers every day across their 400 brands globally, they will still need a lot of help to deliver on that big promise. They will not be able to achieve it alone. One impressive example of how they bring **O**utsiders in to help them succeed is in their laundry soap portfolio. Unilever developed a campaign called "Dirt is Good" to market its regional laundry soap brands such as Omo, Skip, Via, and Persil.[111]

Here's the thing about dirt: Way too many people have started to believe it's bad. It's got germs and cooties and who knows what else in it. Parents get that idea in their heads and suddenly kids aren't allowed to jump in the mud anymore. That's not good. We already know that today's generation of children is the least active in history. In some developed countries, they're even showing up with previously eradicated diseases like rickets because they aren't getting as much sun as they used to. So play really is serious business.

But Unilever's laundry soap brands aren't just about getting kids dirty so that their parents will buy more laundry soap. They're serious about getting kids dirty in the long run. They wanted to solve the "play deficit," as one of their campaign partners called it. So, they launched a website called dirtisgood.com and offered up an Explorers App for filthy kids everywhere to use on the go. They also told parents "the truth about dirt" - basically summarizing the research supporting the idea that kids should play outside.

All of this is well and good, but it's pretty easy for a laundry soap company to argue kids should be dirty. To be credible, they needed to pull in **O**utsiders. And that's exactly what they did. Their expert advisors include Sir Ken Robinson and Dr. Stuart Brown, both world-renowned experts on play. They also partnered with Australia's Nature Play to embed their programming into parks and local governments. There's even a documentary film in which incarcerated people talk about the importance of their two hours of daily outdoor time, which is twice what the average kid gets.[112]

Unilever shows us that an everyday product like laundry soap can find its place to change the world for the better. Unilever also figured out that a campaign of this magnitude couldn't be theirs alone. Outside stakeholders would need to be part of the solution. It sounds simple, but not all companies understand when they can go alone and when they can't.

Finding and pursuing ideas that enable shared benefits, as Unilever does, should be every company's obsession. It's the biggest reason we decided to write this book.

Starbucks gives us some great examples of *crowd*-led campaigns. Some went really well, others didn't. To start with, we love Starbucks' mission *to inspire and nurture the human spirit – one person, one cup and one neighborhood at a tim*e. They see themselves as the 21st-century coffeehouse where people connect, converse, and debate. This is an *Inspired Mission* that promotes democracy and dialogue at a local community level. Regardless of whether you like their coffee, this concept is very cool – and they've adjusted the way they think about their campaigns and communications as a result of it. With this mission, conversations are part of their core business.

Starbuck's #HowWeMet is just one example of how they create campaigns to celebrate their core commitment to "conversations." #HowWeMet was about people sharing their stories of . . . well, you get the idea. Starbucks connected a simple but very compelling social concept directly to their mission. They didn't try to sell extra cups of coffee. They just tried to engage people in a natural conversation about connection. And it worked. Its success demonstrates how Starbucks has effectively transitioned to a place where they can deliver a steady drumbeat of campaigns that resonate because they are inspired by something not meant to change that often – their mission.

At the same time, as companies push new boundaries in campaign design to create more direct and authentic connections with the *crowd*, there may be some hard lessons to learn along the way. Starbucks discovered this when the "conversation" stakes got much higher – when they decided to address racial equality in the U.S.

The resulting campaign – called Race Together – is an important example of good intentions with not-so-good execution. It's a pioneering example of what happens today if you exclude key parts of the *crowd* when you engage in topics they really care about. Here's what happened: When racial tensions escalated across the U.S. in 2015 over police officers shooting unarmed African-Americans, Starbucks wanted to tackle the conversation head-on and publicly. This decision followed several months of internal "town hall" meetings during which the company's leadership discussed race issues with employees. That was a great start. To expand the conversation beyond their own internal walls, they partnered with *USA Today* to produce an eight-page supplement on race that included conversation-starters, fill-in-the-blank statements, vignettes from real people, stats about progress (or the lack of it), etc. All in all, it was accessible and easily digestible content – perfect for an impromptu conversation in a coffee shop ...

Starting on March 19, 2015, the supplement was available at Starbucks retail stores across the U.S. At the same time, any customer who walked into Starbucks to buy a coffee received a cup with "#RaceTogether" written on the side.

Cue a nuclear explosion. Or maybe a coffeehouse implosion.

Despite really great intentions, the company was roundly mocked and criticized. The *crowd* – consumers and Starbucks employees alike – made their opinions known, after the fact and without reservation. In fairness there are probably several reasons for the largely negative initial outcome. The first misstep was perhaps overlooking the importance of creating a "safe space" when delving into a topic like racial injustice. Starbucks had created this space for their internal town halls, which is no small achievement in itself. But the broader public was a different story. An "impromptu conversation in a coffee shop" between strangers about one of the U.S.'s most divisive and painful social issues was really ambitious. While Starbucks had done *some* work with *some* employees, more could have been done to deliberately and practically integrate civil society stakeholders into Starbucks' hopes to expand the conversation. Baristas weren't trained to lead this kind of conversation and, not surprisingly, communities found themselves unable to self-navigate. Had Starbucks worked much more closely with traditional **O**utsiders – civil society actors and other experts – the campaign execution and outcomes might have gone very differently.

Getting something like this right could have been a matter of *bringing the outside in*. More likely, though, Starbucks might have benefited from a little self-reflection before designing the campaign. A company with a white chairman, a white CEO, and only one person of color on its board was trying to lead a conversation about race. We are not saying they shouldn't have done something – particularly when Starbuck's mission challenges them to. It might have been more effective, however, to find ways to leverage their assets and infrastructure to enable *others to lead* the conversation. Perhaps starting with the woman who wrote "I don't have time to explain 400 years of oppression to you and still make my train." That's April Reign – an activist, attorney, and social media influencer with more than 125,000 Twitter followers. She also created the #OscarsSoWhite movement. Reign is just one of many people with the potential to lead a meaningful discussion. But she needed to be recognized and invited first.

Another insight brought to us by Starbucks' Race Together is the risk associated with creating your own message for a social movement already in play. When you're standing up for an issue that's bigger than you are, think twice before creating your own hashtag, tagline, website, or symbol. One Starbucks customer made this point quite elegantly on the side of her coffee cup:[113]

Sabrina Hersi Issa
@

Nope to #RaceTogether. But here Starbucks I fixed your hashtag. #BlackLivesMatter

12:52 PM · 17 Mar 2015 ·

235 Retweets 243 Likes

We don't particularly enjoy picking on Starbucks. We love their willingness to take risks and bring up issues that most corporate legal or PR departments would have axed. Indeed, after the campaign, Starbucks' Howard Schultz called out his fellow chief executives for hanging back: "I have not heard from one CEO in America, black or white or Hispanic, to say, 'Is there anything I or my company can do to help, assist, or support what you're trying to do as a result of Race Together?' Not one."[114] Starbucks is blurring the lines of established roles. That's exactly what is needed for effective brand-marketing campaign design today.

That's why our final lesson from Race Together is this: Starbucks tried, failed, and kept trying. They don't shrink away from big issues, as you'll see in the next couple of pages. Turns out they were forgiven pretty quickly for it anyway. That's a sign of an *Inspired Company.*

So far, we've covered what happens when you let the *crowd* inside and empower them to make a mark across a company's operations – from what a company makes or offers, to how a company shows up in the world. We close this section with a look at the *crowd* influencing the very rules inside a company itself.

2.5 Crowd-led policy development

Workplace policies are reactive. We all know this. If a problem arises, a new rule is written. Eventually, so many rules are written that most people can't remember any of them. We plan for the worst of people without ever acknowledging the best. That's the norm. This is about everything from expense policies to how suppliers are selected.

Inspired Companies operate under a different set of principles. Policies are influenced by the legitimate needs of the *crowd* and legal requirements, not reactive decisions based on isolated internal and external events. They are designed in a way that signals and expects mutual trust.

Trust Employees to self-regulate and create bottom-up policies

Inspired Companies engage employees directly on important issues and in developing policies that directly impact them. When employees are an integral part of decisions that matter to them – diversity, equal opportunity, accountability, responsibility – the results speak for themselves. Netflix is a great example. HR departments are notorious policy factories. Something goes wrong, write a policy. Netflix decided they'd rather HR leaders spend their time finding great talent who aligned with their vision. So they ditched the rules and focused on hiring the right people.[115] That means their expense policy amounts to "act in the best interest of the company" and their vacation policy says "take what you need."

Netflix's position is they're designing for the vast majority who will do good, instead of imposing oppressive rules based on the smaller fraction who will do bad. These (non)policies remain revolutionary, but they've been effective enough for other companies to follow suit. In fact, GE, Virgin Group, and LinkedIn[116] have all adopted unlimited PTO (paid time off) policies. These kinds of non-policies might not work for every company due to the nature of their work, but this approach is worth considering in the right environments. The point is, rules are far more effective when they are co-created, not imposed or imported.

Is there a lawyer in the house?

No one likes legal problems. Most companies "lawyer up" at the first sign of trouble. CrossFit isn't most companies. Over the course of 10 years, CrossFit completely turned the modern fitness industry upside down and in doing so, attracted a *crowd* so loyal it would be any company's envy. According to members of the CrossFit *crowd*, when the company realized they needed a more robust set of liability agreements and protections to cover their community of affiliates, they put the call out to their community to help. Shockingly, it turned out a community united by a love of highly competitive, aggressive, and painful activities contained a lot of lawyers. Within a few days, the community mobilized and CrossFit had an improved set of liability agreements for the entire network to use.

Hiring policies that take a stand

In 2017, Starbucks made a global commitment to hire 10,000 refugees by 2022. Crises in Syria, Sudan, Afghanistan, and Iraq (to name a few) triggered one of the greatest refugee crises we have seen in our lifetime. While displaced people have many immediate needs, Starbucks saw that long-term stability for families doesn't happen without jobs.

With a presence in 72 countries on six continents,[117] Starbucks recognized its unique ability to play a critical role in the ongoing refugee crisis. As they put it, "Starbucks will focus our initial efforts on markets where the refugee need is greatest and where we have a store base to meet the need."[118] They also knew there was no way they could make a dent in the problem on their own. So they partnered with the International Rescue Committee (IRC), UNHCR (the UN Refugee Agency), and the nonprofit No One Left Behind to ensure the program was designed in a way that best served the needs of refugees and local communities. These agencies have a stake in Starbucks' strategy – so why wouldn't they help them? Everyone wins.

This type of public–private partnership isn't new in the corporate sector, although it could be argued that effective ones are relatively rare. What is certifiably rare are co-created policies between a company and its *crowd,* united behind shared values.

Find your path

These are all great examples of the *crowd* leading the way when you let them inside. Whether they're at the center of policy change or integral parts of creative and campaign design, the *crowd* will bring authenticity and flair you wouldn't otherwise see. Having said that, this is not about crowdsourcing cheap labor. This is about trusting the *crowd* with the things you would have traditionally held close. When they're inspired, the *crowd* will do amazing things, but you can't plan on the amazing things from the outset. The Obama campaign team didn't drive toward Shepard Fairey's stylized image of a future president. When Nike launched NIKEiD, they didn't have "Get a consumer to reimagine a sneaker" as a metric of success. Instead, these efforts sought to bring **C**onsumers, **E**mployees, and **O**utsiders inside to mobilize them around big mutually inspiring ideas.

We also don't provide these examples for anyone to outright copy (although no one's going to stop you, and you'll see in a minute that we're rule-breakers). Still, you should know that *Inspired Companies* are by definition uniquely inspired. What works for one brand and organizational culture may not necessarily work for another. The key is to burst your corporate bubble and figure out how your *crowd* can lead you into the future.

Strategy 3: Break rules

We've seen how more *Inspired Companies Shake up the System* by reimagining how their top leaders lead and by bringing their *crowd* closer to the inside. Not surprisingly, companies on this path won't have the patience for industry practices that get in the way of their mission or of the things their *crowd* cares about. They'll break the rules if they have to.

But we get it. The current system has been in place for a very long time. Some pretty powerful forces rely on its very existence. It is established, it is predictable, and it has a set of rules that you just don't break.

That is, unless you want to deliver on really big, inspired ideas.

An authentic commitment to a bigger purpose will lead you to consider breaking the rules. It will force you to question norms and start to recognize where established systems might be getting in the way of progress. *Inspired Companies* will question the established, unwritten rules of their industries. Eventually, they'll figure out how to completely defy standard operating procedures in favor of their big idea and the *crowd*.

3.1 Question industry norms

Industry-wide norms dictate a lot of the policies and procedures companies put into the world. Although they're often arbitrary, over time they establish standard operating procedures and people stop questioning them. These are things like 30-day return policies, one-year warranties, and all of the fine print most of us don't have time to read but are accustomed to accepting. *Inspired Companies* ignore arbitrary standards and create their own to be true to their mission and their *crowd*.

Tesla brings its *Inspired Mission* to life through its daily decisions. One of the ways that shows up is through actions that completely fly in the face of decades-old norms in the auto industry. For example, Tesla created an eight-year infinite-mile warranty in a world that mostly guarantees its product for three years and 36,000 miles. That's gutsy. They also put their showrooms in luxury malls, bypassing the traditional standalone dealership model. Why force their potential customers to come to them when they can just as easily go to their customer (and no doubt save significantly on capital costs at the same time)? Both are great examples of a company completely ignoring industry norms to show up more consistently with their inspired idea to *accelerate the advent of sustainable energy*.

Challenging norms can be done in the ordinary course of business when you are inspired. This is the kind of thing that surprises customers and creates loyalty. It's also the kind of thing that challenges the whole industry to follow suit. And that is Tesla's ultimate goal. If this sounds crazy, remember there once was a time when a lone wireless carrier (AT&T in the U.S.) decided to offer unlimited minutes.

Let's go back to the insurance industry. This is an industry built on stockpiles of data and loads of questions. "It was not unusual for us to ask your birthday five different ways, it was so ridiculous," says Mark Wilson, who most recently led Aviva's turnaround. In recent years, the company invested heavily to make sure all of Aviva's products, services, and IT systems shared customer information seamlessly. Those efforts, combined with big data analytics, means Aviva can now price insurance products at an individual level. Two norms busted for the price of one. Aviva customers no longer have to pay for the daredevils who drive our insurance premiums up, and the company commits to "only ask once, or not at all."

Another reason to question industry norms is that sometimes they can perpetuate broader social and cultural norms that are just flat-out wrong. Nike, for example, has never liked the idea that particular groups of people aren't allowed to run. Until the 1970s and '80s, you might be surprised to learn that there were no women's marathons. Not in the Olympics or anywhere else. The completely unscientific assumption was that women lacked the stamina and physical strength to run marathons. We were excluded, ostensibly, for our protection. That was the norm. Doctors, lawyers, marathon planners . . . It seemed as though everyone accepted it.

It was total crap, of course. And Nike said as much.

The company was especially inspired by Joan Benoit Samuelson. Joan is an elite runner and advocate for girls and women's sports. When she started running, women didn't run outdoors in the U.S. Want to know why? Because they might get spat on. When the folks at Nike heard that from Joan, they vowed it would never happen again. Joan was a Nike athlete and no one would tell her she couldn't run. During a time when society thought women should not be running, Nike was part of influencing the International Olympic Committee to ensure the women's marathon would become an Olympic event. It was first included in 1984. And in case you're wondering, Joan Benoit Samuelson took the gold.

3.2 Defy norms altogether

This is where startups thrive in particular. Big, established companies don't usually spend a lot of time questioning norms. They've been following (and making) them for decades. Startups count on this. They're set up to disrupt the status quo. In fact, it's usually the first slide of an entrepreneur's venture capital pitch deck.

When you're clear on your core and your core is an idea, not a business model, it becomes easier to recognize where rules can be broken. CrossFit defied virtually every norm in the fitness industry (not to mention the branding norms we covered earlier). While others focused on expensive equipment and fancy workout spaces, CrossFit created something pretty much anyone could do in their garage or garden. And any cross-fitter will tell you it's a harder workout than anything a US$6,000 piece of equipment will provide. When asked if the intensive CrossFit workout might be risky, as some have claimed, CrossFit CEO Greg Glassman had this to say: "Dangerous? Maybe to the rest of the industry. I think we are a threat." Why are they a threat? Because they're doing business differently and their *crowd* loves it.

The thing is, defying norms doesn't need to involve industry disruption in the traditional sense. It's just a matter of doing things differently and putting big ideas ahead of anything else.

REI is a powerful example of a company that puts its mission first. It seeks *to inspire, educate and outfit for a lifetime of outdoor adventure and stewardship*. In 2015, the company closed all of its stores the day after Thanksgiving, widely considered to be the busiest shopping day of the year in the U.S. Traditionally, this is the day when retailers move from losses (red) to profit (black) – hence the name Black Friday, and the aggressive competition for customer dollars. For any retailer, closing shop on this day would be considered completely insane.

But REI didn't think it was insane at all. In fact, they went a step further and didn't process any online orders either. Instead of a big sales push, REI is encouraging people to . . . wait for it . . . go outside. And then they asked people to share their experiences with #OptOutside. Yes, this is one day, but closing on Black Friday sends a clear signal about the company's priorities. This is one of the gutsiest moves we've seen a retail company make in pursuit of its mission.

The move certainly didn't seem to hurt REI's financial performance. In fact, the company reported record annual revenues that year. Meanwhile, 1.4 million people participated and the company launched an #OptOutside platform for people to share favorite outdoor spaces and explore what it means to get outside. #OptOutside was so successful that it became an annual Black Friday event for REI.

Inspired Companies go against the current when defiance is in service of their mission, values, or *crowd*. Once you've become practiced at looking at everything through the lens of the ideas that underpin your bigger purpose, it becomes easy to see which industry standards or social stereotypes are getting in your way. It's also a bit easier to see what some of the companies we discussed here already know: Norms aren't laws. There's no reason you have to follow them.

Strategy 4: Play offense with shareholders

There's one last norm that we'll cover here – and it's a big one: shareholder primacy.

Shaking things up and leading with purpose without working with shareholders is a sure way to get yourself fired. And if you're an inspired leader, we'd like to keep you in the top job.

Many companies, and by extension their executive leaders, spend a lot of time *on defense with shareholders*. They provide the information shareholders want according to the schedule on which they demand it. It hardly matters that the average stock-holding period on the NYSE is somewhere between four and eight months (down from eight-plus years in 1960).[119] This idea that a company has a greater duty to a day trader or high-frequency trading platforms than it does to its mission is long past expired.

It's time to reorient actions toward the best interest of the company.

To be clear, shareholders are obviously really important. They are part of an *Inspired Company's crowd* and essential to fueling a robust corporate sector. Shareholders, partners, and investors of any other kind need to be on board. They need to believe you and they have the potential to be inspired. The key here is to change the dynamic from a focus on pandering to short-term investors to a focus on recruiting long-term investors.

So how do you make that happen? During the dot-com boom, companies were notorious for throwing lavish parties to impress investors. You know the stories, maybe you were even there – flying everyone to Bermuda to hang out with a famous band. Or, possibly the most famous: Tyco CEO Dennis Kozlowski's US$2 million birthday party/shareholder meeting on an Italian island featuring a private Jimmy Buffett concert (one of many reasons Kozlowski served a lengthy prison sentence).[120] That's not what we're talking about. We're talking about changing how you communicate with investors and their intermediaries – brokers, analysts, and commentators – and finding ways to work around the limitations of traditional financing models.

We talked a bit about short-termism early in this book. While it's true that short-termism exists in trading communities, it's actually a far more systemic issue. Executive compensation structures and plain old bad hiring decisions have just as much to do with a culture of short-termism as day traders do.

There's another way. *Inspired Companies* take the best of what accountability to shareholders has to offer, while minimizing the busy work.

4.1 Break the cycle

If you cater to short-term investors, you'll attract short-term investors. While that might be beneficial to a one-day share price, it does nothing to serve a company or its broader *crowd* in the long run. To become inspired, companies will need to change the dynamic.

While serving as Unilever's chief executive, Paul Polman famously questioned the need to keep incentivizing a short-term approach to business decision-making. Instead of killing themselves to meet numbers every 90 days, they announced they'd no longer be providing quarterly reports. In an interview with *Forbes*,[121] he describes his thinking:

> Well, first what we said was, in order to solve issues like food security or climate change, you need to have longer-term solutions. You cannot do that on a quarterly basis. They require longer-term investments.
>
> It's the same for companies. A lot of companies are driven by the short-termism of the markets. [They] make short-term decisions that

often go against the long-term viability of the company. Before I came, we were making a lot of short-term decisions to make the quarterly numbers, [and these decisions were] actually driving the company, over time, downwards.

It's very easy to show more profits, if that's what you want, by cutting investments in training and development of your people or your IT systems. And you can do that for a few years but in the long term, you erode your company. So what I said when I came here is I need to create this environment for the company to make the right longer-term decisions. So we stopped giving guidance. We stopped doing quarterly reporting. We changed the compensation for the long term.

Aviva also announced during their September 2017 results period that they would no longer be doing quarterly reporting. "I want shareholders who want long-term results . . . a focus on the short term was what got this company into a mess a few years ago. If you want short-term results, don't invest in me," said Mark Wilson over dinner with one of us in London. The topic annoyed him so much he promptly asked for the check, and the interview (and dinner) was over.

As frustrating as this topic is for chief executives, leaders must be smart about when to make this kind of a move. Wilson picked his moment to announce the new reporting cadence when all of Aviva's key performance indicators had been on the rise for several consecutive quarters. His leadership approval rating was high and the company's pipeline of new innovations impressive. A good time to strike.

As more corporate leaders push for long-term strategies over short-term gains, we can reshape the unrealistic expectation that good business and sustainable growth happens in 90 days. Elon Musk has no problem telling the world that he will make decisions that serve the best long-term interests of the company. Take this example from Tesla's 2014 shareholder letter:

This also is a legitimate criticism of Tesla – we prefer to forgo revenue, rather than bring a product to market that does not delight customers.

Doing so negatively affects the short term, but positively affects the long term. There are many other companies that do not follow this philosophy that may be a more attractive home for investor capital. Tesla is not going to change.[122]

Defying established norms of the financial system, as Polman, Wilson, and Musk all have done, takes a fearless level of courage and conviction. Decisions of this magnitude won't be without backlash, particularly during this moment of transition when the norms and practices of the financial system have not yet adjusted to the growing power and accelerating impact of the *crowd*. Change is right around the corner, however, and leaders willing to take a stand will be on the right side of history.

4.2 Proactively leverage your culture

In the end, an *Inspired Company's* best investor offense is often its corporate culture. All of the recommendations and suggestions in this book are really about transforming the culture of your organization to be inspired. Of course, you know the challenge here as well as we do. Culture is notoriously hard to define and quantify. You have to see it or experience it for yourself to believe it and understand its power. For shareholders, the key is to open your doors, let them see it for themselves and have them get to know and trust the people who bring it to life.

Show what you're made of: Use investor events as opportunities to inspire

All public companies and many private ones have to communicate regularly with investors. The quarterly report. The investor call. It's a job unto itself. They can also be painfully boring. Why not use it as an opportunity to inspire?

That's exactly what Tony's Chocolonely does. You remember them. The folks who want 100 percent slave-free chocolate. First, Tony's doesn't just do an annual report. They do an annual FAIR report. It covers the state of their business and the state of their industry.

And they do it in a way that not only draws in shareholders, but also delights their *crowd*: They throw a really big party.

The way Tony's leadership describes it, the annual meeting is a combination of "serious" (a day-long public meeting, sharing results and the state of slavery in the industry) and "crazy" (a cultural event that includes bands, artists, and thousands of attendees). It's a perfect reflection of their "crazy about chocolate, serious about people" tagline. As a privately held company, Tony's has four equity shareholders, all of whom take an active role in decision-making and are in it for the long haul.

When we were at Nike, the company brought the investment community closer to the inside by inviting them periodically to the Nike campus – its world headquarters in Oregon. The company showcased innovation from across markets and functions, and provided access to leaders who knew Nike's consumers best and were aligned to the future strategy of the company. Leaders as excited about the company as they want investors to be. For Nike, where design and innovation are everything, it was also an opportunity to inspire visually. Most of all, it was a demonstration of the quality of leadership and depth of succession. It told investors the company is a good bet – not just for today, but tomorrow.

Apple is a good example of a company that knows how to get people excited about its plans. Everyone knows about the company's annual product events. They're wildly popular, eagerly anticipated, invitation-only gatherings that are covered heavily in the press. They're also designed for investors. For years, the message has been the same – something along the lines of "we innovate ahead of the curve with products that make consumers' lives better." Of course, not everything ever announced by Apple has been a success[*] (or makes life better), but enthusiasts of the splashy product events don't seem bothered by that because, on balance, Apple stays true to its ability to innovate and make elegant, intuitive products.

---

[*] Remember Pippin and Macintosh TV? Yeah, neither do we.

Tony's, Apple, and Nike are pretty cool, but being cool is not
a prerequisite to attracting the right investors. Being authentic is.
Berkshire Hathaway was one of the original companies to bring
together shareholders and have the chief executive talk to them openly
and directly. It's an old-school example that's unflashy, humble, and
brave. Just have a look at the 2017 agenda:

Saturday, May 6	
Annual Meeting	
Doors Open	7:00am
Company Movie	8:30am
Q&A	9:30am – 3:30pm
Business Meeting	3:45 – 4:45pm (approximation)
NFM Picnic	5:30 – 8pm

Berkshire Hathaway's Annual Meeting in 2017

Nope, no danger of smoke and mirrors here, distracting investors
from the business at hand. What Berkshire Hathaway does brilliantly
is to say, "Here's who we are, here's what we believe in. If you want
to be part of this community, come on out and we'll work together."
Berkshire seems to be doing okay and anyone who's ever attended a
Berkshire shareholder meeting knows there are plenty of people who
plan to hold onto their stock for a long, long time.[123]

Seek out investors who understand the link between strong culture and results

It's common for a company's leaders to talk about their culture and
purpose with one set of words and for everyone else to talk about it
differently. That's why investors like Stewart Investors do onsite visits
and interviews. Amanda McCluskey, Investor at Stewart Investors
Group, says it's time for companies to get real about where they're
at. When asked about how they make decisions for investment she
emphasized, "We don't go to road shows or read sustainability
reports. Those are marketing tools. Pictures of smiling children and
lists of CSR awards don't do it. Instead, we encourage companies to

come up with ways of articulating the true challenges they face and [to] communicate about them in an honest way."

Stuart Investors assess the strength of a company's culture by talking to as many people as possible. And when they're evaluating a potential investment for their portfolio, one critical thing they want to know is, "Does the company have good *dharma*?" (That's the Sanskrit word for "purpose".) "Is everyone telling the same story as the chief executive?" If they aren't, there may very well be a problem.

The managers of this high-performing fund also look carefully for how a company translates words about culture and purpose into action. They look for "signals of a good moral compass" and examples of "how a company responds" when it makes mistakes. McCluskey adds: "Most large companies lack *dharma*. A company with good *dharma* has an added layer of protection from making decisions that will undermine long-term performance."

Evaluating investments through that lens has led the fund to disproportionately invest in companies like Unilever, as well as Novo Nordisk and Wärtsilä, a Finnish company that's moving the shipping industry toward sustainability. Stewart Investors is not a niche investor. According to Lipper Data from Thomson Reuters, the Stewart Investors' Asia Fund is the best-performing fund in its category over 10 years. Their Emerging Markets and WorldWide funds have also been consistently in the first and second quartiles relative to other investment funds. This is against all investment products, not just sustainability products.

Of course, the folks at Stewart Investors aren't the only ones making this connection. Alex Edmans, a highly regarded professor of finance at London Business School, has made a practice of proving that a) to be profitable, businesses must take a multi-stakeholder view and b) the connection between profit and purpose can be quantified.[124]

Edmans spent four years putting together a study to show that companies with higher employee satisfaction perform better. He used the data associated with Fortune's "100 Best Companies to Work For" because it extends back to 1984 and includes a large repository of quantitative data (e.g., pay, benefits) and qualitative data (e.g., trust in management, pride in your job, etc.). Controlling for industry, size, growth opportunities, past performance, etc. and layering on tests to prove causation, Edmans looked at the effect of being a "best company to work for" on future stock market returns. The finding? Best companies to work for had returns of 2 to 3 percent higher than their peers. That's 2 to 3 percent per year. For 26 years.

Edmans also argues that fund managers and investors more generally all have access to the same information. As a result, the only way to gain an edge is to look at the information differently and find the measures of things like corporate culture, loyalty, and innovation. While everyone else is looking at P/E ratios and market cap, or so the theory goes, the smart investor is layering on more purpose-related intangibles linked to performance. From the returns data currently available, it looks like Edmans is onto something.

When investors are onside

Attracting the right investors (i.e., those with a long-term interest in your *Inspired Mission*) is essential for an *Inspired Company's* capitalization. And they just might come to your defense when you need them to. When Kraft made a "friendly" US$143 billion bid for Unilever in 2017, Unilever rejected the offer. The bid followed calls from some analysts for more aggressive growth strategies. Jack Nelson, a fund analyst with longtime Unilever shareholder Stewart Investors, published a letter defending Unilever's approach in the *Financial Times.* Here's some of what he had to say:

> The cacophony of voices from "the market" seeking to pressure Unilever's management into action seems premised on the misplaced notion that the company has been underachieving.
>
> In reality, Unilever has been particularly successful at striking the right balance between present and future needs and ambitions. This has enabled the company to deliver not only for its shareholders but also on its broader social purpose.

Investors in Unilever's London listed shares have been rewarded with a return of just under 13 percent a year over the past decade, vs. a little over 5 percent a year in the FTSE100. Sustained for ten years, this has meant a 230 percent return vs. 66 percent in the index. This is a company which has delivered handsomely for its shareholders. ...

As a significant shareholder in Unilever on behalf of our clients, Stewart Investors will be encouraging Unilever's allegedly "chastened" management to resist short-term pressures to take corporate action in the wake of the Kraft-Heinz approach.

Instead we will be supporting them to continue doing what Unilever has been for 130 years: pioneering responsible capitalism and combining sustainability leadership with ample rewards for long-term, patient shareholders.

How often do you see a fund manager publicly standing up for a company's long-term interests? We think it's time for more of that. Imagine a future where investors routinely come to the defense of the companies they invest in. With the *new C.E.O.s* firmly in charge, companies that behave and perform consistently over longer periods of time will have whole *crowds* coming to their defense.

And that includes their investors.

4.3 Find financing workarounds

No matter how great the mission or how deep the commitment, almost all *Inspired Companies* have to operate within the current financial market and capital-raising system to access serious funding and increase capitalization. When they do, the stakes get a whole lot higher. More influencers come into play, the light of scrutiny gets brighter and leaders become responsible for more money belonging to more people. The possibility of making a mistake becomes very scary and leaders may find it easier to fall in line with the existing system. The good news? There are other ways to go.

Inspired Companies find workarounds to reduce or diffuse the pressures associated with the profit-at-all-costs shareholder primacy dynamics to ensure their core inspiration takes priority. While some workaround efforts could be seen as luck, others are deliberate and strategic. This is an area where silver bullets and perfect solutions do not exist. However imperfect, here are a few approaches that can help:

Founder as the majority shareholder:
When a founder owns the most significant portion of a company's stock, the founder could have more leverage when it comes to strategic decisions that serve the company's original inspiration. As long as they are an inspired leader, this can serve as a protective force. See: Nike and Phil Knight.

Committed family stewards:
Companies with a committed family at the helm and a majority (or at least very large) shareholding tend to take a longer-term view of their business and are less likely to prioritize short-termism. For example, Indian IT giants Wipro and Tech Mahindra are steered by the Premji and Mahindra families, respectively.

Investment funds with aligned interests:
As noted, Stewart Investors is a great example of an investment fund that is wired to look for *Inspired Companies*. The company is broadly focused on long-term investments and fiduciary duty. Their sustainable investments group invests exclusively in companies that are "positioned to benefit from and contribute to the sustainable development of the countries in which they operate."[125] Funds such as Marathon or Generation Investment Management are also well regarded for seeking out long-term hold positions in companies committed to big ideas with strong sustainability leadership and governance practices. When these funds are authentically committed to the long term, they can be important backers for *Inspired Companies*.

Stay private, or return to it:

The fact that *Fortune* now ranks the 25 most important private companies is telling in and of itself. Major companies are shedding their publicly traded status in exchange for freedom from compliance and regulation costs. ARM Holdings, for example, was delisted from the London Stock Exchange when it was bought outright by Japanese telco giant Softbank for US$31 billion in September 2017. Others are choosing not to go public in the first place. A study of the U.K.'s most trusted brands in 2016 ranked LEGO and IKEA at the top of the list.[126] What do these two companies have in common? They're both privately held. We're not saying all companies should stay private. Instead, we're suggesting a closer look at what gives those companies the freedom to behave in ways that make them the most trusted.

Employee-owned:

Huawei is 100 percent owned by its employees – allowing them to deliver long-term value when they see it. David De Cremer and Tian Tao, both business professors in China, put it this way: "Being privately held has allowed Huawei to work on its 10-year plans, while its competitors struggle to follow near-term fluctuations of the capital market."[127] Huawei is now the third-largest smartphone company in the world and the only Chinese telecom company with significant business success outside of China.[128] Having the freedom to prioritize things that create long-term value is why this employee-owned firm took the unique stance that an IPO would diminish the work they do – enriching a few while causing the rest to lose motivation.

Expense offset:

Inspired Companies are finding creative ways to finance mission-driven decisions. One example is the CEO of Gravity Payments, who personally absorbed the cost of company-wide pay raises. Another is a public–private partnership in Seattle that sought to bring professional basketball and hockey teams to the city. The lack of adequate facilities has always been a stumbling block, so the group secured a city government commitment to finance a new stadium with repayment coming in the form of future tax revenue from the project.

Crowdfund:

Consumers don't mind funding cool stuff. Indiegogo and Kickstarter have certainly figured this out. For that matter, so has Tesla. After creating a few relatively expensive and unbelievably cool electric cars (that work!), the company set out to make something for the masses. Enter the Model 3, Tesla's US$35,000 entry-level electric car. Problem was, the company needed about US$1.4 billion to bring the car to market. A good chunk of that came from 455,000 pre-orders[129] of US$1,000 each. All from customers who were willing to wait a few years to get their cars.

Selective private equity investment:

Companies that remain private are sometimes lucky enough to have equity shareholders who value the inspired core and are aligned with the overall mission. One outcome of this is unexpected investors, like the Bill & Melinda Gates Foundation's US$52 million equity investment in CureVac, a biotech company that's developing a promising approach to more efficiently and cost-effectively deliver vaccines to the world's poorest. This model of staying private – whether the company is inspired or not – is appearing more and more. Companies like the business intelligence firm Domo, for example, receive massive amounts of private funding and, so far, aren't seeing the appeal of public markets. (Domo originally planned to go public in 2015. By 2017 they had been successful enough at raising money privately, saying "You can't be as aggressive when you're public as when you're private."[130]) Heck, even investment firms like Vanguard and Fidelity Investments have opted to remain privately held.[131]

Align to new structures:

In Chapter 6 we covered the idea that new legal structures are emerging – like public benefit corporations and certified B corps. These structures are designed to more deliberately acknowledge and drive accountability to a broader set of stakeholders and promote social return. These structures logically attract long-term sustainable investors. One well-known example is Ben & Jerry's.

Capital alternatives:

Private companies often seek alternative forms of capital, including co-operatives, membership dues, program-related investments (below-market loans designed to support social outcomes), etc. REI is probably the best-known and most successful co-op in the U.S.

There are a couple of key takeaways here. First, leading companies are already starting to reject the very powerful and magnetic pull toward the short-termism pitfalls of traditional corporate financing and capital raising. Second, some combination of workarounds is essential to staying focused on an *Inspired Mission,* especially as the company grows and is by default leveraging the existing system. Third, the list above represents several promising ideas. We're certain that *Inspired Companies* of the future will create entirely new workarounds that have yet to be imagined.

Are you ready to shake a few things up?

This whole chapter is about moving a company from the internal work of *Obsessive Alignment* to mobilizing the *crowd* and showing the world you mean business. If you've read this chapter and feel like you don't have to *Shake up the System* to achieve your big idea, your big idea probably isn't big enough. Showing that you have the courage and follow-through to question norms, break rules, and bring the outside in shows that you're serious. These are the things that will give people reasons to believe you. It's what helps you grow your *crowd* and it certainly gives them a better reason to get behind you.

The next step involves taking things to the next level and leading with *Bold Conviction*. It's a phase in the journey with opportunities to further differentiate your brand through increasingly assertive ways of pursuing purpose and standing up for your values. This is where you'll create even greater distance between your brand and less inspired competitors. It's also a part of the journey where you'll really need your *crowd's* support – and if you show them that you are brave enough to shake things up, there's a very good chance you'll get it.

Chapter 7 Summary

The corporate system has been gearing itself toward an
uninspired way of doing things for about a hundred years.
Turning things upside down means you'll have to break some
rules and get on the offense. Key strategies include:

- Reimagine the top job
  - Lead with Purpose. Always.
  - Be accessible. Let the *crowd* get to know you.
- Bring the *crowd* inside. Create a more participatory business model.
  - From innovation to branding communications and internal policy
    development – the *crowd* can be your most inspired innovators,
    content creators, and storytellers if they can be trusted to
    participate directly.
- Break rules
  - Question industry and social norms. Or defy them altogether.
- Play offense with shareholders. Change expectations for the better.
  - Break the cycle by challenging investor community norms that
    perpetuate short-termism
  - Proactively leverage culture to build confidence in the long term
  - Find financing workarounds

Finding ways to *Shake up the System* will unlock opportunities to
surprise and delight the *crowd*. Following through on this part
of your *Inspired Company* journey increases the chance that a
broader base beyond your employees will also know that you are
serious about pursuing big ideas.

Chapter 8

Inspired Action:
Bold Conviction

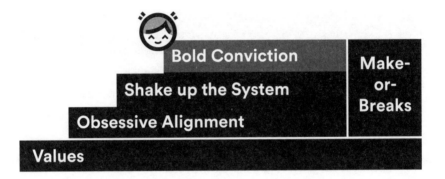

Lead with Conviction

Leading with *Bold Conviction* is where *Inspired Companies* separate from the pack.

Once companies have committed to the ongoing work of *Obsessive Alignment,* and lived through the trial and error of doing things differently by *Shaking up the System*, this is the fun part. The commitment to mission will pay off with newfound agility, new competencies, and increased clarity about the path forward. With growing support from the *crowd*, a new kind of self-assured confidence will emerge as organizations learn how to identify, create, and respond to opportunities in real time.

At this stage, leaders of *Inspired Companies* show the courage to lead, not follow. They will do things on behalf of the company that will be thoughtful, authentic, and entirely unexpected. There are many ways we have seen the more *Inspired Companies* bring this to life. Here are a few frontrunners:

- Fight when you have to

- Disarm

- Do something unexpected

In This Chapter

- How you can take unimaginable risks for your *Inspired Mission*, with speed, clarity, and creativity – enabled by an aligned organization and permission of the *crowd*

- Step off the sidelines: your *crowd* expects you to stand up to political challenges and join broader movements, and will be inspired when you do

- Surprise your critics and competitors: always find a way to make things right, be radically transparent, find common ground, and share the spotlight (as well as some of your trade secrets)

- Here's when you can truly create distinction (and what happens if you don't get your *new C.E.O.s* onside first)

Remember when Apple stood up to law enforcement by refusing their request to break into the iPhone of a terrorist attacker? When companies around the world united to visibly celebrate marriage equality? Or when American chief executives resigned en masse from federal business councils in protest of Donald Trump's tacit support for white supremacist groups in 2017? *Inspired Companies* are bold enough to lead when others won't. They're committed enough to big ideas and a strong set of values that they're able to take a stand without checking in with focus groups.

Inspired Companies show a brand of courage and creativity not traditionally seen in the corporate world. Every once in a while, they will demonstrate their commitment to their bigger purpose in ways that blow people away. They have so much faith in their mission, values, and unique ability to create value that they do things others would consider unthinkable. Like giving away IP, co-branding great ideas or . . . not doing any branding at all so that big ideas become shared ideas. The point is, these leaders make decisions that serve big ideas and shared values, and aren't afraid to double down when the decisions aren't popular.

This type of *Inspired Action* typically happens fast, especially when it plays into current events or social movements. Moving quickly and effectively takes confidence – and what can give a company that confidence? Everything we've covered in previous chapters: Once a company has done the work to articulate an irresistible mission, driven alignment internally, and questioned existing systems, they build trust with the *crowd*. This groundwork ultimately enables a company to accelerate further and lead with bold levels of conviction. It might be tempting to step over the other *Inspired Action* building blocks and jump right into it. The only problem being that the *crowd* doesn't grant that kind of permission.

Remember Pepsi's widely mocked, tone-deaf ad we started this book with? If you wondered how Pepsi might have found itself in that place, it's likely they skipped the advance work necessary to build a strong base, and jumped ahead to join in on what looked to them like a trend: standing up for what you believe in. What's especially interesting about the Pepsi example is the company's chief executive at the time, Indra Nooyi, was well known for her efforts to transform Pepsi into a more purposeful company. Like many companies, Pepsi has been wired over a long period of time to pursue profit-as-purpose. Perhaps not explicitly, but certainly implicitly. The failed 2017 advertisement just goes to show that realigning an established company to a more *Inspired Company* is hard work. We suggest taking it seriously.

One final thought before we dive into our frontrunner strategies for *Bold Conviction*: The best ideas in this phase will almost always come directly from your *crowd* – and because you have now learned to bring them inside and really listen – it's possible for you to turn their ideas into even more creative forms of *Inspired Action*.

And now's the time to make it happen.

Strategy 1: Fight when you have to

Thirty years ago, there was a distinction between who a chief executive was personally and who they needed to be professionally. Likewise, there was a wall between corporate brands and politics. Those lines no longer exist today. *Inspired Companies* understand that brands no longer have the luxury of being neutral in a world where a powerful *crowd* expects so much more of them. They know when something's not right and they aren't afraid to do something about it. They'll venture into uncharted waters to stand up when their big idea or the values, rights, or needs of the *crowd* are threatened. More and more frequently, that can mean entering the political fray or weighing in on controversial issues. Oh, and they don't always wait until everyone else has stepped up to say something – they move first with conviction. They don't ask for permission or paralyze themselves with analysis of potential blowback because they know when it's the right thing to do. Their secret weapon? They've already been consistently earning the trust of the *crowd* and have them onside.

1.1 Take a stand when no one else will

Inspired Companies stand up for their **C**onsumers, **E**mployees, and **O**utsiders every day. And they fight hardest and loudest when true injustice threatens their *crowd* or the idea they are in pursuit of.

Nike takes a stand against ignorance

An *Inspired Company* is set up to rally quickly. It knows what it stands for, so it doesn't require three months of approvals from 12 different departments to move. That's why Nike was able to respond rapidly to radio host Don Imus' obscenely racist and sexist comments about the Rutgers women's basketball team following their exit from the NCAA tournament in 2007.

After the *crowd* (including sponsors) spoke, Imus was fired. At Nike, the outrage ran deep. 'Every athlete' in Nike's mission applies to 'every athlete,' regardless of race or gender. Nowhere does the mission say that black female athletes should be excluded, or that race should be a factor in Nike's commitment to deliver inspiration and innovation. To put it in less fancy terms, pretty much everyone at Nike thought Imus was an asshole and they wanted to respond.

Within a week or so, Nike released a full-page ad in *The New York Times*. It didn't mention Imus by name. Instead, it thanked "ignorance" for bringing a conversation to the forefront that sorely needed to be had. Here it is:

Thank you, ignorance.

Thank you for starting the conversation.

Thank you for making an entire nation listen to the Rutgers team story.

And for making us wonder what other great stories we've missed.

Thank you for reminding us to think before we speak.

Thank you for showing us how strong and poised 18- and 20-year-old women can be.

Thank you for reminding us that another basketball tournament goes on in March.

Thank you for showing us that sport includes more than the time spent on the court.

Thank you for unintentionally moving women's sport forward.

And thank you for making all of us realize that we still have a long way to go.

Next season starts 11.16.07

This ad was covered by almost every news outlet at the time. It didn't require extensive testing or layers of approvals. And it wasn't like Nike had creative folks waiting in the wings ready to write the perfect ad for the perfect time. While that might be how the public perceives it, that brilliant response wouldn't have been possible without significant and authentic efforts and belief systems leading up to it. That is, Nike couldn't have run that ad if it hadn't already demonstrated a sustained commitment to women's sports.

Nike's history with girls' and women's sports, while not perfect by any means, set them up to speak with credibility when the Imus issue arose. This was not a one-off – and that's what allowed them to act swiftly and confidently (at least by *Fortune* 100 terms) during the Imus debacle.

As highlighted in Chapter 7 with Joan Benoit Samuelson's story, Nike had been advocating for women's sports participation since the early 1980s. In the 1970s, a federal law in the U.S. called Title IX was enacted to prohibit sex discrimination in educational programs or activities receiving federal funding – including for sports programs. While it eventually closed the funding gap for girls' and women's athletics, it didn't address attitudes and perceptions. That's where Nike (and others) filled a void by sponsoring female athletes, expanding women's athletic wear businesses, and launching advocacy campaigns like "If You Let Me Play," which showed the world just how much better off girls would be if they had the chance to play sports. And by "better off," Nike meant less likely to get breast cancer, be beaten, or have an unintended pregnancy, and more likely to grow into healthy, strong, and confident women.

Beyond great product and powerful storytelling, what separated Nike from others was that they dared to move during a time when men still dominated organized sports and gender stereotyping was still alive and kicking across mainstream media. Nike recognized injustice and stood up to say and do something when others shied away or viewed it as someone else's job to fix.

Levi's protects its customers

In 2016, a customer in a Levi's store in the state of Georgia accidentally shot himself with his own gun. He sustained an injury but it was not fatal. The incident disturbed Levi's chief executive, Chip Bergh, enough that he subsequently issued guidelines asking that customers refrain from bringing guns into any of their stores anywhere in the world.

Bergh went public with the decision in an open letter to its customers posted on LinkedIn. Keep in mind that these new guidelines came hot on the heels of a deeply divided U.S. Presidential election. So it was subsequently picked up by a wide range of media.

In his letter, he didn't take sides in the gun debate. He simply explained that it was in the interest of safety: "while we understand the heartfelt and strongly-held opinions on both sides of the gun debate, it is with the safety and security of our employees and customers in mind that we respectfully ask people not to bring firearms into our stores . . . " He went on to explain, "you shouldn't have to be concerned about your safety while shopping for clothes or trying on a pair of jeans."[132]

Firearms are widely accepted in Georgia, so Bergh knew he'd face a backlash. As expected, the social media response ranged from "I'm buying more Levi's today!" to "This is how someone can shoot himself in the foot without a gun." Nevertheless, Bergh did what he felt was best for his employees and customers and he stuck by it. The decision doesn't seem to have hurt the bottom line, with net revenue in the quarter following Bergh's letter up 4 percent from the prior year.[133] When a company knows what it stands for and authentically defends its place in the world, *fighting when you have to* will take courage but can also be fairly simple.

Apple protects your privacy

Apple is another company that knows how to fight when it has to. Apple's stance against the U.S. government's request to unlock the iPhone of a terrorist after a mass shooting in San Bernardino is a great example. The company could have handed the phone over without incident, registering barely a blip in that week's news cycle. Instead, they refused to comply with the FBI's request to unlock the phone, as well as an eventual court order to do so. Apple's decision made a strong statement about the company's desire to prioritize freedom over fear, and privacy over potentially bad publicity.

Some people thought Apple should turn over the data, while many others respected the company's stance on data privacy. Defenders made a compelling case that Apple wasn't being asked to unlock a phone at all. Instead, they were being asked to *create software* that could unlock the terrorist's phone – but in doing so could also unlock millions of others like it. Would it also weaken Apple's position when another government makes a similar request?

All of this tells us that the situation was a complicated one. Apple was in a tough spot. Nevertheless, by staying true to their core beliefs, Apple sent a message to their customers (and everyone else) that their customers' privacy comes first. They showed conviction in the face of an order from one of the most powerful law enforcement agencies in America. The trust that conviction built simply cannot be bought. They showed us all that Apple will be bold enough to fight for their consumers when it has to. For the big idea in their mission or for the shared set of values they have with their *crowd*.

Don't mess with our people

Starbucks founder and former executive chairperson Howard Schultz was quick to act when it came to the company's employees. "Coffee is what we sell as a product, but it's not the business we're in. We're in the people business. I'm passionate about human connection."[134] If you've paid any attention to Howard Schultz at all over the last two decades, you know this is the kind of thing he shouted from the rooftops on a daily basis.

So, when Trump issued an order in January 2017 that made major changes to America's policies on refugees and immigration, there was no question as to where this company founder would stand. The order came on top of an already volatile political climate that raised questions about the availability of health insurance to U.S. immigrants and conditions of trade between the U.S. and other countries – two issues core to Starbucks' business and its culture. Schultz stepped up within two days, sending a letter to his employees in which he addressed the inevitable concerns and fears that many Starbucks' employees and their families were dealing with. In the letter, he communicated unwavering support for employees (Starbucks calls them "partners") in Mexico, as well as for the Mexican farmers whose coffee the company sources.

In the letter, Schultz showed empathy and concern, but more importantly, he laid out exactly what would happen and who employees should call if their access to health insurance coverage changed. While his decisive action at this point was already impressive, he took it a step further. As we covered in the previous chapter, Schultz committed to working with the United Nations to hire 10,000 refugees in 75 countries served by Starbucks. That's taking a stand and fighting for your people. Here's how he closed the letter:

> We are in business to inspire and nurture the human spirit, one person, one cup and one neighborhood at a time – whether that neighborhood is in a Red State or a Blue State; a Christian country or a Muslim country; a divided nation or a united nation. That will not change. You have my word on that.

Racism has no place on the sports field

This type of conviction doesn't only unfold in the U.S. In the early 2000s, European professional football games were marked by a particularly ugly series of racist acts committed by "fans" toward players on the field – insults, banana skins thrown at black players, and the like. While European football has long battled racism, these events compelled French superstar Thierry Henry to team up with Nike in a mutual desire to act. Together they envisioned a call to the vast majority of fans who celebrate the beautiful game and *all* who play it. The result was "Stand Up Speak Up," a campaign that eventually involved players across Europe's club and national teams. The players encouraged fans to wear intertwined bracelets – one black, one white. With this visible sign of anti-racism, fans let others know they could be counted on should they be confronted with acts of racism. Five million bands were sold to raise funds for anti-racist initiatives in football communities.

Don't be afraid to *fight when you have to* if there is something to do or say that your company believes in. It shows conviction and will build trust with the *crowd*. While the examples we've used here are from larger companies like Nike, Apple, Starbucks, and Levi's, it is a transferrable concept for small and medium-sized organizations. There are many ways to *fight when you have to* – for any size budget. When you stand up alone and in advance of others, be prepared to face backlash and be available to deal directly with it in non-defensive ways.

1.2 Unite with others

While there will be times to stand up and fight for your big idea or *new C.E.O.s* alone, there will be other times when it'll be essential that you become one of many, and stand beside others rather than to try to get in front of them.

The corporate sector is not traditionally good at sharing credit, talking points, or the stage, but there are a few companies around the world showing us how to do this well. Whether it's the BT Tower in London lighting up alongside other organizations for gay pride, or Black Lives Matter banners on buildings from a city hall to Facebook, organizations of all sizes are showing who and what they stand for in bold, creative, and visible ways. Importantly, they're uniting around established (or at least rapidly emerging) social messages and movements – and not trying to falsely create their own.

We're not talking about cause marketing here – the practice of selling products with vague claims that "proceeds will be donated to [insert cause here]." That may have worked in the 1990s, but today the *crowd* can quickly find out where those funds are going (if anywhere) and whether the company's ever done anything else remotely connected to the cause. The bar is higher now. What we see are businesses stepping up to play a powerful and exciting role, demonstrating who they uniquely are and what they and their *crowd* stand for along the way.

Love Wins: A global movement to support gay marriage and pride
In 1978, an artist named Gilbert Baker created the rainbow flag as a symbol of gay pride and unity. He refused to trademark it because he wanted it to belong to everyone.[135] And now it does, along with messages like #LoveWins (created by the nonprofit Human Rights Campaign) and the broader concept of *Pride* (a word popularized by activists in the early 1970s). This is an issue where companies around the world have become quite adept at joining a movement that's bigger than they are while still showing up in distinctive and creative ways.

In 2015, Coke celebrated the U.S. Supreme Court's decision that made gay marriage legal nationwide. The company honored marriage equality with #LoveWins. It wouldn't have been quite so powerful if they had tweeted #CelebrateLoveWithCoke. Also in celebration of the decision, companies from Smirnoff and Mentos to Oreo and Apple customized their products in rainbow colors to honor #LoveWins. Apple's rainbow watchband was designed as a gift to employees who were marching in the San Francisco Pride parade. Once everyone else saw it, broader demand quickly followed. Apple didn't approach the watch design with a mass consumer product push in mind. Who knows? Maybe that's why people ended up wanting it so badly.

Among all the color and creative expression, it's important to recognize that there's a fine line between uniting with others and commercializing an important moment. With Pride, for example, there are plenty who feel the celebration is over-commercialized. From rainbow burritos and advertising by major banks to parades sponsored by airlines and floats created by defense contractors, it's fair to say they have a point. *Inspired Companies* handle their engagement with issues they care about differently. While they may well make a product (and we are big supporters of anything that moves a disenfranchised group from being invisible to valued customers), they also wave the flag without a primary profit motive and find other ways to press for change. For example, it was reported that 379 corporations – Coke, Smirnoff's parent company Diageo, and Apple among them – filed an amicus brief with the U.S. Supreme Court in support of legalizing same-sex marriage.[136]

The most *Inspired Companies* familiarize themselves with the issues and become authentic allies to the community. They support local groups and create safe, welcoming environments for their *crowd.* Their authentic engagement gives them permission to commercialize as an integral part of the celebration.

The timing of the 2015 U.S. marriage equality ruling happened to occur in June – Pride Month in many countries, when buildings around the world now light up to celebrate. Coincidence or not, seeing cities from Hong Kong and Helsinki to London and Tel Aviv mark Pride during this critical moment in big beautiful ways was something else. Companies, nonprofits, universities, and governments opted for incredibly bold rainbow demonstrations – creatively illuminating their buildings, towers, and cities to show the world where they stand.

From BT's rainbow tower in London to the rainbow "oo" in "Google" emblazoned on its Silicon Valley HQ to HSBC's rainbow skyscraper in Hong Kong: none of these brands felt the need to take out a separate ad or issue press releases to solidify their statements. They didn't need focus groups to determine how many of their customers or employees would give the thumbs-up. These companies are all clear on who they are and happy to share it with the world in living color.

By the way, we are not saying that all of the brands mentioned here are fully *Inspired Companies*. We are saying that they do a great job of working alongside others for the same cause. Pride is a great example of companies all over the world standing up together. They find unique and creative ways to join in, but remain united under a single banner. Doing something bold and distinctive and alongside others can be one of the most impressive things a company can do.

When discrimination is not one of your corporate values
It is increasingly common to see companies voting with their checkbooks to take a stand. This has been particularly evident in circumstances where discriminatory legislation is passed. For example, when the U.S. state of Indiana passed a 2015 "Religious Freedom Restoration Act," which effectively allowed businesses to discriminate against individuals based on religious grounds, companies across the country reacted swiftly – and together. Salesforce and Apple canceled events and corporate travel to the state. Performers canceled shows, and cities and states banned non-essential travel to the state. The city of Indianapolis visitors' bureau says the city lost more than US$60 million in convention-related revenue.[137] The message from these brands was clear: You mess with our values or our *crowd* and we'll mess with you.

Apparently, the state of North Carolina didn't learn from the Indiana experience. In 2016, North Carolina passed a law that removed all anti-discrimination protections of LGBTQ citizens and mandated that people use the public bathrooms that correspond to the sex listed on their birth certificates. The legislation has no shortage of opponents. Several states banned publicly funded travel to North Carolina. Companies like PayPal canceled plans to locate there and, as in Indiana, a long list of performers canceled shows in the state.

Perhaps the most surprising of all the collective action, however, was the National Basketball Association's decision to move its long-planned 2017 All-Star Game to another state. This was unexpected, partly because professional sports leagues in the U.S. tend to stay out of political debates, but also because elite-level men's sports have long had a reputation for intolerance when it comes to LGBTQ players. This is something the four major leagues (hockey, basketball, baseball, and football) have slowly started to combat in recent years. We say "slowly" because it's largely been a matter of supportive words without much action. That changed when the NBA announced it would be moving the game from North Carolina to Louisiana. This was done with only six months' lead time – unheard of for an event of that magnitude.

It's worth noting that the NBA did this with a lot of pressure from fans, former players, media, and several U.S. senators – in other words, the *crowd* mobilized to express their expectations. And the NBA, in an unprecedented move, responded.

What's interesting is that, while there was plenty of outrage at the decision,[138] it wasn't directed at the NBA. It was directed at the North Carolina governor for signing the bill into law.

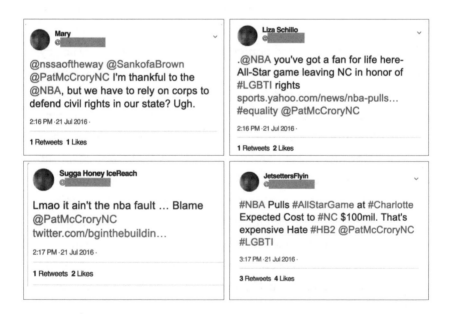

So, in this case, the NBA, after being a comparatively slow mover on this issue, made up for some lost ground with this very visible and financially material boycott. After a partial repeal of the law, North Carolina was awarded the 2019 game.

None of these entities sought to individually rebrand anti-discrimination efforts or to become an outright symbol of civil rights. They simply saw something that was at odds with their values and not in the interests of the *new C.E.O.s*, and they took a stand.

Standing together to say Black Lives Matter

In a time when the majority of Americans now support LGBTQ rights, you could argue that sporting rainbows for Pride is a relatively safe corporate choice. The stakes get much higher when tackling racial inequality and structural racism. It's worth having a closer look at how a few U.S. companies responded to Black Lives Matter. As a reminder, this is a movement that was created in response to injustices surrounding police violence against black citizens in 2013 and has rapidly expanded since. In Chapter 7, we highlighted what can go wrong when you move alone on a social movement already underway through Starbuck's Race Together campaign. Here we review what standing together on this issue looks like.

Let's start with Facebook. It might be easy to assume they have no greater connection to Black Lives Matter than any other large corporation, but that's not true at all. The phrase "Black Lives Matter" has its origins in a conversation between two black women – one in Oakland and the other in Los Angeles – in 2013. That conversation happened on Facebook.[139]

Fast-forward a few years and a slogan has become a movement, and it continues to have unique meaning at Facebook. The company's buildings, for example, are well known for their "Facebook Walls" – chalkboards that employees and visitors can write messages on. In February 2016, several "Black Lives Matter" messages were altered to read "All Lives Matter." Mark Zuckerberg, Facebook's CEO, was not happy. He issued the following statement to all employees[140]:

> "Black lives matter" doesn't mean other lives don't. It's simply asking that the black community also achieves the justice they deserve. We've

never had rules around what people can write on our walls – we expect everybody to treat each other with respect. Regardless of the content or location, crossing out something means silencing speech, or that one person's speech is more important than another's.

A few months later, the world watched Philando Castile get shot to death by police when his fiancée live-streamed the incident on Facebook. Zuckerberg responded with his own Facebook post – a message of sympathy and support – within 24 hours. In the three years from that original Facebook conversation to Castile's death, Facebook had shown itself to be an ally and credible supporter of the movement, not to mention a platform for its growth.

As several other killings unfolded in that same week, Facebook installed a "Black Lives Matter" sign on the side of its U.S. headquarters,[141] accompanied by a moment of silence to honor all who had been affected. The letters in the sign were made up of the names of people who have given their lives for civil rights.

Because of the authentic commitment of Facebook's leadership on this issue, the image was seen as a sign of solidarity and support rather than appropriation and opportunism.[*]

Nike is another company that moved to action as the series of 2016 killings continued to dominate the U.S. news. The situation had worsened with the ambush of a group of police officers in Dallas, killing five. While many chief executives remained silent, Mark Parker didn't. Sitting idly by wasn't an option and he wrote a letter to all 32,000 employees.[142] Here's part of it:

Like many of you, I'm struggling to make sense of the incomprehensible. We have experienced heartbreaking, disturbing and

---

[*] Facebook took a clear and compelling leadership position in its commitment to Black Lives Matter. The company is currently under extensive fire for issues we will cover in Chapter 9 *Make-or-Breaks*.

challenging times in the United States. I have watched with sorrow the events that took place across the U.S.

Nike has a long history of supporting the marginalized and those whose voice is not always heard. In many cases our athletes have eloquently argued for change and to stop the situation. Last night, at the ESPYs, we heard athletes like LeBron James, Carmelo Anthony and Chris Paul powerfully speak out about the issues facing society. Others, like Serena Williams, have also made their voices heard.

As a company, I'm proud that Nike takes a stand on issues that impact all of us, our athletes and society as a whole. And I am proud that Nike stands against discrimination in any form. We stand against bigotry. We stand for racial justice. We firmly believe the world can improve. We are a diverse company and, as we stated in our recent Sustainable Business Report, are firmly committed to making it more diverse and inclusive.

Remember when employee letters were internal documents? If the media got hold of them, it constituted a "leak"? Those days are over. In fact, Mark's letter ended with "#blacklivesmatter." and "#stoptheviolence."* That way employees could easily tag the letter when they shared it on social media. How's that for taking a stand?

Ben & Jerry's support of Black Lives Matter polarized a lot of ice cream eaters. In October 2016, the company tweeted a statement (retweeted by the Black Lives Matter Global Network the next day) about racism: "Black Lives Matter. Choosing to be silent in the face of such injustice is not an option."

Here's what Chris Miller, Ben & Jerry's social mission activism manager, had to say about the tweet: "In order for us to begin to create a society that is not built on a foundation of institutionalized racism, it requires us to admit that it exists."[143]

---

* A hashtag originally associated with domestic violence that emerged organically during that time.

Folks who are threatened by the idea that black lives should matter immediately called for boycotts. Given the topic, the company surely knew it would face some backlash. But Ben & Jerry's knows where they stand and who they stand with, so they went ahead anyway. They walk straight into controversy with fearlessness, and their parent company Unilever seems to be smart enough to leave it to them to decide when they should do that.

Ben & Jerry's is not new to holding strong and controversial points of view – it's been a visible part of their culture and brand strategy for years. Just recently, they banned their Australian stores from selling two scoops of the same ice cream until the country legalizes marriage equality. Thankfully it was legalized at the end of 2017 and we can all go back to doubling up on our favorites.

As for Black Lives Matter, Ben & Jerry's responded to backlash as follows:

> We understood that by speaking out on a highly charged
> and controversial issue, we would hear from those who don't share
> our point of view, and we were prepared for that. We've never
> shied away from controversy, and we don't intend to start now. We
> understand that doing the right thing is often not the easiest thing.[144]

A few other interesting notes about Ben & Jerry's: first, the title of the guy in the first quote. Have you heard of a "social mission activism manager" before? We hadn't, but that kind of staffing is exactly the kind of role to think about as you build the internal capabilities to deliver on ideas that matter. And second, recognize the font in the Twitter image? It's the same one they use on their ice cream cartons, in their ads, throughout their stores. Ben & Jerry's didn't try to create their own movement or their own hashtag. They aligned the company's branding directly to the message of the movement. That is about as big a statement as the company can make, short of giving the movement its own ice cream flavor (although you might argue that "Empower Mint" – a flavor launched in partnership with the civil rights organization NAACP – did just that[145]).

Finally, it doesn't take much time in front of a computer to see that Ben & Jerry's commitment to civil rights goes beyond talk. While admitting that "we are a predominately white company based in one of the whitest states in the country and we sell a lot of ice-cream to white people," the company has revamped its internal hiring practices to increase its own diversity, and has embarked on an employee learning journey around systemic racism and implicit bias.

These are all strong examples of companies uniting in support of a common cause that's bigger than they are. In every case, it wasn't without risk of a backlash. These were (and still are) turbulent times in the social and political landscape. They were also relatively early days in the Black Lives Matter dimension of the civil rights movement. All of these companies – and others, like Starbucks and its Race Together campaign described in the previous chapter – moved early, with conviction and faced their critics head-on. They had all done work over time that had built a level of credibility that allowed them to engage authentically. That brings us to our last point about standing up for your mission and your *crowd*.

If you're joining a movement, make sure your own house is in order.

You can't jump into really important issues without engaging the right partners, understanding the dynamics at play, and doing the work to build credibility. Notwithstanding that, none of the companies we covered have a perfect scorecard on the issues they stepped into. Ben & Jerry's knows the diversity (or any lack thereof) in their own leadership and organization is public knowledge. In 2017, Facebook's employee base was 2 percent African-American while Nike's boardroom was mostly white and male, as was its executive committee – all facts that the *crowd* has been quick to point out. Perhaps the reason these companies weren't completely mocked for their support of Black Lives Matter is they're all actively working on the realities of internal bias within their own organizations. It's sometimes more important to say something publicly and trigger more work internally than to stay silent and wait. *Inspired Companies* know when to do it.

If you're looking for a poster child of what not to do, just look at the color pink. As the symbol of breast cancer awareness, pink is one of the most successful cause-marketing vehicles of all time. You'd be hard-pressed to think of a product or packaging that hasn't been dyed pink at one time or another. Since the introduction of the pink ribbon in 1992 by *Self* magazine, companies have piled onto this very safe social bandwagon, and it's fair to say that some important progress has been made around the basic issue of awareness. The problem is that many companies that participated and benefited also stretched their actual financial "support" for breast cancer so thin that investigative books were written, documentary films were made, and the New York State attorney general had to issue consumer protection guidelines for buying pink.[146]

But false advertising is only part of the problem. Activists define "pinkwashing" as "A company or organization that claims to care about breast cancer by promoting a pink ribbon product, but at the same time produces, manufactures, and/or sells products that are linked to the disease." They point out the cancer risks of ingredients found in pink-labeled cosmetics, perfumes, cleaning products, soups, snack foods, and alcohol. A company that aligns with a social issue for marketing gain while perpetuating the problem as part of their business will eventually be called out. And it won't take years to be called out – it will take just minutes under the regime of the *new C.E.O.s.*

Now, the difference between selling pink-branded cancer-causing lipstick and making a call for racial equity without your own diversity policies in place might seem clear to you, but the *crowd* may have a different idea. Here's the good news: If you're aligned around a big idea and are already engaging the *crowd* in its delivery, there's an excellent chance your house is already in fairly good shape and will stand up to the scrutiny.

If you've done the work, you'll know what to do

Standing up to *fight when you have to* isn't new (Henry Ford did it when he went to court to pay his workers better), but it hasn't been common practice in the corporate sector. However, in today's connected world, where every choice you make happens under a spotlight, the moments will come when you'll need to stand up for what you believe in. When the moment or the issue calls for it, you'll find creative ways to let the *crowd* know they are respected and valued. Hold your ground in the toughest of times and let the world know where you draw the line. Sometimes you'll need to take a stand alone. Other times you'll unite with others and be part of a groundswell. If you've laid the groundwork with a consistent commitment to the pursuit of an *Inspired Mission* and built credibility by showing you're serious in the way you *Shake up the System* to deliver, you'll know which way to go when the time comes to emerge with *Bold Conviction.*

Strategy 2: Disarm

There's a good chance you'll find yourself in crisis mode at least once in your corporate life. An honest mistake, technological problem, or system failure can create a lot of unhappy *crowd* members (including employees!). When the hate mail comes in, *Inspired Companies* respond differently than others do. They find authentic ways to disarm critics with transparency, bringing more of the *crowd* onside with each bona fide effort to own and resolve whatever it is they screwed up on. To prevent critics from taking up arms in the first place, *Inspired*

Companies work with traditional outsiders proactively – watchdogs, regulators, media, activists, and so on – to identify shared missions, create shared value, and deliver collective impact. In moments of criticism or crisis, you can deliver a response that is just enough to get you out of hot water or you can act in a way that further reveals your authenticity and conviction.

Here, we explore ways to disarm your biggest critics by standing up for the idea you are pursuing and not compromising on your values. Some of these might seem like no-brainers, but you'd be surprised how often they're overlooked or poorly executed.

2.1 Make it right

With some screw-ups, words might be enough: a genuine apology and a commitment it will never happen again. Other times words will be entirely insufficient. Historically when mistakes have been made, the trajectory of how companies show up has gone something like this:

Make a mistake, try to hide it. This evolved to: Make a mistake, make an immediate apology, and then do a tightly held internal investigation before offering anything else. Today, if you make a mistake, make it right. Fast.

Like these guys did:

- When British Airways' computer system went down in May 2017, stranding thousands of travelers globally with flights in and out of London, the company played offense. The chairman and chief executive Alex Cruz sent an apology email to affected passengers within about 48 hours. His message was empathetic and believable. He accepted full responsibility and gave no excuses. Ordinarily, that might have felt like little more than lip service, but the email included tangible ways for impacted customers to feel much better about the situation: resources for lost baggage claims (and a promise to deliver via courier), flight rebookings, and an easy process for expense reimbursement. Speaking of compensation, expenses were reimbursed via direct deposit within a few short weeks and with a personal email confirming the transfer.

- On January 2017, a tech company called UxPressia sent an email to its subscribers that accidentally included some broken links. It shouldn't have been a big deal, but their follow-up "apology" included a tongue-in-cheek reference to firing the guy who sent the original email. While some recipients read it as a joke, others didn't. When UxPressia received email replies criticizing their decision, the chief executive, Yuri Vedenin responded within hours, copying the "content ninja" who had written the original email with the broken link. In addition to apologizing and explaining the ninja was in on the joke, he also asked for advice on how they might rectify the situation. Humility, immediacy, and an unequivocal no-excuses apology go a long way in building trust.

- Hyundai's European operation released a digital ad in 2013 that depicted a man trying to commit suicide with car exhaust. The ad eventually reveals that the car has 100 percent water emissions, so the man's attempt was unsuccessful. This was a wildly insensitive move on Hyundai's part and could have turned into a sustained public relations disaster. How they handled it, however, is what's most impressive. They apologized profusely and pulled the ad after just one complaint. One.

When faced with one of these moments, don't sit on it. Get on it.

Sometimes making it right means righting the wrongs of others in support of your *crowd*

We've already noted some of the impact of the U.S. 90-day ban on travelers from seven Muslim-majority countries in early 2017. The subsequent emotional and practical impact on individuals and families was very real and traumatic: husbands separated from wives, and parents from babies, abruptly and indefinitely. While the swift action of the courts provided some relief, it was chaotic and stressful for those impacted. Many airlines around the world

issued immediate statements of support and offered refunds
and rebookings to those affected. Likewise, Airbnb offered free
accommodations to those in need. These decisions aren't necessarily
related to these companies' missions and they'll likely cost more
than they return (at least in the short term), but it was the right
thing to do in a moment where everyone was caught completely off
guard. The public's response indicated they thought
it was pretty awesome:

As with all of these examples it is important to note how quickly these organizations move. In this case, most reacted within 24 hours of the travel ban's announcement. When it comes to making it right, you need to make it right, right now.

2.2 Embrace radical transparency

As we've noted, companies typically give in to the impulse to close the blinds when fingers are pointed at them. *Inspired Companies* have a different way of dealing with the watchdogs and critics that are a fact of corporate life. In some cases, *Inspired Companies* will pull back the curtain and give their scrutinizers a front-row seat to the action. It's hard to imagine a better way to *disarm* a critic than that.

Every company, no matter how conscientious, will face public criticism related to the way they do business. Sometimes the issues will be known to the company. Other times, they will come as a complete surprise. Sometimes the accusations (and realities) will be deeply systemic and impossible for any single company to solve alone. Other times, a company can get a handle on solutions and take action for their own footprint fairly quickly. Either way, the key is how that company responds – because everyone is watching. To retreat, go dark, and shred the evidence (we mean that figuratively, though we imagine there are many literal examples) is not only unethical, it's exhausting, ineffective, and may eventually bury your company. As the saying goes, it's not the crime that kills you, it's the cover-up.

As with most major decisions, *Inspired Companies* do the opposite. They aggressively investigate the criticism or issue and respond with radical levels of transparency.

Take a look at Tony's Chocolonely. When they discovered they couldn't fully trace their cocoa butter and confirm it was made slave-free, they didn't hold focus groups to see if consumers would be okay with that. They didn't sweep it under the rug and ignore the report until it became a really big problem. They decided right then and there to stop producing white chocolate – their product that relied most heavily on cocoa butter. And then they told their stakeholders everything.

This is the kind of transparency that builds trust and demonstrates authenticity. It's not always easy, but it pays off in the end. Here are more examples:

Nike publishes its global supply chain
Nike's response to an industry-wide factory crisis was far from a quick fix. In fact, it evolved over more than a decade. When the market leader was pressed for answers about its supply chain in the 1990s, there weren't many responses to offer. The company had to undergo some trial and error in deciding what action to take. Among the errors, thinking the problem would eventually go away and commissioning a report on factory conditions that was seen as biased toward Nike are two standouts.

By the late 1990s, however, Nike had started to figure it out. Phil Knight acknowledged the problem publicly and in more open and less defensive ways. Another big shift came in the early 2000s when the company conducted hundreds of factory audits. Then Nike did something no one in the industry had done before. It published a complete list of all of its contract factories worldwide, along with a report focused on pay and working conditions that gave visibility to widespread issues. This radical level of transparency shifted the industry into a new era and changed the dynamic with Nike's most vocal critics. The company went from being a whipping post of human rights, labor, and student organizations to being a standard bearer of transparency.

Changing the dynamic took a decade of learning and hard work, but radical transparency ended up being the turning point for Nike at the time. College students went from burning Nike product on campuses across the U.S. to this: "What Nike did is important," said Eric Brakken, an organizer for United Students Against Sweatshops, a coalition of campus groups. "It blows open the whole notion that other companies are putting forward that they can't make such disclosures."[147] Human rights organizations also moved to publicly praise Nike for the unprecedented move while acknowledging the work ahead to fix system-wide issues.

Nike managed to do what no one in the early 1990s ever would have predicted: They turned (most of) their critics into their partners.

This example provides an important lesson for *Inspired Companies.* When trouble finds you – and it probably will at some point – open the door, turn the lights on, and invite the world in to help you fix it.

Google goes toe-to-toe with regulators over the gender pay gap
In April of 2017, Google announced it had closed the pay gap between men and women across the company. Not many companies have made such a bold claim and anyone who's looked at the issue closely knows there's a lot more to it than "John gets paid more than Sally." You have to look at experience, employment gaps, education, whether people have similar titles for similar work, etc. Put another way, Google can claim to close the gap and academics will line up to poke holes in it. The company probably expected that – and may have even welcomed it, given that's how methodologies are improved upon. What Google might not have expected was the federal government slapping them with a lawsuit citing "extreme" pay discrimination.

Google hit back. Hard. In addition to inviting the federal government to publicly share the methodology that led regulators to such a conclusion, Google also published its own methodology.[148] The company also published a guide based on its methodology for other companies to assess their own pay practices. The folks at Google knew this would expose the company's approach to even more scrutiny. They're also savvy enough to know it's how they build credibility and get the science to be taken seriously.

The lawsuit was still in place in 2018, and throughout it Google seems to have struck a good balance between having high levels of transparency while upholding the privacy of sensitive information about its employees. So, after having an unexpected lawsuit filed against them, the big windfall has been the fairly limited media attention, with much of the coverage equally focused on Google's efforts to achieve pay equality, alongside discussion of the lawsuit. Imagine if a company like Walmart faced similar accusations. Do you think coverage would be quite so balanced? (Do a search for "Walmart wage gap" and find out.)

2.3 Activate shared goals

Another way to *disarm* your critics is to prevent them from taking up arms in the first place. Anyone who pursues big ideas will quickly find out how important it is to work with others. Whether it's researchers, customers, regulators, or anyone else, you'll probably need to find common ground to move the needle.

For example, plenty of people support Tesla's mission (the pursuit of sustainable energy) because they'd like to leave their children a world that's conducive to human life. But the thing is, Tesla's mission is such a big idea it will require everyone's participation to get it done. That includes people who may not have bought into the idea of sustainable energy just yet.

Tesla needs as big an audience as possible. To reach that bigger audience Musk hasn't spent time trying to convince the non-believers, he spent time creating customer demand for things that will make it happen anyway: beautiful high-tech cars that have a gasoline cost of zero dollars. Even those who believe climate change is a hoax are likely to want a car like that.

He started with expensive versions of the Tesla (necessary for R&D purposes and likely to build cachet). Within a few years, the company figured out how to build a less expensive model. Pre-orders on that version hit 300,000 within a few days of its 2016 announcement.[149] For a car that wasn't expected to hit the market until the end of 2018,* we'd say shared goals were activated.

---

* Tesla ultimately beat expectations and delivered the first ones in 2017.

If you've got a big idea, there's a good chance plenty of other people will want to see it realized too. If your big idea is transformative (and it should be), others will always have a critical role to play. In addition to finding powerful demand-driven approaches, the corporate sector must go beyond transactional relationships with traditional "outsiders," and engage in effective cross-sector alliance building if they want to achieve big things.

Activating shared goals (and the coalition-building and total industry transformation it can require) takes work. There's no getting around that, but there are several factors that will make life a whole lot easier should you pursue or participate in them. For the most part, we're trained as business leaders to elevate our company brands at every turn. *Inspired Companies* aren't so insecure. When *Inspired Companies* pursue ambitious missions, they know when to invite others in and jointly unleash a big idea on the world.

Tackling a global physical inactivity epidemic
Physical inactivity trends globally are a major threat to people's health and wellbeing. While this human downside accelerates some industries (like weight loss), it's a concerning issue for others, like the sports industry. As with many of society's greatest challenges, this is a systemic issue impacted by more factors than we can count. It's not just about individuals getting off the couch and away from their screens. It's about schools, transportation, infrastructure, and health policies, quality of coaches and teachers, early sports experiences, parents' activity levels. The list goes on (and on, and on). Obviously, this isn't something one company or organization can change on its own.

As we mentioned in Chapter 6, Nike learned all of this in 2010, when we started looking much deeper into global physical inactivity. Of course, we weren't the first to realize there was a big problem. We would never have understood the true magnitude of the problem if it weren't for the collective contributions of nonprofits, government agencies, and researchers in several countries all working together to get a better handle on the truth. In Nike's case, identifying and activating shared goals across all these players not only increased the chance that we could make things a lot better for the world, but it also created powerful new alliances that would eventually be counted as friends.

Surprisingly at the time, most governments had not been tracking population-wide physical activity levels in any sustained or consistent way, and the medical research on physical activity was splintered into specialist areas. So the first step was to work openly to share information and mobilize around a common set of facts. How do you move from a shared view of the facts to a united force for action? Well, build the answer together.

Nike did it in partnership with more than 80 organizations that collectively supported the framework for action, Designed to Move, cited earlier in Chapter 6. We started by synthesizing the facts on physical activity, but the most important thing that came out of this collective effort was co-creating and publishing a shared action plan that boiled down to just two "asks" for everyone to deliver on:

1) Create early positive experiences in sports and physical activity for children (to shape their preferences for life)

2) Integrate physical activity into everyday life (in school, at home, at work, and in cities)

They are what we call "irresistible propositions." No sane person (or member of the Designed to Move alliance) could disagree with them, and all of us could immediately act on them alone or together in ways that furthered our individual missions and organizational goals. The partnership mix was unusual and unprecedented: Nike, the American College of Sports Medicine, Chinese research agencies, Brazil's School system, the IOC, Special Olympics, Adidas, and Under Armor, for goodness' sake. Altogether, hundreds of organizations that care about movement and physical activity to sustain the human race agreed on how to approach a very big problem together. The development of what looked like a report had suddenly become a global alliance.

Shared goals are the only way to solve a problem as big as poverty
Participating in coalitions is never easy. You know how they say marriage takes a lot of work to succeed? Coalitions are like that, but usually with a dozen or more partners.

As we were developing the Nike Foundation's strategy to alleviate global poverty by investing in the potential of adolescent girls, our external partners had many ideas about what Nike could do. "If only the Nike Foundation could do for girls what Nike has done for running, we could solve poverty a whole lot faster," said one advisor, speaking for pretty much all the experts we spoke to. It was clear they wanted the full force of Nike's communications and creative resources to elevate the issues they had been fighting for decades.

So that's what we did. But to make sure that it would ultimately work for a broader coalition, we had to do it in a very non-Nike way. Ordinarily, Nike's communications brilliance doesn't come from focus groups or testing; it comes from smart, creative people trusting their gut, talking to real athletes, and taking risks. Most of the time that works. The idea of sharing a creative process with anyone outside Nike's brand team – much less outside the company – was considered career suicide. But since the rest of the company knew relatively little about solving poverty, we were given more leeway than usual. Civil society partners and other experts were engaged at almost every stage of the process. From taking our advertising agency, Wieden+Kennedy, into the fields of Bangladesh to meet girls who were central to solving poverty in their communities, to reviewing and deciding the final creative direction – we had our partners in the room with us.[*] Together, we landed on a shared communications concept called the Girl Effect.

---

[*]   Key founding partners such as Jennifer and Peter Buffet of the Novo Foundation and Kathy Bushkin Calvin, CEO of the United Nations Foundation.

In the creative execution of the Girl Effect (mostly videos to start with) we did something very simple and also very non-Nike: we didn't brand anything. The company had already learned that taking Nike's swoosh off the yellow wristband for the Livestrong campaign allowed the wristband's core message – the strength of cancer survivors – to shine through, and connected with millions worldwide. When the Girl Effect launched without any swooshes, it became the property of any girl champion who could use it to advance his or her work.

Our best days? When someone would forward the Girl Effect videos to us at the Nike Foundation with a note saying, "Hey, I know you all are working on girls, have a look at this." That's when we knew it was working. We weren't doing for girls what Nike had done for running; the whole coalition was.

Google finds common ground with cities
Shared goals aren't always obvious. Sometimes it takes a while to find them. Take Google Fiber for example. Google rolled out a plan to offer significantly faster internet connection speeds than anything previously available across U.S. residential markets. And by "significantly faster," we mean speeds 5 to 200 times faster than typical offerings. Sounds great, right?

Here's the catch: Google needs to lay fiber optic cable under city streets. On top of that, most cities offer monopolies on cable and phone service (the other internet providers). These companies can often have vested interests and longstanding donor relationships in city politics to effectively ensure no other competition enters the market.

Google faced the challenge by activating shared goals with cities. Broadband access is a difference-maker in communities. It's how homework gets done, jobs are found, businesses are promoted, social services are accessed, health information is researched . . . the list goes on and on. However, in the U.S., the gap between the broadband haves and have-nots is wide. So Google offered free Wi-Fi for seven years in the cities it partnered with. Local regulators cleared red tape and streamlined the permit process.

Considering the cutthroat environment internet providers operate in, finding shared goals and making friends with regulators turns out to be a pretty smart move. This is a place where small and medium-sized organizations can participate and leverage resources and efforts of other like-minded organizations.

Shared goals create shared benefits and new friends

We get it. Building coalitions and activating shared missions doesn't sound like the most fun you'll ever have. In fact, if you've tried to build cross-sector partnerships before, there's a good chance it involved exasperating levels of frustration and an astounding lack of follow-through. Here's the thing, though: When it comes to delivering on a big idea, investing in the right alliances is really important. We know this from our experiences at Nike and we know it from everything we've seen since. They take work, but they'll keep you from shouldering the (frankly impractical) burden of solving huge problems alone.

Because the most effective alliances take significant time and resource investment, prioritize the ones with shared agendas that further your mission. And learn how to let go of those that don't. When you get it right, you'll have more friends in more places than you ever thought possible.

And you'll change the world along the way.

Strategy 3: Do something unexpected

Over time, *Inspired Companies* develop the expertise to respond to events and unforeseen opportunities in real time in ways their competitors simply can't. They know who they are and they know how to rally. We've seen the speed with which *Inspired Companies* can move when they need to fight for their mission or values. We've also seen them be incredibly transparent when faced with criticism. This last set of strategies demonstrate what can happen when speed and transparency are applied together in ways that surprise and delight the *crowd*.

This is how *Inspired Companies* distinguish themselves.

3.1 Accelerate – especially when others back down

Life moves quickly. Opportunities to engage with the *crowd* and express who you are present themselves every day. Sometimes it's for fun. When Donald Trump released a letter from his lawyers saying that his tax returns didn't reflect income from Russia "with few exceptions," the internet had a field day. So did RC Cola,* which jumped on the viral hashtag by announcing it had outsold all other soft drink brands #withfewexceptions.

Of course, some moves are incredibly serious, like AT&T removing all charges for calls to the Philippines following Typhoon Haiyan. Either way, when opportunities arise or tragedies hit, companies should be able to immediately recognize where they uniquely fit and find new and surprising ways to lead.

A fashion brand co-opts a hashtag
You don't have to be an established *Fortune* 100 chief executive to get this right. Take a look at Wildfang. You met them in previous chapters – they're the brand that celebrates feminists and tomboys. It was started by two women who liked the look of men's clothes but were frustrated that the fit never worked. Wildfang filled the gap and made a whole *crowd* of *new C.E.O.s* ecstatic in the process.

In early 2017, it was revealed that the Trump administration had a dress code for female staffers. This policy was summed up by White House sources in media reports as, "Trump likes the women

---

* The RC Cola brand is now part of the Plano, Texas-based Dr Pepper Snapple Group.

who work for him to dress like women."[150] Social media erupted and #DressLikeAWoman took off. Immediately the world saw pictures of uniformed women in combat, scientists and doctors in lab coats, judges in robes. Firefighters, police officers, race car drivers, and astronauts all lined up to show Trump and the world how to #DressLikeAWoman. Wildfang saw this as a unique intervention point for their point of view. Here's how co-founder and chief executive Emma Mcilroy describes the moment:

> We look for those unplanned moments that have raw energy. We want to be the first to strike. So I was in the bath. Tara [Taralyn Thuot, Wildfang's creative director] was at a karaoke bar. I happened to be on Twitter and I saw #DressLikeAWoman. I started to read into it and realized we had to take a point of view. I texted Tara – who's so purpose-driven she answered at 9:30 p.m. when most people wouldn't. I said "Let's take women wearing Wildfang-styled apparel and overlay the phrase and then let's do an Instagram takeover." And she said "Brilliant. I'll make it real quick." She made it on an app on her phone. She made six assets in 15 minutes, sent them back to me and I posted them. From "should we respond" to "what should we respond with" to "here's the decision" to creating the assets and executing was about 20 minutes. It cost zero dollars. We went viral on HuffPost, Forbes, and Refinery.

Within days of the Instagram takeover and mainstream media coverage, Wildfang took it a step further and rebranded its entire seasonal line with the DressLikeAWoman hashtag. Total marketing budget? Zero. Mcilroy's reflection about going on the offense? "It wasn't a campaign, but we made it one. It was speed and authenticity versus perfectionism."

When faced with hate, celebrate who you are
The graham cracker brand Honey Maid got plenty of reactions to their "This is Wholesome" ad campaign about what it means to be a family. When the campaign ran a spot that featured two gay dads with their

son, the hate mail came in. Rather than backtrack or make excuses for their ad, Honey Maid took it all a step further – and higher. They hired two artists to carefully roll each piece of hate mail and arrange the rolled papers into the word "love." And then for good measure, they used all of the positive mail they received as a backdrop. According to the company, and as you can glean from the image below, the love:hate ratio was 10:1.

Honey Maid could have backed off when the hate mail started coming in. They could have quietly moved toward something that might be less offensive to the delicate sensibilities of people who don't believe in everyone's right to love. But Honey Maid didn't back off. They stepped on the gas and let the whole world know where they stand.

Honey Maid's celebration of love over hate.

Accelerating in the midst of controversy is not for everyone. Chief executives who spend their time trying not to rock the boat too much or whose primary focus is keeping their job into the next quarter need not apply. This is for leaders who possess a special kind of confidence. It's a confidence that comes from taking the
role of custodian of their company's values and mission very personally, and a conviction that comes from having a *crowd* onside who's counting on you. These leaders believe in a big idea and the

path forward, and they're going to accelerate toward it when there is a crossroad.

3.2 Give away the answer

If you want to surprise consumers, disarm detractors, and distinguish yourself from competitors, consider doing the unthinkable: share your answers. Or at least the bits of it that can make life better for everyone if your whole industry knows them. It'll push everyone forward – and likely put you in front.

Japan Taxi gives away the answer and boots Uber out of Tokyo
Inspired Companies are ready for anything a startup has to throw at them. When Uber started making waves around the world, Nihon Kotsu (Japan Taxi) invested in software that could compete with Uber by the time it had arrived. Japan Taxi is the largest taxi service in Japan and is almost 90 years old. Despite their legacy and history of success, they weren't lulled into the idea that they couldn't be rendered obsolete. They weren't married to their business model. So they proactively commissioned their own software development and served it up with Japan Taxi's famous white glove service. Then Japan Taxi did something entirely unexpected: They shared their software with the rest of Japan's taxi industry.

This is how you go on the offense, *do something unexpected* – and carry your whole mission with you. Japan Taxi had generations of taxi drivers grow up with their company and families who had been connected to the company over the course of decades. They saw a threat to their industry and they neutralized it. That involves a ton of foresight and the skillset of an *Inspired Company*.

Nike responds to criticism with innovation for the whole industry
In 2011 Greenpeace issued a report that called into question Nike's environmental waste and toxification in its supply chain. Most of

what the company was doing was industry standard, but as the market leader, Nike has always been at the top of the watch list for environmental activists. Here's the thing though: Greenpeace was right. So Nike publicly committed to change things. They put a huge team against it (changing practices in 900 factories across 50 countries isn't easy) and they innovated across the design process so they could ensure suppliers could actually deliver on what was being asked of them.

This could easily be seen as a way to simply disarm critics with radical transparency, and it certainly had that effect. But there's more to it than that. What Nike did differently in all of this was to share the tools they developed with the wider industry.

To start, they shared the IP (intellectual property) for a water transparency tool that helps improve water usage levels in factories. That's nice, of course, but some might say "It's not like you handed them the formula for a shoe." Nike thought the same thing, so they handed the industry the formula for a shoe (or parts of it, anyway). Nike reformulated the rubber used across its footwear line – an effort that reduced toxic chemicals by 96 percent. Nike then shared this patent and 400 other sustainable innovation patents for competitors and others to use. How's that for *Bold Conviction*?

Tesla shares its secrets to accelerate sustainable transport
We've talked about Tesla's interest in transitioning the world toward sustainable energy. They're inspiring words, but they don't mean much if all the company does is sell expensive electric cars to well-off people. Not that we have a problem with wealthy folks or fancy cars. It's just that there aren't enough of either to move the needle on sustainable energy.

What Tesla did was prove that an electric car could be powerful, reliable, and attractive to mainstream buyers. While the company was in the midst of developing its more moderately priced Model 3, Elon Musk figured the best way to deliver energy innovation to the masses would be to let others access the firm's IP via its website. So in June 2014 he did. As he put it, "We believe that Tesla, other companies making electric cars, and the world would all benefit from a common, rapidly evolving technology platform."[151] Legally, Tesla still holds patents on its work, but Elon Musk publicly committed to allowing appropriation of its IP. As Elon Musk wrote in a blog[152] published on the company's website, "Tesla will not initiate patent lawsuits against anyone who, in good faith, wants to use our technology." That's game-changing in a country that's considered one of the most litigious in the world.

By July 2017, somewhat out of nowhere, Volvo announced that by 2019 it would only be making electric and hybrid cars. Likewise, BMW announced plans to more than double the number of hybrid and electric cars between 2017 and 2019. Who knows if they're using Tesla's IP? Who cares? That's industry transformation if we've ever seen it.

This kind of collaborative IP sharing isn't actually that novel. Many of our parents and grandparents survived long enough to make sure we would be born because five different pharmaceutical companies contributed to research that would increase penicillin production in the 1940s.[153] Open-source IP is also how we mapped the human genome, which sought to sequence all of human DNA. Imagine a scientist in 1990 considering a seemingly infinite number of sequencing possibilities. There was a ton of work involved, more than one organization could take on. The Human Genome Project promised a map and then they delivered it – two years ahead of schedule, through a massive public–private partnership. That's as big an idea as we've ever seen and the corporate sector could use this type of thinking much more often to do much bigger things.

Now what?

Acting with *Bold Conviction* can set your company apart from the masses. You can take risks because you've made genuine and strong connections with your *crowd*. When your decisions spark excitement, support, and action from the *crowd,* you'll know you're doing it right. By that point, you'll have done a lot of hard work to lay the foundation. Your efforts will not need to be perfect nor finished in order to move to this phase confidently – but they do have to be authentic and sustained enough for you to be believable. Success at this phase of your *Inspired Company* journey means you're in a place to deliver on ideas people love, inspire your employees' most amazing work, and secure the endorsement of the regulators, watchdogs, and researchers you once dreaded.

Let's say you've gotten everything right so far. You've got a big idea with many winners; you've built the internal culture and leadership needed to align a dynamic organization; you lead rather than follow; you defy industry norms with creativity and courage; and you've developed the confidence to lead with bold levels of conviction to surprise the world even more. Your employees believe you and the world is behind you – hoping that it might actually be true.

What we've just described is an *Inspired Company,* and the potential payoff on so many levels is huge. But before we dig into that, we need to address one final piece of being *inspired:* making sure you stay that way.

Chapter 8 Summary

Companies that have laid the groundwork by *Aligning Obsessively* to mission and who've found ways to do things differently by *Shaking up the System* will naturally build the confidence to emerge with powerful forms of *Bold Conviction*. They'll stand up for their mission and values and embrace radical transparency. They'll own mistakes and fix them fast. The best part? If you've made it this far, you'll have the *new C.E.O.s* onside. And that means you'll be able to do entirely unexpected things at a moment's notice and become a brand that the world remembers. *Bold Conviction* forms of *Inspired Action* include:

- *Fight when you have to*
  - o Take a stand when no one else will
  - o Unite with others
- *Disarm*
  - o Own mistakes. Make them right, right away.
  - o Embrace radical transparency
  - o Activate shared goals
- *Do something unexpected*
  - o Accelerate in pursuit of your mission. Especially when others hold back.
  - o Give away the answers. Especially if it achieves your *Inspired Mission* faster.

Chapter 9

Inspired Action:
Make-or-Breaks

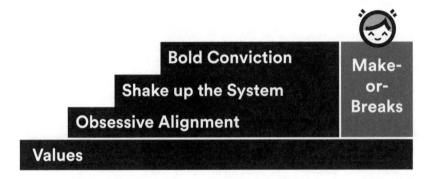

The moments that define you

There are times in the life of a company or in your role as a leader that are the real moments of truth. *Make-or-Break* moments that reveal who you are and what your company stands for.

We started this book with a painful reminder that the *crowd* doesn't trust us today. Not just a little bit. A lot. When trust is as low as it is, the impact of *Make-or-Break* moments is amplified many times over. You might have been doing a lot of things right with your business up to now: great customer service, strong environmental, social and governance practices, you may even be an employer of choice already. Then a moment of truth arrives.

How you show up in these moments will either lift you up and earn trust and support from the *crowd* or push them further away. They can happen anytime and more regularly than you would ever plan for. So be ready.

In This Chapter

- How companies harness the power of their *Inspired Mission* and the *crowd* to transform moments of abrupt change into visible proof of commitment and trust

- Your *Inspired Mission* as the North Star: navigating new leadership, funding, acquisitions, and unexpected developments

- Opening up when others shut down: prioritizing the *crowd* when facing regulatory changes, bankruptcy, or wrongdoing

- Bite-size case examples that demonstrate how these moments can pull the *crowd* even closer – or push them further away

You can anticipate some *Make-or-Break* moments if for no other reason than that they are inevitable: new leadership is appointed, major investors step in (or out), growth milestones are achieved, margins come under pressure. Others may not be inevitable, but they are common: mergers, acquisitions or divestments, the threat of bankruptcy, regulatory changes, scientific discoveries, or the surfacing of new material information.

And some *Make-or-Breaks* will come at you like a big slap in the face. This is especially true in the moments when the business fails in some way and a PR crisis hits. In these moments it's common practice for the CFO, chief legal counsel, VP of communications, and the chief executive to huddle first. And that might just be your first big mistake. These are not the moments to make your decision through the lens of short-term stock price impact, minimum legal requirements, or defensive messaging strategies. These are the moments to go back to your *Inspired Mission*, the values you committed to, and the wisdom of the *crowd* for direction. Then go ahead and call in a broader set of VPs and act quickly with courage and confidence.

So how do you protect yourself? There's one thing that characterizes the "breaks" of *Make-or-Breaks* more than any other: Companies have grown accustomed to ignoring the relationship between their business outcomes and the interests of the *crowd*. That won't cut it much longer.

Everyone's watching. What will you do?

New boss, new mission

Let's start with something that's inevitable: a leadership change.

When Satya Nadella took the Microsoft helm from Steve Ballmer in 2014, he did what a lot of incoming chief executives do: He looked to make his mark with a new mission. This isn't always a good idea. If the mission is inspired to begin with and the company culture seems ripe with potential, there are many other ways for a new leader to put their stamp on a business than changing the mission statement.

On the other hand, if the mission is full of red flags – for example, focused on narcissistic and internal goals, narrow competencies, or promises to do the right thing – it's time for fresh thinking. When Nadella became Microsoft's third CEO, he inherited the following mission: *To create a family of devices and services for individuals and businesses that empower people around the globe at home, at work and on the go, for the activities they value most.*

In 2015, Nadella gave this much simpler, much bigger gift to the world: *To empower every person and every organization on the planet to achieve more.*

Now that's an inspired idea to get behind.

Growth milestones

From leadership changes to growth milestones that raise the stakes, the transition from startup to small-cap to mid-cap are significant moments in the life of a company. When an entrepreneur is in startup and small-cap mode, they are driven, passionate, and liberated by the pursuit of their big inspired idea. Communication is simpler and angel investors stay largely out of the way.

The moment a company moves into mid-cap size or you accept a material amount of funding from investors who weren't on your "friends and family" investor list, higher expectations emerge. That's when it's time to work within the larger financial system. The benefits of sourcing the additional capital are significant, but the pull away from the inspired idea toward short-termism will be strong. Almost any leader of any business that has experienced growth from small-cap to mid-cap will know this transition well.

Alexis Bonte, co-founder of eRepublik games learned this first hand. In 2007, video games were still sold in boxes. They cost a fortune, took hours to install, and often didn't work. Bonte – a self-proclaimed gamer and already a successful entrepreneur – knew there had to be another way. "The market was ripe for disruption. The internet was finally powerful enough to deliver games to everyone and make them fun again."

Bonte launched eRepublik – an online virtual world that players would continue to build over time. It was supposed to be the company's only game – a completely new type of game on a completely new platform. Talent was easy to attract. Games are notorious for their reliance on copycat mechanics; it seemed like just about everyone wanted to work on something new and different.

It was a great time to be a gamer. eRepublik's business function was set up in Spain, while the more creative design and tech function was established in Romania, essentially establishing the small gaming company as a multinational overnight. Within a year, eRepublik had 1 million players. By year three, it had 3.5 million players and the game was turning a profit.

Investment came easy, and so did attention. And that's when things really started to fall apart. Rapid growth brought plenty of tech problems, creating what Bonte calls, "a precarious situation. Profitable, but precarious."

"There was pressure to replicate our success. The market was more competitive by then and investors wanted the next big thing." In very raw terms, Bonte explained, "Every week on the App Store or Google Play, 3,000 games come out. Of those, two or three will make money. Now it's harder than the movie industry." The financial burden and urgency were forcing them to focus on games that drew on existing work – something that their innovation-minded developers weren't excited about. Bonte started pushing back. The board wanted to sell the Romania studio – and all of its passionate game designers – to finance the next big hit. Bonte refused. "And eventually, the team we didn't sell actually made our next big hit."

"We had reached a mid-cap point and there was a significant step change in pressure that came with it. I needed to figure out how to give everyone a common direction as we grew. It's easy to innovate. It's hard to innovate and make money."

For Bonte, the key has been to let go of control: "I'm the least powerful chief executive on the planet." He found people to run the day-to-day operations so he could go back into observation and learning mode, spending far more time with his team. Here's where he landed:

"The reason we make games is because we love games and we play them and it gives us joy. We had gotten far away from that. I started asking colleagues, 'How do we get back to a place where there's a common purpose in the company that we all believe in?'" Bonte figured it would take a year to get the company where he wanted it to be – but spending the time to find out what inspired his team in the first place was where he found the answer. "Sticking to a more inspired purpose and pushing back against investors to protect it isn't easy, but it's necessary."

A decade after the company was founded, eRepublik Labs was acquired by Stillfront, a portfolio of digital game creators, in a cash-and-stock exit deal. eRepublik's investors cashed out with a *very* positive return. Meanwhile, the team was able to keep the Romanian studio, where Bonte felt all of the passion resided. He also agreed to stay on as chief executive and was able to share a significant portion of the exit proceeds with the team in Romania, all of whom have stayed with the company. The combined entity (eRepublik and Stillfront) now has a market cap of US$400 million on the Swedish Nasdaq. Revenues at the eRepublik Labs more than tripled between mid-2017 and mid-2018 and profits grew 500 percent.

Most importantly, as Bonte puts it, "We found our purpose and are living it every day."

When the nature of funding threatens the core of a company, saying no might actually be the best option
As the chief executive of Wildfang, Emma Mcilroy is fiercely protective of her company's mission to let people be themselves and be their best. "Everything on our roadmap is aimed at pursuing the mission. It's not a partial commitment. It's not a balance. It's everything." She goes on to say that profitability is super important – because it allows her to have control to fuel initiatives that drive the mission. As Wildfang's success started to hit the radar of venture capitalists, she and other company leaders knew they were facing a turning point. They could take an infusion of capital and pay the bills, but the trade-off would be that they'd have to operate under the direction of the VC. They said no. "If you have shareholders invested for the wrong reasons, they can make your life hell. Ours are not in it for the wrong reasons."

Mcilroy has stayed on the offense and focused on attracting a profile of investors who believe in Wildfang's mission and who are willing to have a two-way relationship. "They let me do my job and they help me do it better. They believe in me and Wildfang's purpose and want to protect me as much as their money."

Now that's what we call bucking the system from the beginning so you don't have to shake it up later.

Going public is a special kind of threat

An IPO is a high-risk proposition. On the upside, going public exposes companies to an entirely new level of scrutiny, which truly *Inspired Companies* will weather better than most. The challenge comes in pressure from shareholders to deliver right out of the gates. Etsy, the online marketplace for handcrafted goods, was celebrated as a collaborative-economy company that put the interests of its artists first and even went so far as to set aside 5 percent of its pre-IPO shares for them.

When the company went public in 2015, it was one of the first certified B corps to do so. It seemed like great news at the time, but by the end of 2017, the company looked to be in trouble. Excessive spending and losses caused the share price to lose a quarter of its original value. Hundreds of people were laid off and the board abruptly replaced the founding chief executive.[154] What went wrong?

Put simply, their mission and intentions were great but their business model couldn't measure up to the purpose or the expectations of investors. One observer put it aptly: "The underlying issue of Etsy's post-IPO devaluation is that its original model of serving as a marketplace for handcrafted goods didn't align with the growth demands placed on publicly traded companies."[155] Etsy's whole value proposition revolved around goods handmade by actual people. For years, there were strict rules about where the materials could come from and whether or not an artist had help. That's great for handcrafted goods, but it doesn't exactly inspire growth. Even the most *Inspired Company* needs the finely tuned strategies and growth milestones you'd expect to see in any successful company. In fact, well-run nonprofits operate with basic good management approaches in place.

The point is, you can't rely on an *Inspired Mission* alone. You still need to be good at running a company. And fortunately, it now looks like Etsy has a good chance to get back on track.

Someone acquires you. Or you acquire them

Hitting growth milestones, however they arrive, tends to have a way of testing a person's character and identity. Companies are no different. Mergers and acquisitions activity will test what your company and culture are made of and determine whether your business is leaning toward the more inspired end of the spectrum or not. What happens before, during, and after acquisitions will have a significant effect on the *crowd* and whether they decide to stick with you afterward.

This is especially true for employees in the early days of a merger or acquisition. They will try to decipher the immediate impact on their lives (do I still have a job?) as well as the potential longer-term impact on their own sense of purpose, motivation, and values alignment. (Does the company acquiring us believe in the same things I believe in and signed up for?) And given the power of their newfound voice, any waves employees create during M&A activity will quickly reverberate across the *crowd,* including with potential investors.

When Ben & Jerry's was acquired by Unilever in 2000, the company's founders publicly objected. The self-described hippies weren't interested in selling out to a conglomerate in fear of losing what had always been at the center of Ben & Jerry's company: *To make the world a better place.* In this case, though, the powerful financial system won. Shareholders sued and the board surrendered.[156] Regarding its acquisition, Ben & Jerry's had no options. This is a situation that could have broken Ben & Jerry's and destroyed the principles it was founded on. Fortunately, it didn't.

Though no one could have known it in 2000, the acquisition ended up working out well since Unilever is pretty inspired themselves. As we touched on earlier, Unilever is one of the largest conglomerates in the world. As with most conglomerates, acquisitions are central to their growth strategy and, after close to 100 years of practice, they've gotten really good at it. Here's where Unilever separates itself from the pack: They take a long-term view of growing their portfolio of brands. In other words, they don't acquire to sell off – they acquire to keep.[157]

And since they're in the business of keeping what they buy, they want their acquisitions to matter.

All of Unilever's brands are expected to contribute to Unilever's purpose *to make sustainable living commonplace.* Holdings in the Unilever portfolio making the most progress are called Sustainable Living brands and Ben & Jerry's is one of them. As they put it, "Such a brand must not only have a clear purpose that, over time, helps to tackle a social or environmental concern; the product itself must also contribute to one or more of the targets we have set in our Unilever Sustainable Living Plan."[158] In 2015, 12 of the top 40 brands in Unilever's portfolio were Sustainable Living brands. By 2016, 18 were and the approach is paying off. In 2017, the Sustainable Living brands grew 46 percent faster than other brands in the company's portfolio and are 70 percent of Unilever's turnover growth.[159]

As for Ben & Jerry's, Unilever showed a commitment to the company's roots from the start. They appointed Yves Couette as chief executive. From the outset, Couette recognized the company's unique value to its employees and customers (who could more aptly be called fans), and strived to maintain it. A decade later, Couette would be hailed as a "culturally agile" leader, who was able to simultaneously navigate the ice cream company's quirky culture alongside the more button-down demands of its parent company. This balancing act has withstood the test of time. In 2012, Ben & Jerry's became the first subsidiary of a public corporation to become a certified B Corp, meaning that they "meet rigorous standards of social and environmental performance, accountability, and transparency."[160] This is one case where the founders' original intent has been embraced and celebrated.

If Ben & Jerry's founders were worried the acquisition would backfire, it's because they often do. This is especially true when the *crowd* objects to the terms. Take a look at Juno. Once billed as the driver-friendly alternative to Uber, Juno rapidly expanded its driver roster when it offered equity to drivers. Juno drivers could choose to make more cash up front or take a portion of their earnings in equity in the company. That was all well and good until Juno was purchased for US$200 million in cash by a company called Gett. The drivers who had sacrificed earnings to own a portion of Juno were offered pennies on the dollar. Understandably, a group of them promptly sued.

And really, with Uber and Lyft on the scene, and technology platforms easy to replicate, wasn't "reputation" Juno's only real value proposition? What Gett failed to realize was the inherent value of Juno being the "good guy" in an industry fraught with employment legality and fairness issues. Gett could have embraced the values that attracted drivers and passengers into Juno's business in the first place. Instead, the buyer (and the sellers, it seems) threw all of that currency along with the *crowd* away.

Making acquisitions to achieve a market leadership goal – or doing it at any cost, to minimize the cost – is likely to inhibit success unless the impact on the *crowd* is handled very carefully. Many studies conclude that the majority of acquisitions fail – in the range of 70 to 90 percent.[161] If a company is doing it solely to achieve efficiencies and amalgamate, that might be all they'll ever find. On the other hand, M&A activity can help a company realize (or reinforce) its big idea. That's why we say these moments will make or break you.

Microsoft is a company that does some good things, but they know they can do better. Their failed acquisition of Nokia cost them US$8 billion[162] (and counting) and only a very small number of Nokia's employees remain at Microsoft following thousands of post-acquisition layoffs. As we noted earlier, it seems their more recent purchase of LinkedIn might signal a shift in Microsoft's acquisition strategy.[163]

We're not so idealistic as to think Microsoft didn't see the potential in acquiring what is arguably the world's largest source of data on human capital (and we can certainly envision nefarious ways to utilize that information). Still, Microsoft's post-acquisition behavior suggests they see the opportunity to bring LinkedIn's knowledge and affinity for working with the *crowd* into their own operational bloodstream. Perhaps the partnership will improve delivery on Microsoft's new mission *to empower every person and every organization to do better.* Uniting around a common big idea.

Now that sounds like an inspired acquisition.

The decision to use science for good (or evil)

As long as you're not asleep at the wheel, you will see leadership changes, growth milestones, or mergers and acquisitions coming. Now that you recognize them as *Make-or-Breaks* – with the *crowd* watching more closely than ever – you'll know to double down on your commitment to an *Inspired Mission* and values to prove you're in it for the long term. Other *Make-or-Break* moments may also be common, but they aren't as predictable and can require a step change in timeliness of your response while testing the depths of your commitment. Like when a scientific development threatens to put you out of business.

When tobacco companies first came into being, they probably didn't know the full extent of the damage their product does. Nevertheless, they added nicotine to make sure their product would be as addictive as possible, along with a bunch of other ingredients that made cigarettes even worse than natural tobacco ever could have been. As that information came to light, tobacco companies quickly realized it had the potential to destroy them. So they did the most uninspired thing possible. They hid what they knew and promoted their own "scientists" to discredit the research that suggested cigarettes kill people. We noted in Chapter 3 that similar tactics have been employed from time to time by the fossil fuel industry (climate change) and professional sports organizations (concussions and performance-enhancing drug use).

You can't argue that tobacco companies didn't see science coming. They did see the data and they squashed it, replacing it with their own junk science. Whether you see it coming or not, an *Inspired Company* has a prerequisite to use science for good and not evil. If that means changing your entire business because you find out your product is killing people, then guess what? You change your entire business.

McDonald's – once celebrated as family-oriented and healthy – has also been hit by science. When the company was launched in 1955, products were sourced from family farms and bakers, and the world believed in four equally important food groups. At the time, burgers were thought to deliver on all four food groups (especially dairy-laden cheeseburgers with special sauce and a bit of lettuce and onions). Nutritional science eventually caught up with the folks at McDonald's as people started to wonder what they were eating and why they didn't feel so great.

In the face of new knowledge, it eventually became clear that McDonald's approach was not serving the best interests of most of its stakeholders – from farmers to families to health systems. McDonald's (and many other large food companies, for that matter) could have shifted as this information became known, but a focus on profit maximization seems to have precluded any material level of change for several decades.

Having said that, some food companies – including McDonald's – now seem to be turning a corner. As of 2016, healthier options became more readily available on the McDonald's menu – apple slices instead of fries, bottled water as an alternative to soda. It would be easy to argue that these shifts are a response to growing backlash and regulatory pressures – and they may well be. Nevertheless, there's little doubt it's a step in the right direction. And it's what an *Inspired Company* would have done in the first place.

Facebook is a company that currently has a chance to turn things around, but they'd better do it fast. Following the Brexit referendum and 2016 U.S. elections, the company came under fire as a platform for spreading fake news. Despite early denials, it eventually came to light that the company had done little to stop advertising paid for by foreign entities meant to sway votes.[164] And Facebook did next to nothing. Now former executives are calling them out,[165] as are regulators.[166] Perhaps the worst news yet is from the court of public opinion, where people have ranked Facebook second (behind Marlboro) among companies that are bad for society.[167]

Earlier we talked about some issues Facebook addressed in a really inspired way. Their handling of fake news is not one of them. Facebook is an example of using science (in this case, data science) in a way that completely ignores the best interests of the *crowd.* Their algorithms were designed and constantly tweaked to maximize advertising revenue, regardless of its source or veracity. And now the company finds itself in the midst of a *Make-or-Break* moment.

This is the time for Facebook to step up.

Those pesky regulations

Any company can be turned upside down by new taxes, reporting requirements, product restrictions, and other regulations. Sure, some are more susceptible than others. Energy companies, pharmaceuticals, financial institutions, and the like will always face the ups and downs of regulatory change. If you're not in those industries and think you're immune, think again. With a more vocal and powerful *crowd* more tightly linked to the email boxes of their political representatives, regulators have more ammunition than ever to come after you.

Even the most hyped collaborative-economy companies are facing regulatory issues that threaten their existence. We talked earlier about how Uber was built as a workaround to an otherwise heavily regulated taxi industry. Regulators brought their business to a screeching halt in many countries when the company repeatedly failed to address concerns. We mentioned in Chapter 3 that in late 2017, the company was stripped of its operating license in London due to a lack of "social

responsibility."[168] Around the same time, the European Court of
Justice ruled Uber should be classified as a transportation company,
not a technology company, opening it up to all sorts of taxi regulations
and labor law. Uber is appealing the decisions and is able to operate in
London as of the end of 2018.[169]

That's all well and good, but we have to wonder what would happen
if Uber actually aimed to work with civil society rather than against
it. What if it joined forces with cities to create jobs, reduce drunk
driving, use technology to reduce traffic and whatever other ills such
a brilliantly disruptive company is in a position to solve? Maybe the
target on their back wouldn't be quite so large.

Of course, it's not only uninspired collaborative-economy
companies looking to benefit from a lack of regulations. DraftKings
and FanDuel are multi-billion-dollar daily fantasy sports outfits
whose entire competitive advantage is based on loopholes in the U.S.'s
online gambling laws. In each of these cases, regulators seem to be
paying close attention. Once available right across the U.S., by mid-
2017 daily fantasy sports were not available in at least 10 U.S. states
due to regulatory restrictions. Another 18 have legislation or lawsuits
pending.[170] As sustainable business models go, this does not strike us
as a promising formula.

When your entire business model relies on laws not applying to you,
what happens when the laws change? Usually the result won't be good.

Many of these companies rely on the gig economy and an army of
non-employee workers. Suddenly there is a new dimension to ever-
present workers' rights conversations. Lawsuits and regulators in the
U.S. have begun to question whether the millions of people working
for these companies are employees. The potential impact of these
developments will completely reshape how the collaborative economy
works. How companies respond will be a signal of just how inspired
they actually are.

Airbnb is an interesting example of a collaborative-economy
company doing things a bit differently. The home-share company

aims to help people "belong anywhere."[171] That's a pretty big idea in a world where connection is usually something we think of as electronic. Airbnb doesn't have the labor law issues other collaborative companies do (the commodity is people's homes and the owners aren't required to be in them), but they have run into trouble related to cities' zoning laws prohibiting short-term rentals and tax collection. The company has spent its share of lobbying money,[172] but it also works with cities and has started collecting taxes and providing legal information to homeowners.[173] All in all, it strikes us as a bit more promising than Uber's historically combative approach.

Another sign that Airbnb may be headed in the right direction is its decision to forgo an expected 2018 IPO. Airbnb ended 2017 with US$5.5 billion in cash and a unique investment fund that contributed 30 percent of its cash flow.[174] So chief executive Brian Chesky announced the company wouldn't be going public. After all, who needs that headache when there's cash in the bank? CFO Laurence Tosi, who hails from the venture capital titan Blackstone Group, disagreed. The two clashed and Tosi was the one to go.[175] For Chesky's part, we hope that he'll keep working *to create a world that inspires human connection*, even if they subsequently decide to IPO in the future. That's their mission, and so far the crowd is behind it.

In many cases, companies that act in the best interest of the *crowd* will be well positioned to respond to regulatory change when the time comes. Take a look at salt. Increased sodium intake is associated with serious health problems like cardiovascular disease and stroke. These come with a massive human and financial cost – so much so that many countries are issuing major salt reduction guidelines for food manufacturers while at least nine countries have enacted specific legislation governing the amount of salt that can be included in food products.[176] So why do food companies use so much salt in the first place? It's cheap, it's addictive, it's a preservative, and it enhances flavor.

Oh, and no one has told them they can't.

This is an important point. In the U.S., the medical costs associated with cardiovascular disease are expected to triple by 2030, to US$818 billion annually.[177] In the U.K., heart disease causes 35 percent of total deaths and costs £30 billion per year.[178] Worldwide, salt is linked to 1.6 million deaths annually.[179] The stats are seemingly endless. The point is, too much salt is bad and it costs society and governments a fortune. It would be naive to think it will continue to go unregulated. Food manufacturers whose customers have come to expect a certain (high-salt) flavor may well face pushback from sodium-loving customers when they're forced to create the same products with different ingredients.

Why wait for regulation? A company that cares about the *crowd* is likely to care about the health of the *crowd*, particularly when its products have a direct influence on health outcomes. Deli brand Boar's Head is getting this right. When the U.S. announced a voluntary salt-reduction initiative in 2010, Boar's Head was among the first group of companies to sign on. As they put it, "For us, pledging our commitment was easy. We began meeting the 2012 and 2014 sodium targets for deli meats over 25 years ago."[180] Boar's Head is a privately held, century-old company with an established brand. And they'll be ready when regulators come knocking. Until then, they're cultivating plenty of fans with quality food that isn't unnecessarily pumped full of salt.

Near-death experiences (aka bankruptcy)

Bankruptcies don't usually come out of nowhere. Many of them are caused by us putting short-term business-model efficiencies first and longer-term pursuit of a big mission or purpose a distant second. If you've had your blinders on for too long, hoping the signals from the *crowd* will go away, you may eventually end up in a near-death moment. There are many war stories about these moments over corporate history, and not many of them have happy endings. Here's one that does, though. The key to its unlikely turnaround? A chief executive who turned to the most grassroots part of the *crowd*, and listened, learned, and then acted swiftly.

In 2010, Japan Airlines filed for bankruptcy. The company was in a shambles after excess spending led to US$25 billion in debt. A government bailout gave the country's largest airline a reprieve, but the leash would be short. New leadership had to turn the ship around – and get the *crowd* onside – fast.

That's where Kazuo Inamori comes in. Before taking over, Inamori's entire experience with JAL was as a customer – and a dissatisfied one at that. "I really hated JAL,"[181] Inamori admitted on Japanese national television back in 2012. If he wanted to get answers, Inamori understood he needed to go to the most important part of the *crowd* first: employees on the front line like baggage handlers and check-in counter staff. He then turned to unit leaders of teams that had been notoriously divided and put processes in place to ensure they met monthly, shared cost-saving ideas and competitive intelligence, and were accountable to put ideas into action.[182]

Inamori is a leader who places employees above everyone else. When referring to his leadership philosophy at JAL, he said, "It wasn't for shareholders, and it wasn't for executives. It was for all the employees working at the company . . . This is your company, and its goal is to make all of you happy."

Here's the thing about Inamori: He didn't turn to fancy strategists or expensive consulting firms. He knew that a company's employees are the smartest, best-prepared people to turn an organization around. He also knew that if any gains made during the turnaround were to be sustained, JAL's employees and leaders would need to be brought into the process and deeply engaged in coming up with the solutions.

In near-death moments like a bankruptcy and restructuring, employees can quickly be reduced to disempowered, scarred victims of harsh and abrupt layoffs and cost-cutting measures. Highly paid consultants typically seek out "redundant" employees, creating a culture of fear and betrayal. That's exactly what JAL did early in the bankruptcy process. Before Inamori came on board, company leaders cut 15,000 jobs. In such a toxic environment, the best talent often leaves early in the process.

Putting employees in charge of the solutions and uniting them with a single philosophy is why Inamori believes the turnaround effort will be sustained. "I believe JAL executives and employees will keep working hard, not becoming satisfied or complacent . . . It won't be like the old JAL."[183] The *crowd*-led approach laid the foundation for a strong comeback. In 2012, the company's US$8.4 billion IPO was the second largest of the year, following Facebook's.

JAL got through the hard times. The government bailout legally limited their growth from 2010 to 2017. Once the restrictions were lifted, JAL came on strong with high operating profits[184] and an eye toward expansion.[185]

The examples we've covered so far are fairly predictable. In some cases, they're inevitable and in others, common enough for your business to plan for and not be surprised by them. They're issues, milestones, everyday screw-ups or miscalculations that we all will face while in leadership positions – only they're happening in full public view more and more often with the acceleration of social media. In each of the examples so far there's a common thread: the best decisions were made by prioritizing an *Inspired Mission*, values, and the *crowd* you want to keep tightly onside. In this era where the *crowd* has more say than you do in your success, these are your compass points. And you'll need them to continue succeeding in this new *crowd*-dominated era – especially when a storm hits.

When *Make-or-Break* moments are wrongdoings with major consequences – this is when *Inspired Companies* truly distinguish themselves.

Big mistakes, storms and scandals

Every company will face a crisis at one time or another. Oil spills, E. coli outbreaks, defective products, mismanagement, ethics and labor violations whether intentional or not. A good gauge of a company's potential is to look at its employees at that moment. They're either saying, "This isn't who we are" or "Oh yeah, I'm disappointed but it doesn't surprise me." From what we've seen, the more invested your employees are in your company, and the more swiftly leaders act in favor of an *Inspired Mission* and a strong set of values, the faster it will recover from a crisis moment. This has never been truer, as these major *Make-or-Break* moments become increasingly visible and the old ways of deflecting, rationalizing, containing, or covering up only serve to dig you a bigger hole.

A crisis-level *Make-or-Break* forces a company to look at what it means and who they are. The holistic framework of this book offers a sustainable and authentic way to protect your company, build resilience, and minimize the downside of inevitable crisis moments. We highlighted in *Bold Conviction* the importance of *making it right* when mistakes, miscalculations, or genuine mishaps in your footprint occur. That approach is more important than ever in moments of real crisis. In these moments when you are fighting to *make it right*, right away, *exceed expectations*. Don't just meet them.

Take a look at Nike. (You had to know that was coming.) Nike has had several crises that it has recovered from – everything from egregious behavior from athletes the company held up as heroes to very real supply chain issues. Even in the darkest moments, you could have predicted the recovery. Why? Because, among other things, Nike's employees were heartbroken.

In 2018, Nike became the first company to directly collide with the #MeToo movement. Up to that moment, only powerful individual men had been challenged – not powerful companies. As we've covered earlier, "Just Do It" was never a gender-specific tagline. So how did a company that celebrates the power of girls' and women's sports – and that openly stands for diversity in all forms – end up enabling a culture that *The New York Times* reported as threatening, unfair, gender-biased, and sexist?[186]

Our take is that this is an example where the company's values were broken, and an increasingly empowered employee base found better ways to be heard than going to HR. Not living up to the values you espouse will not only cost you a few employee complaints to manage today, it will cost you a crisis-management plan to manage. A crisis that emerges from the inside.

Nike's had its share of *Make-or-Break* moments and fighting to do the right thing – and, in this instance, it seemed to have learned from them. The actions were immediate and very public. Firings were swift, some announced via press release. All-employee meetings were immediately arranged where unequivocal apologies and commitments to make it right were made.

Nike could have launched an internal investigation or settled quietly with those making the complaints. Instead Mark Parker and co-founder Phil Knight acted quickly and decisively. There were no jumbled talking points. Just leaders who love the company and what it stands for when it is at its best.

We've talked a lot about Nike in this book – some of it inspired and some of it not. Our cumulative experience there totals more than 30 years, so it's fair to say we know more about the ins and outs of that company than any other. We can both say that Nike provided us with some of the best opportunities and greatest moments of our professional lives. We believed in the mission and still do. This issue is by no means over for Nike, but with a track record of successfully tackling big issues, we are confident that Nike's *crowd* of *C.E.O.*s, including current and former female employees, will support them to figure it out.

That's how the *crowd* works when they are onside.

BT provides another example of how values conflicts will not – and cannot – be contained internally today. BT fights hard to pursue a big *Inspired Mission to use the power of communications to make a better world.* In 2016 it got smacked upside the head with a scandal that rocked the company to its core: a whistleblower triggered an investigation into fraudulent accounting practices in the company's Italian operations. All told, the financial cost was estimated at £530 million. It caused the company's shares to fall 21 percent for a total book value of £8 billion.[187]

The financial fallout of this sort of thing is obvious, but it's also a critical moment in the life of an *Inspired Company.* For BT, the shock and devastation of the findings were felt at every level.

The natural reaction in these situations is to retreat. It would be easy to revert to the silos, cover up details, obsessively try to control the narrative, fixate on cost-cutting, freeze headcount, etc. Or you could do what BT's chief executive at the time, Gavin Patterson, did: use it as a lightning rod. Get out in front of the world and talk about it. Recognize your role in rebuilding trust. Be disappointed. Be appalled. And most of all, be transparent and take ownership. Patterson continued to do that internally and externally. He met with executives and employees at all levels to reinforce who the company is and why they must remain committed to their purpose. He was willing to talk about his feelings about the scandal and what it says about the company to any media who will listen. In BT's 2016/2017 annual report, he says:

> I'd be the first to say that 2016/17 has been a challenging year, and one that has been humbling for us all at BT . . . The behaviours and practices we found in our Italian business . . . have no place in BT. We take these extremely seriously and have reviewed all aspects of our governance, putting in place new measures and controls to prevent them from happening again.

More than ever, companies need to pay attention to internal values conflicts and be prepared to step up quickly when they do.

Let's take crisis *Make-or-Breaks* to another level and see what more *Inspired Companies* do. In 1982, when Johnson & Johnson found out some of its Tylenol capsules had been laced with cyanide, resulting in six deaths in Chicago, the company didn't wait for regulators to come knocking. They spent US$100 million pulling every bottle off the shelves nationwide and set to work to design a tamper-proof bottle.[188] It's an easy decision to make when you live by a credo to "put the needs and wellbeing of the people we serve first." It's also now hailed as one of the smartest business decisions of all time.

Johnson & Johnson's action in relation to Tylenol bottle tampering is a clear example of how a significant business decision can be driven by an *Inspired Mission* and lead to positive outcomes overall. Their swift action created enormous levels of trust enjoyed by the brand for many years that followed. In 2018, allegations surfaced about Johnson & Johnson suppressing decades-old scientific evidence linking ovarian cancer with the use of their baby powder products. In 2018, the company was ordered to pay nearly US$5 billion in damages, with the potential for more lawsuits on the horizon.[189] In this serious *Make-or-Break* moment, it remains to be seen whether their mission will guide their final decision-making.

Kao Group has similarly faced a moment where everything was at stake – and they were smart enough to exceed expectations with their response. We introduced you to Kao in Chapter 6 on *Obsessive Alignment* – they're the large Japanese conglomerate with a portfolio of businesses ranging from soap toiletries to baby care and health food products. To deepen their investment in beauty products, in 2006 they acquired a well-known Japanese cosmetics company called Kanebo. For this story, it's important to know that, post-acquisition, Kanebo maintained a high level of brand autonomy, separate from Kao. Six years in, a crisis emerged: One of Kanebo's skincare products caused white spots on the skin of 1 to 2 percent of users – that's 20,000 people, some of whom have not fully recovered even today.

Given the low brand association between the two companies and the tangible risk to the broader Kao portfolio, a very real option for the executive board was to isolate the incident to Kanebo. That's what most companies might have done, but Kao isn't most companies. Kao's chief executive Michitaka Sawada moved with extraordinary conviction, took full responsibility, and put the impacted customers' interests first by committing to solve it. Kao created a special organization that at its peak had 200 dedicated staff. They visited each impacted individual, one by one. Counseling resources were provided and tailored solutions were developed, including 20 different skin foundations. Kao still follows up with individuals today – four years later.

While a few lawsuits were filed, many more were avoided. Major media outlets supported Kao instead of attacking them. Kao's board and 33,000 global employees were proud, not embarrassed. Chairman Sonosuke Kadonaga recalls, "In the middle of this regrettable crisis, Sawada's decision, taken with no hesitation, was nothing short of inspiring. He knew the decision would cost a lot, but he simply said, 'This is The Kao Way' – and we all supported him."

And if you don't face the storm head-on, expect to pay
Remember the United Airlines Flight 3411 overbooking case, where the doctor was forcibly removed from his seat? This was United's first response:

> Flight 3411 from Chicago to Louisville was overbooked. After our team looked for volunteers, one customer refused to leave the aircraft voluntarily and law enforcement was asked to come to the gate. We apologize for the overbook situation.

Chief executive Oscar Munoz's response did nothing but fan the flames; it read in part, "I apologize for having to re-accommodate these customers." By that time, the man they had dragged off the plane was in the hospital with missing teeth and broken bones, getting prepped for surgery. That is not a situation most people would characterize as "re-accommodated." Of course, the people of the internet happily served up their own definitions.

United didn't lose US$250 million[*] in book value in one day[190] just because they violently forced a customer off a flight (although it certainly didn't help). This is a company that ranks last among airlines in customer satisfaction.[191] United's troubles are a symptom of a much bigger problem that starts with employees feeling disempowered to make decisions for the good of the customer and the company. They have no clear path toward making it right. They obsess their business model, not a bigger idea, purpose, or set of values. And it ends with a world full of fed-up consumers who have cameras in their pockets and social media networks to spread the word.

TOP DEFINITION

re-accommodate

to beat up and violently **drag** paying passengers off an **airplane** in order to make room for airline **crew** on stand-by.

*"I apologize for having to re-accommodate these customers." (***Oscar*** Munoz, **CEO**, **United Airlines**, April 10, 2017)*

by Wim2600 April 10, 2017

Niall Stanage ✓
@▮▮▮▮▮▮▮   ▼ Follow

I remember when a young Mike Tyson re-accommodated Trevor Berbick in short order. #united #reaccommodate
youtube.com/watch?v=WAWU1d...
2:46 PM - 10 Apr 2017

💬   ⇄ 4   ♡ 12

---

* $1bn in market capitalization was immediately lost in the first part of the trading day, which eventually settled back to $250m by the end of the trading day.

In the end, United's brand equity took the final beating with an entire spectrum of action taken against them. Everything from calls for the chief executive to be fired and a boycott, to competitors openly mocking them – and, of course, a very expensive lawsuit from the "re-accommodated" passenger.

Handling crises doesn't have to be as hard as companies try to make it. The United case came up in a conversation with Emma Mcilroy of Wildfang. Her advice to every chief executive who finds him- or herself under fire is simple. And yet, it seems just about everyone needs to hear it. The first three steps are *so* basic, every communications department should know them:

1. Firstly, thank you for caring enough to call us out.
2. You are 100 percent right. (Do not make ANY excuses. Ever.)
3. From me personally, I am deeply sorry. This will never happen again. (Take responsibility like a grown-up. Deflection never works.)
4. Fix it. Make it right. Exceed expectations.

On the fourth point above, coming up with the actual solution is a matter of who you are as a company and how the problem came about. One option is to take immediate action and let the public decide what the right plan of attack is. In *Inspired Companies*-speak, we'd say that's about "bringing the outside in" and counting on the *crowd* to give you the right answer. This also ensures they feel valued at a time when you'll need to reinforce that most.

When a storm develops into a global catastrophe

In 2009, Mark Wilson was the CEO of AIA Group, a life insurance company owned by AIG. He's often quoted as saying, "You can have all the plans in the world, but events will occur that blow you off course." Or "punch you in the face," as he more candidly puts it.

When the global financial crisis hit, it's fair to say Wilson might have seen it coming. After all, he had plans in place that others didn't. He stockpiled cash, for example. Enough to cover AIA's liabilities and payouts to individual shareholders should something big unfold. AIA's parent company, AIG, hadn't done things quite the same way.

"Picture it this way: I was sitting at home in a leather chair on the phone with the New York Fed and the Bermuda and Hong Kong monetary authorities all at the same time. I hadn't been to bed and it was 4:30 in the morning. When that happens, you know you've got a problem."

In an effort to make itself whole, the chief executive of AIG was demanding Wilson surrender AIA's cash reserves. "They did things they shouldn't have done and destroyed a legacy for many generations of management and leaders before it." Wilson refused to hand over the cash, and put a ring fence in place.

The global financial crisis had hit, and the world had gone into a panic. This is where inspired leadership kicks in.

"I called my team and said, 'We need to meet. Our parent company has collapsed and I don't think they'll be around by the time we get into the office.'" He arrived at the entrance to AIA's offices in Hong Kong and was swarmed by media, customers, employees, security, you name it. "No books have been written about how to handle this type of crisis. I'd never dealt with this type of situation before," he said in a Bloomberg interview.[192] All he knew was that he had to come up with a different solution than the one AIG was proposing.

Because AIA was in a good cash position, Wilson started to prepare for a public listing – a courageous move in the middle of a financial crisis. At the same time, after refusing to hand over the cash, he came under enormous pressure to sell AIA to a large U.K. insurer as another way of bailing out the parent. That's a deal Wilson looked at and declined, despite extraordinary pressure to accept it.

Why was Wilson pushing back so hard? Because he knew the fallout would land on ordinary people. To put things in perspective, AIA had material holdings in the long-end government bonds of several Asian countries at the time. Practically speaking, that means several economies were leveraged to the company Wilson was responsible for. Twenty-five million customers also depended on him to do the right thing, as did 300,000 employees. As Wilson tells it, "No one went home for weeks." If he had handed over the cash reserves to AIG, he'd have sold out employees, pension-holders, and millions of innocent bystanders of several different countries. The stakes don't get much higher than that in leadership.

Wilson left the company just before the successful IPO he'd positioned it for. Both AIA and AIG survived the crisis. He eventually took the reins at Aviva, the 300-year-old U.K.-based insurer we've talked about previously. You probably won't be surprised to hear that Wilson continued to do very well post-AIA: "Wilson Disrupting U.K. Insurance With Turnaround at Aviva"[193] and "Aviva Turnaround Ahead of Schedule as New Business Climbs"[194] are just a few of the headlines celebrating his inspired leadership. This is what happens on the other side of *Make-or-Break* moments.

Put simply, a real leader knows when to say "no," and under extreme pressure shows what they're made of.

Navigating the turning points

Anyone who runs a company knows the pressures are constant. No matter how inspired you or your company may be, there will always be *Make-or-Break* moments that, left unchecked, can lead to abrupt changes in the level of trust you enjoy with the *crowd.* Truly *Inspired Companies* understand that these moments, while hard, don't have to be dark.

New leadership, scientific developments, regulatory pressures or changes, hitting growth milestones, and unforeseen events from your business footprint are the moments that show what a company is made of. *Inspired Companies* don't run from these moments. They pursue, recognize, and embrace them.

The important thing here isn't whether or not you'll face a *Make-or-Break* moment (you will). It's how you respond when the moment slaps you in the face. A decision to take the easy money, turn a blind eye, or cover up missteps and misdeeds will always be tempting. It will probably even seem like a smoother path than the alternative. Trust us, it only seems that way. But it isn't the only way. Of course, companies need to have their fingers on the pulse of the macro trends – the science, regulations, public sentiment, etc. Even more importantly, they need to keep the best interests of the *crowd* at the heart of decision-making. If Facebook cared as much about the average user as it did about cost-per-click, or if Marlboro put its customer ahead of the customer's wallet, those companies would have handled their crises a lot differently.

Inspired Companies and their leaders are ready for these moments. Their decision-making is guided by an *Inspired Mission* and a commitment to their *crowd*. They know what to do when faced with a *Make-or-Break* moment. They double down on their big idea and show everyone what they're made of.

If you've come this far, you've gotten a good look at what it might take to become the kind of company that the *crowd* will support. You've seen what we mean by putting a big idea at the center of all that you do, and reinforcing it with an ever-present set of shared values. You've covered a range of strategies and tactics that more *Inspired Companies* employ to ensure they authentically deliver on their mission, from obsessing alignment to challenging the system when it gets in their way, to stepping out with *Bold Conviction* when circumstances call for it. You've probably thought: That's a lot of work.

And it is.

Getting the *crowd* onside after a century of disconnection will take some doing. The trick is to do it now. Get the world onside by leading with *Inspired Action*. Create a company everyone wants to be part of and proud of. Then watch them fuel your success.

Inspired Companies – the ones that never gave up the pursuit of their big idea even though it turned out to be really freaking hard – will make good money.

Really good money.

Chapter 9 Summary

Every *Inspired Company* will have *Make-or-Break* moments. New science, new leaders, new regulations, or new growth milestones are just a few of the existential threats to your *Inspired Mission* and the support of your *crowd*. How leaders react in these moments will disproportionately impact everything else that follows.

Here's what *Inspired Action* in these moments looks like:

- Plan for the predictable:
  - o Leadership transitions, growth milestones, new funding sources
- A better approach for common *Make-or-Break* moments:
  - o Acquisitions and divestments, scientific developments, the temptations to benefit from regulatory loopholes, bankruptcy
- Show who you are when things really blow up:
  - o Act quickly and decisively, guided by your mission and shared values when you've made a big mistake and are facing a storm or scandal

Chapter 10

Inspired Profit:
Value Created when the Crowd is Onside

INSPIRED *Mission*	INSPIRED *Action*	INSPIRED *Profit*
Stand for a big idea. A promise with many winners.	**Authentic Pursuit.** The idea is everywhere - all the time.	**Good money.** Value created when the *crowd* is onside.

Inspired Companies make good money

It costs a lot to be uninspired. As we covered in Chapter 3, uninspired companies face a downward spiral of headwinds from the *crowd* for a host of reasons, but mostly because they are not trusted. Employees, customers, regulators, civil society, media, and investors are very real and very expensive threats when they are not onside. They could even cost you your business or your career if they decided to work against you together.

Inspired Companies, on the other hand, have a decidedly different profit-making experience than uninspired ones. They make "good" money - in both senses of the word.

"Good money" is the way you keep the *crowd* onside.

> ## In This Chapter
>
> - The payoff for *Inspired Companies*: brand distinction and sustained financial success in a world controlled by the *new C.E.O.s*
>
> - How getting that *crowd* onside and authentically pursuing an *Inspired Mission* translates into three big competitive advantages
>
> - How those advantages – expanded playing fields, *crowd*-fueled tailwinds, and resilience – create lasting brand distinction and superior financial performance
>
> - The result: profit to invest more of what the *crowd* wants – a vibrant organization delivering on big ideas and creating a virtuous cycle of success and the ultimate 21st-century competitive advantage

Ernst & Young and Harvard Business School found that 85 percent of companies with a clearly articulated and well-understood purpose experienced revenue growth, while 42 percent of purpose-starved companies saw a decline.[195] When LinkedIn explored what this data meant for their company specifically, they discovered that purpose-oriented employees were more engaged and fulfilled by their work.[196]

It's really very simple: deliver something people care about, do it amazingly well, and focus everything you do on that inspired idea. Commit to a set of values shared with the rest of the world and always do the right thing. Profit will follow, and so will the passion, loyalty, and resilience required for sustained success. This has always been a formula for success in business.

Only now it's not optional.

Inspired Companies make "good" money because they create real connections with the *crowd* of *new C.E.O.s*. In this chapter, we'll explain more about how focusing on big ideas over narrowly pursuing business-model efficiencies and short-term profits expands the playing field of business opportunities. We'll also show how the active support of many stakeholders translates into competitive advantage and superior financial performance.

We call that *Inspired Profit*.

And really, doesn't that sound a lot more interesting than setting up another department, or writing another policy to see if they might make the headwinds you're facing go away? When *Inspired Companies* articulate an *Inspired Mission* and are authentically pursuing it, they stand a good chance of making very good money. Here's how:

Inspired Companies **expand their playing field.** They are free to evolve, expand, and innovate in ways that uninspired companies are not. A big idea inherently attracts a bigger proportion of the population to innovate for, and a greater chance you'll be granted "permission" to expand beyond narrowly defined product or service offerings.

Inspired Companies **leverage historically untapped stakeholder value and experience powerful tailwinds.** By driving toward a mission that benefits many, our *new C.E.O.s* will deliver unprecedented levels of value in the form of accelerated sales referrals and positive PR, reduced red tape, lower transaction costs, and diminished need for things like crisis management.

Inspired Companies **bounce back.** Thanks to the trust that has been earned, the *crowd* protects *Inspired Companies* from the aftermath of missteps and unexpected events. They enjoy resilience that their uninspired counterparts do not.

Inspired Companies **create brand distinction and a virtuous cycle** that delivers superior performance that compounds to further separate them from peers.

This kind of competitive advantage will leave uninspired companies far behind.

1. Expanded playing fields

The unlimited potential of big ideas

Over the course of this book you've seen various ways the power of the *crowd* plays out. An *Inspired Mission* delivered with *Inspired Action* creates shared goals and builds trust. Together, they have a way of determining how big your business will be. The *crowd* seems fine for some companies to expand their horizons but not others. Consider this:

Would you trust Yahoo! to drive your car?

Would you let Chrysler power your home?

Would you be happy about getting a medical scan from Kodak?

These questions seem absurd, until you consider what their "industry peers" are actually achieving: Google is bringing self-driving cars to market, Tesla is mass-producing renewable home energy, and Canon is making medical imaging devices.

The reason these companies can do this is because they are driven by big ideas. Through their everyday actions and priorities, these companies show they aren't limited to a narrowly defined set of internal goals or set of existing business models as their implied purpose. As a result, they are not constrained by preconceived notions of market size, market potential, or delivery models. They see the unlimited potential of very big ideas, and they believe in the infinite growth and agility that an *Inspired Mission* can bring about. This allows *Inspired Companies* to expend their energy creating bigger and new pies, instead of obsessing about the size of their slice. And, to state the obvious, investors pay premiums for companies that demonstrate potential for growth beyond single products or industries.

The reason consumers buy into the concept of a car manufacturer like Tesla powering their homes is because Tesla's not a car manufacturer. They may have started out that way – with a focus on transforming the car industry. But the pursuit of mass-market sustainable energy is the bigger idea they pursue.

It wasn't that long ago that people thought electric cars would amount to little more than golf carts. Handy for environmentally minded celebrities to scoot about the studio lot, but not very practical for real people to get from point A to point B. In fact, it was only 2010 when the head of Total, the French oil conglomerate, said, "People say they are inventing electric cars. Well, where is the electricity coming from? Flowers? Maybe someday. But what is available now is oil and gas."[197] Cars allowed Tesla to show the world what's possible; that all of the assumptions about sustainable energy were wrong. In other words, their real business is making sustainable energy work for people across their lives. That's why a "car manufacturer" like Tesla would create a system for low-cost, battery-powered home energy.

Tesla demonstrates how consumers are much more likely to give an *Inspired Company* permission to invest in business adjacencies than they would a profit-as-purpose company. This is also why both Apple and Google are allowed to play in spaces like payments (Apple Pay, Google Pay), which have traditionally been the purview of financial institutions. Meanwhile, most large telecom companies missed the opportunity to lead in the payments business – despite having all the data, capabilities, and infrastructure to do so. They were too busy obsessing over their existing business-model products and services to see bigger ideas that a more *Inspired Mission* and *crowd* of active supporters might lead them to.

Agility that comes from a focus on bigger ideas

Organizations that are driven by a big idea are able to take advantage of opportunity when it arises. These are companies that have mobilized the *crowd* (starting with their employees) around ideas rather than around things. In so doing, these companies are afforded the agility they'll need when it comes time to grow, change direction, and innovate. The research is starting to bear this out. A recent study looked at companies that self-identified as having a strong sense of purpose and those that don't. "Prioritizers" of purpose were much more likely to have expanded geographically and launched new products. Additionally, 50 percent of them "engaged in a major transformation initiative," where only 16 percent of the study's purpose "laggards" said the same.[198]

Let's go beyond the big brands and look at a lesser-known company, APX Alarm Security Solutions, Inc. Their business model and related goals focused on providing alarm systems. Not surprisingly, that's what people expected of them. In 2011, the company became Vivint Smart Home and a new mission was re-envisioned: *to help you create a smarter home with intelligently designed products that simplify your life*. As we know, it takes a lot more than changing a few words to be inspired, but a compelling purpose like "simplifying life" is a great starting place.

For Vivint Smart Home, authentic pursuit of their mission pushed them into residential solar energy and cloud storage solutions to complement their original line of security products and services. By aligning against a bigger idea, they've also been able to partner with big players – like an Airbnb deal that allows hosts to link their accounts to offer keyless entry and security features, and a partnership with Google to connect products to voice-activated Google Home Speakers. Vivint Smart Homes was named one of Fast Company's Most Innovative Companies of 2017. Not bad for folks who used to sell security systems.

In addition to pursuing a big idea, their ability to pivot is predicated on happy employees. Vivint employees believe in what they're doing, they like their boss, and they seem to like working there. The company's chief executive, Todd Pederson, has a 90 percent Glassdoor approval rating from employees and almost 70 percent recommend it as a good place to work.[199]

If we look at this from the opposite vantage point, consider Uber (yes, they have continued to be an easy target). Its US$66 billion valuation (implied by a US$12 billion raise in 2016)[200] was cut by 20 percent with a Softbank offer at the end of 2017.[201] Even so, the company has the resources to enable continued global expansion and movement into adjacent lines of business – and they actually are, with food delivery and pet transportation. However, the company's reputation and workforce problems in many countries underscore its lack of purpose. It remains to be seen if the *crowd*, including regulators, will actually let them.

Earlier, we called out Ford Motor Company's mission statement as being rather uninspired: *People working together, as a lean global enterprise for automotive leadership.* It's interesting to consider what might have happened if Ford Motor Co. had stayed laser-focused on Henry Ford's original vision to connect people to opportunity instead of aiming for automotive leadership. The latter forced them into a position they share with most other automakers – as a lobbyist that impacted the entire public transportation system in the U.S. to serve automakers' interests. Their approach to business and their mission made the company – and the country – completely dependent on cars. Now life is full of traffic jams and smog.

Imagine if Ford's model had remained focused on connecting people to opportunity.

They might have invented the internet.

2. Crowd-fueled tailwinds

Companies that have the *crowd* onside create a set of benefits that more uninspired companies don't: They enjoy *crowd*-fueled tailwinds. We're not talking about giving away profits here to buy more employee benefits, loyalty programs, or make donations to get them onside (although done right they certainly help). We're talking about profitable growth that arises when you have the *crowd* onside from being an *Inspired Company*. A *crowd* that buys, refers, advocates for, and defends your business.

A *crowd*-fueled tailwind is a positive force exerted by the *new C.E.O.s* when they believe you and are inspired by you. The *crowd* will create more value and reduce costs throughout your value chain.

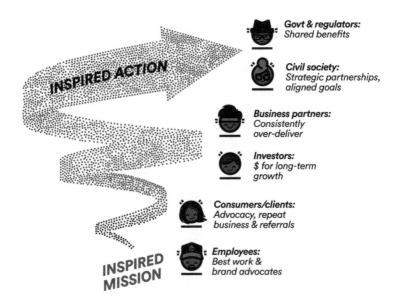

INSPIRED ACTION

Govt & regulators:
Shared benefits

Civil society:
*Strategic partnerships,
aligned goals*

Business partners:
*Consistently
over-deliver*

Investors:
*$ for long-term
growth*

Consumers/clients:
*Advocacy, repeat
business & referrals*

**INSPIRED
MISSION**

Employees:
*Best work &
brand advocates*

Figure 7: *Crowd*-fueled tailwinds enjoyed by *Inspired Companies*

Viewed almost as a bonus in the past, this dynamic will now make or break your profitability and, at its most potent, your viability.

Tailwinds in action – how they work

By now we hope it has become clear that everything starts with having an *Inspired Mission* – the shared purpose others will get behind.

As a headline recap to Chapter 4, creating shared goals by framing your *Inspired Mission* in the right way is a powerful way to cut through bureaucracy, draw in powerful friends, and encourage the sharing of resources and expertise across sectors to get stuff done:

To help people discover things they love and inspire them to do those things in their daily lives (Pinterest)

To make clean, reliable energy affordable for everyone in the world (Bloom Energy)

To create a world where people work to make a life, not just a living (WeWork)

These are the kinds of mission statements that draw others in, not confuse or push them away. When executed authentically, they give these companies a shot at keeping the *crowd* onside and in your corner.

Here's how it plays out when you do:

Employees: United by a common sense of purpose, their success is your success

When employees are onside they are loyal and deliver their best work. They love being asked where they work. They're proud of the company and its products and services and have a strong sense of purpose to their everyday. Want to reduce unwanted turnover by up to 59 percent? You can do that by having more engaged employees. You can also expect productivity to increase by 17 percent, while shrinkage drops 28 percent, and – here's one that surprised us – a 70 percent reduction in safety incidents.[202] Another study found that people who have high levels of trust in their employers have "74 percent less stress, 106 percent more energy at work, 50 percent higher productivity, 13 percent fewer sick days, 76 percent more engagement, 29 percent more satisfaction with their lives, 40 percent less burnout."[203]

Put simply, that's lower healthcare and turnover costs, and much higher productivity and ingenuity driven straight to your bottom line.

Excellence from business partners

Business partners love working with *Inspired Companies*. One simple reason is because they know they'll be treated fairly. But more than that, your mission can drive business partners too. It can connect their work to a greater sense of purpose and give them something to be proud of. When business partners are onside, it can mean preferential treatment across a range of business-critical items and great service. When they believe in what you're doing and are treated fairly, it may even inspire them to advocate powerfully on your behalf.

We've already talked briefly in earlier chapters about how Huawei and BT work together on a number of shared purpose

opportunities. Fiserv and ANZ* provide another example. Fiserv
is a provider of financial services technology whose employees are
passionate about how banks like ANZ are using their technology.
Fiserv enables this large multinational bank to deliver mobile
banking to some of the hardest-to-reach places on Earth. In
practical terms, that means a teacher on the island of Vanuatu no
longer needs to close the school and travel for a week to get paid.
As a business partner, Fiserv – without request or payment from
ANZ – used its own PR machine to promote ANZ's efforts through
media, advertising, and awards.

That type of public advocacy is invaluable for anyone, let
alone heavily regulated industries like banking. For too long B2B
partnerships have been undervalued, limited to transactional
relationships, and seen as a zero-sum game. *Inspired Companies* create
partnerships with benefits.

Loyalty and passion from consumers

Consumers know how to spot an *Inspired Company*. They may not call
it that, but it's the brand they love and speak favorably about. It's the
brand they believe cares about them.

Nike is an example of a company that figured this out. Twenty years
ago (back in the days of its narcissistic #1 mission), the company had a
very small women's business. To oversimplify (though not by much),
the women's business back then was mostly about repurposing men's
product in pink or lemon yellow. At the time, Nike was rather lucky
that no other company was doing a particularly good job for women's
and girls' athletic apparel (with the notable and unfortunate exceptions
of the Lycra and legwarmer brands of the 1980s – which at least one
of the authors admits to being a victim of). As for athletic footwear,
Reebok took the prized market-share leadership position from Nike for
part of the 1980s – largely due to Reebok's efforts to design and market
directly to women.[204]

---

* Australia and New Zealand Banking Group.

The happier end to this story (at least for us) is that Nike made some very big shifts as part of aligning to its new mission statement *To bring innovation and inspiration to every athlete* in the world. (*If you have a body, you're an athlete.)* Many Nike employees knew that the new mission certainly must include girls and women and, as such, more commitment than color-palette adjustments might finally follow.

And it did.

Nike invested in R&D to better understand girls and women, the sports they love, their activity needs, busy connected lives, and shopping preferences. A whole range of changes throughout the company emerged over time to deliver much more authentically to these athletes – dedicated sales floor environments, women's designers, as well as things like girls- and women-only marathons and training clubs with charitable fundraising components. The results have been extraordinary for Nike across the globe. By 2005 – in just the first few years of a more authentic focus on women – the women's business grew by 20 percent. This outpaced the company's overall growth, and that deeper level of commitment was then replicated in every region the company operated in.[205] Profitability, innovation, and growth – but also a huge and valuable social network of inspired female consumers globally who became champions for Nike.

And here's another important point: At face value, you could look at this example and say, "it looks like they did a good CSR thing to reach women by making sure they have incorporated some good charity and cause marketing elements, so we should do that too." That's the wrong way to think about it, and it's not why Nike succeeded. That was just one insightful and meaningful tactic. Nike succeeded because they turned their attention to their new mission and applied it more deliberately. They got serious about a huge portion of the world's "athletes" that were being underserved and they decided to commit. And that's also why none of the work – even for the cause marketing and charitable fundraising elements – came out of the CSR budget. It was all considered core.

In 2015, the company announced plans to grow the women's business from US$5.7 billion to US$11 billion by 2020.[206] That's a big pie that just seems to keep expanding as women decided to wear their new athletic gear all day long. Who knew? Perhaps product designed for women fits us better than the men's product does – what a newsflash.

A group of unlikely stakeholders committed to your success

Inspired Companies strive to achieve things other people care about. Reduce physical inactivity, bring about financial security, increase access to justice, nourish generations of growing children, efficient transportation systems, and ubiquitous access to knowledge. These are ideas that many actors across society can get behind. They may not sound catchy but, as we've mentioned, wordsmith later. The important concept here is that a big idea expressed as a relevant corporate mission statement does not have to be narrow and exclusive to be powerful. The more widely inspiring it is, the more powerful the potential results. This is particularly true for large populations of **O**utsiders.

National governments, for example, are more likely to be open to supportive regulation and infrastructure when they share your goals. Kenya's M-Pesa is a mobile money-transfer service used by more than two-thirds of adults in the country. The service is cheaper than that provided by banks, far more convenient, and can be used during turbulent times. When traditional banks complained about the lack of regulation, the Kenyan government awarded M-Pesa a special license to continue its operations and worked with the company to ensure customer identification standards could be realistically met. M-Pesa had community goals at the heart of their business mission, and the government went as far as changing the rules to support them. That's game-changing value creation and someone else fighting for your way of doing business. *Local governments* can decide to grant permits and provide access to infrastructure and support quickly - or really, really slowly. Let's look closer at Google Fiber again. When Google was looking for new locations to launch its low-cost (and sometimes free) Wi-Fi service, many cities submitted proposals. Kansas City was one of the winners because they were able to offer access to public rights of way, expedite permits, and offer Google city facilities and marketing resources. Kansas City rolled out the red carpet because they saw Google's entry as an economic development asset that could facilitate equal access to important information and opportunities for city residents.

Could Google have paid for all the things local governments were doing for them? Maybe, but why not share resources when you share goals?

Academics will help *Inspired Companies* get the right work done. The more they are at the table understanding a root issue and contributing to the solution, the more supportive they will be of the ultimate business solution and model. Nike's work on physical inactivity, for example, brought together experts from all walks of life: brain researchers, skeletal experts, chronic disease experts, program practitioners, and teachers to name a small handful.[207] They were also the ones who testified before government officials, giving evidence on the policies that needed to be in place to get inactive populations moving again – something fairly crucial to a sports company's future growth prospects.

Civil society will also want to forge collaborations with *Inspired Companies* if they believe there are shared goals and united interests. Group Danone, a global food manufacturer known mainly for dairy products, has a mission to *bring health through food to as many people as possible*. That's a goal that speaks to many throughout the world, and Danone is actually delivering. In fact, that mission led to a joint venture in Bangladesh called Grameen Danone. It's a social business enterprise that delivers key nutrients – through yogurt, of course – that are missing in the diets of many rural Bangladeshi children. The enterprise is completely self-sustaining and draws on Danone's competencies as a food manufacturer and distributor, alongside Grameen's reach in rural communities and understanding of the complexities associated with extreme poverty there. This was not something Danone did to make extra profit. It was an investment that paid for itself, pushed them to innovate, generated goodwill with customers, business partners, civil society, and government, and that ultimately served their bigger corporate mission of *health through food to as many people as possible*.

Working with researchers, government, and civil society may not seem like a natural step for profit centers outside CSR and government affairs teams, but pool all of this together and the value created becomes irresistible. Federal and local governments, NGOs, and academics actually wanting you to succeed. Imagine that.

Investors who value the mission and are in it for the long term
As the tailwinds from **C**onsumers, **E**mployees, business partners, and other **O**utsiders builds, your investor community will start to pay attention to new ways of measuring value. Intellectual property consultant Ocean Tomo's research on companies' market-to-book value suggests investors reward intangible assets. The research found that in 1975, 83 percent of the S&P 500's value was based on tangible ("book") assets. By 2010, only 20 percent of equity was tangible, while the other 80 percent was intangible.[208]

In very recent years we've seen the emergence of new types of valuation indices that measure intangibles in increasingly sophisticated ways. For example, Enso's World Brand Value (mentioned in earlier chapters) proposes a new metric to measure brand value. It factors in a range of people's awareness of a brand's purpose, along with how that awareness translates to public action and bottom line. Specifically, the four dimensions they use are:

1. **Awareness of purpose:** What does the brand stand for, beyond making money?

2. **Alignment with purpose:** Is the company's purpose something that aligns with what people care about?

3. **Active support:** Is the company's purpose something that people would publicly support?

4. **Impact on purchase:** Does the company's purpose motivate people to buy from the brand?

(Source: https://www.enso.co/worldvalue)

Enso describes its approach as "The brands that do the most and least good for the world measured by people not shareholders."[209] This way of viewing and valuing brands directly aligns with our view that the *crowd* holds the power today to dramatically influence the outcomes of your business. This index places a value on whether or not your purpose or mission stands for a clear, bigger idea that resonates with what others care about. It then places a value on whether the public is committed enough to act in favor of the brand. It ranks corporate and nonprofit brands together, so you'll see a combined ranking that includes everyone from Save the Children to Amazon, Google, PayPal, and Wikipedia. Is it comprehensive of the whole value equation for *Inspired Companies*? No. But it's a great start that did not exist before 2016.

In short, when a tidal wave of traditional and untraditional stakeholders are working with you rather than against you, this support creates more value and reduces costs throughout your value chain. All of this because you've succeeded in recruiting a *crowd* that wants to help you and is onside.

This is a tailwind – and it's more valuable to your business than ever.

3. Resilience and the art of being forgiven

The third element of *Inspired Profit* is your insurance policy. *Inspired Companies* are much better equipped to weather storms because the *crowd*'s got your back.

That's your policy, right there.

Let's go back to Uber and Tesla. When people turned up at U.S. airports in droves to protest the Trump Administration's Executive Order that banned travel from seven Muslim-majority countries, Uber announced it wouldn't charge "surge pricing" in New York, where a taxi strike was already taking place. If Uber had any trust in the bank, consumers might have seen this as a good thing. Instead, it was viewed as an attempt to capitalize on the situation and the #DeleteUber campaign was launched. This came at the same time as now former Uber CEO Travis Kalanick was named to Trump's business council. All told, more than 200,000 people deleted their Uber accounts, and Kalanick was pressured into quitting the council. Kalanick said he resigned because people perceived his participation as "somehow endorsing the administration's agenda."[210]

Compare that to Elon Musk's experience. The Tesla and SpaceX chief also faced scrutiny for participating on the business council, but no one called for boycotts and he seemed to be afforded the opportunity to explain himself. He did so in true Musk-like fashion with a public letter that said, in part, the following:

> Advisory councils simply provide advice and attending does not mean that I agree with actions by the Administration. My goals are to accelerate the world's transition to sustainable energy and to help make humanity a multi-planet civilization, a consequence of which will be the creation of hundreds of thousands of jobs and a more inspiring future for all.[211]

Apple's 2015 blunder involving a free trial of a new music service is another good example of the forgiveness effect and the impact of brand trust. Taylor Swift publicly took the company to task for refusing to pay artists during the trial period. Even in her letter, she referred to the situation as "completely unlike this historically progressive and generous company." Apple quickly pivoted, and all was right with the world again. (Not to mention the publicity Apple got for a pretty much unheard-of new service.)

Earlier we talked about TOMS' brand value – specifically that it ranks 22nd among millennials (ahead of Nike at 26th). This is due in large part to the company's easy-to-understand, easy-to-get-behind purpose that actively engages regular people. The willingness of TOMS' founder to learn and pivot (and also be open about it) is what gave the company the resilience it would need as it grew. For example, when TOMS started, regardless of their very good intentions, they didn't know much about global poverty. It turns out their production model was not only inefficient, it also didn't produce shoes in the countries they were donating in. This was both a missed opportunity and a crushing blow to anyone actually making shoes in those places. TOMS took the criticism well and they are now working toward producing a significant percentage of shoes locally. And of course, they're telling that story.

You're going to make mistakes. We all do. The difference is whether or not you'll be given the chance to bounce back relatively unscathed. If you're driven by profit and profit alone, the chances are pretty good that people will leave you in droves (kind of like 200,000 people deleting their Uber accounts in the span of a few days). On the other hand, if you're guided by a big idea that the *crowd* is behind – and better yet is a part of – you'll be given a lot more leeway when you make inevitable slip-ups. Like Apple and Tesla, your *crowd* is more likely to give you the benefit of the doubt. And like TOMS, you'll be given the chance to make things right.

And of course, that's the key with *Inspired Companies*.

We know they will make things right.

4. Brand distinction and a virtuous cycle

Here's where expanded playing fields, *crowd*-fueled tailwinds, and resilience combine to deliver powerful, sustainable, and profitable growth for *Inspired Companies* (Figure 8). These competitive advantages work together to create a compounding and virtuous cycle.[*]

Brand distinction flows when decisions across the business are guided by an *Inspired Mission* and embrace a common set of values with the *crowd*. When an inspired idea sits at the core of the company and is authentically pursued, when everyone involved is free to make decisions in service to a greater goal (as long as there are checks and balances in place to ensure focus and prioritization), the brand will emerge from the inside out. Once the *crowd* knows the mission and the actions of a company are legitimate, missteps are far more likely to be forgiven and you'll have more positive unofficial company spokespeople than you ever imagined in the form of loyal employees, customers, and political advocates.

---

[*] We are exploring the creation of a formal index that quantifies the market performance of *Inspired Companies* under this expanded definition.

Superior performance is the result. We've laid out how an *Inspired Company* creates incremental profit and resources for reinvestment based on its expanded playing field, compounding tailwinds from the *crowd*, fewer complaints and issues, and faster recovery from missteps. When combined, these create a cycle of compounding returns that profit-as-purpose companies cannot compete with.

Research is starting to bear out the importance of this. In a survey of global companies who say they have a stated purpose, those who made purpose a priority were far more likely to have experienced growth of more than 10 percent over the last three years than those who say their purpose is not well understood internally.[212] Another global study of 50,000 brands by brand consultant Millward Brown found that "the brands that serve a higher purpose deliver stronger financial performance and build deeper relationships with consumers. The key to their growth was defining themselves not around a particular product or service, but around an Ideal; a higher-order reason for being that articulates 'why' the brand exists and the impact it seeks to make on the world." [213]

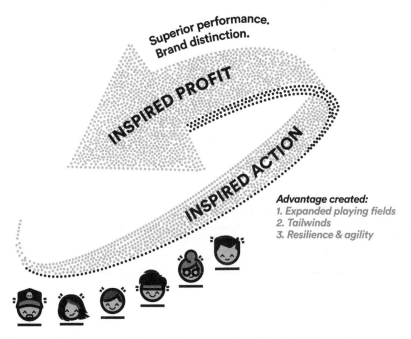

Figure 8: The compounding and virtuous cycle of *Inspired Companies*

A virtuous cycle

It makes sense that a company striving toward a big idea that people care about is probably going to have more satisfied stakeholders – whether those stakeholders are customers, employees, neighbors, or whomever. The result? Far fewer obstacles and unnecessary expenses, and more growth opportunities. The additional profit generated by *Inspired Companies* can then be reinvested to create further distinction and separation from competitors to create compounding returns – namely in areas like business-model innovation, new business and customer acquisition, and retention of the brightest and best leaders.

Welcome to a new era of *Inspired Profit*.

The basic payoff principal for *Inspired Companies* is this: The company is thinking about its market differently because it's solving a bigger problem than trying to be #1. The revenue base expands and a whole range of stakeholders are now working with you not against you. Everyone supports an *Inspired Company*'s big idea and, as such, they are in a unique position to harness historically untapped value from the growing and powerful *crowd* of *new C.E.O.s* that believe in the mission you are pursuing. Employees and business partners deliver their best work. Consumers act like the company matters to them because it does. Governments are more likely to roll out red carpet than red tape. Civil society will help you solve problems, not picket outside your corporate headquarters.

Oh, and when the going gets tough, the *crowd* will come to your defense, not bury you in spectacular style by working together and turning headwinds into a cyclone.

The business of an *Inspired Company* leads to greater returns for everyone. And because of who has the power today, it's a model that can be sustained into the future.

It turns out being a force for good pays pretty well these days. That and the fact that it might just be the corporate sector's only option for the next 100 years.

Chapter 10 Summary

Inspired Companies make good money. With the *crowd* onside they have permission to evolve, expand, pivot, and innovate. That's why Google can make driverless cars (and why Yahoo! can't).

With the *new C.E.O.s* onside, *Inspired Companies* experience more tailwinds and far fewer headwinds. Consumers are advocates and brand ambassadors, Employees deliver their best work, business partners over-deliver, and traditional Outsiders throw in their support. And that's just the start. *Inspired Companies* are more resilient and the *crowd* will be more likely to forgive the occasional screw-up.

All of these things combine to deliver brand distinction, fueled by a virtuous cycle of invaluable support from the *crowd*.

Conclusion

A New Legacy

Four years ago, we set out to define *Inspired Companies*. We wanted to understand why a handful of companies seem to enjoy so much support (and forgiveness) while the rest of the corporate sector appears to be under constant attack. What dynamics are at play? What are they doing right? And, most importantly, what would a company need to do to become a company the whole world will get behind?

We were as surprised by the answer as anyone. Sure, we knew that **C**onsumers, **E**mployees, and **O**utsiders – what we now call the *new C.E.O.s* or the *crowd* – had a louder voice and a bigger platform than they'd had in the past. We knew they had more information than ever before and that trust was in short supply. What we didn't fully realize was just how much momentum they had gained. Suddenly, ordinary people from ordinary places now had the potential to bring the corporate system crashing down, one uninspired company at a time.

Fortunately, a few companies are starting to figure things out. The key features of these companies are that they have a completely different view of why they're in business, what values they want to live, and who they need on board to deliver their promise to the world.

Getting on the right track

The population of urban commuters in China is somewhere in the neighborhood of 800 million people. For a rideshare company, that's a lot of potential customers. We can hear the investor pitch now. Ten million drivers in cars leased from the company deliver nearly a billion fares – many of them during surge-pricing hours. Once the customers are locked in, who would dare to question the brilliance of a business model that connects millions of people to private rideshares for their long daily commutes?

To start with, the company that pushed Uber out of China questioned it.

Didi Chuxing is the world's largest rideshare company, clocking around 25 million rides per day. (By comparison, Uber does less than half that globally.) If you listen to Jean Liu, Didi's chief executive, for a few minutes, you're likely to hear about quality of life in China. More specifically, you'll hear about what Didi is doing to improve it. You'll hear about carpooling programs and minibuses, bicycle shares, and a designated-driver program that sends a driver to meet you and then deliver you safely home in your own car. You'll hear about reductions in carbon emissions, predictive analytics that know you need a ride before you do, and the company's vision to literally end traffic jams. What you won't hear is an obsession with the ridesharing business model, KPIs she commits to hit, or that Didi is "only a technology platform." That's because Didi's chief executive knows exactly why she's in business. It's to solve one of China's most vexing problems: how to efficiently, affordably, and safely move nearly a billion people.

Similar to other rideshare companies, one of Didi's biggest threats is regulation. Instead of paying massive sums to lobbyists, they decided to find common ground with the communities they work in. Government officials are just as interested in cutting congestion as the private sector is, so Didi has partnered with 20 different cities to apply Didi's technology to otherwise outdated traffic management systems. In other cities, they've partnered with taxi companies to provide their technology to drivers free of charge. It gives Didi's customers an additional transportation option and gets taxi drivers on the company's side.

Didi understands the influence of the *crowd* of *new C.E.O.s*. The company spends most of its time doing things that will make life better for everyone. The closer Didi gets to realizing its goal of ending traffic congestion, the happier everyone is. And not just governments and commuters: everyone from Didi employees and their families to other businesses and their workers benefit. All because Didi's leaders are visionary enough to articulate a world-changing mission, courageous enough to do things differently, and smart enough to know they'll need a very large and diverse *crowd* onside.

By the end of 2017, Didi had a valuation of US$56 billion thanks to blue-chip investors that read like a who's who of big capital: Apple in the U.S., Alibaba in China, Softbank in Japan, and Mubadala in the United Arab Emirates. This is the kind of growth we talked about in *Make-or-Breaks*. It's a risky time. Large-scale capitalization can make it easy for a company to forget why it's in business in the first place. On the other hand, it can be the time for a company to double down and show the world what it's made of.

We have no way of knowing what the future holds for Didi or any other company, but we do know what's possible. We also know that companies like Didi appear to be on the right track. Here's why:

Jean Liu is finding new ways to harness the power of the *new C.E.O.s* and bring meaning to their lives. Didi is looking to solve what Liu calls "a world-class dilemma": how to move 800 million people around China. If they solve that problem, then they'll improve quality of life for everyone. In other words, when Didi wins, everyone wins.

So far, she is succeeding where others have not because she understands a fundamental truth: This new era of *Inspired Companies* is here to stay.

The crowd of new C.E.O.s is here to stay

Consumers, Employees, and Outsiders are gaining strength. They increasingly recognize their own influence and seek to hold companies accountable to higher expectations. If anything, the dynamic that shifts power to these new players will only get stronger and more sophisticated.

Sharing control with the *crowd* probably feels like uncomfortable territory for a lot of business leaders. It ought to. The profit-as-purpose regime we operate in today has been fine-tuned over the last century. The rules were written, roles were defined, and functional expertise was shaped to ensure efficiencies and profitability comes first.

And then it all fell apart.

Companies know they're under attack. Leaders sense a loss of control. Some will fail under the weight of decisions that were once standard operating procedure. The support they felt as they pursued a singular goal to be #1 will wane. The profits they once enjoyed from arbitrary fees and penalties, monopolies, and extractive business models will be their demise.

Power is definitively in the hands of those who do not trust us. The forced transparency of the digital revolution, the higher expectations of those that buy from us, a war for talent, the failure of other institutions, and the politicization of everything have shifted power to the *crowd* and they aren't giving it back.

We'll say it louder for the folks in the back:

This is a good thing.

As businesses, we've already seen the worst of it

Most leaders are beginning to realize there's nowhere left to hide. When *The New York Times* revealed that Bill O'Reilly, host of Fox News Channel's highest-rated program, paid out US$13 million to settle multiple sexual harassment lawsuits over the years, advertisers left the show in droves. (The figure has since swelled to US$45 million.) Within a week of the *Times*' original story, 70 advertisers had bolted, leaving only a handful of companies to sell stuff during prime time. These included such blue-chip advertisers as a "no gimmicks, no hassle" seller of gold coins, and a company that offers a cash advance on your life insurance.

The point is that companies didn't always have to worry about their media buys. The people who didn't watch *The O'Reilly Factor* probably wouldn't ever know if you bought 60 seconds of airtime. Now we can all easily access social media feeds that chronicle which companies are taking a stand and which are not. And then make decisions with our wallets and voice accordingly.

We've reached a point where even other companies are putting the pressure on. In Australia, companies have boycotted YouTube advertising, pressuring Google (YouTube's parent company) to implement better controls for the types of YouTube videos a company's advertisements can appear on. Companies from McDonald's to Audi waged a boycott of Google's Display Advertising network until the company could confirm their ads wouldn't appear alongside objectionable content. A similar boycott occurred in the U.K. when it was discovered that hundreds of brands were being displayed next to ISIS propaganda videos and pornography.

In response, Google changed its policies to guarantee brand safety and give advertisers more control over where their ads appear. The overhaul also included new rules on the types of content that could be monetized (no more financing terrorists with ad dollars) and created options to blacklist certain types of content.

This is what *Inspired Companies* do. In the face of new information, they don't run and hide. They don't ignore what they don't want to see.

And we're starting to get a better view of what *good* looks like

When we started this work, there wasn't much in the way of measuring or identifying companies who are doing things differently or, more to the point, who are doing things better. That's not true anymore.

Brands are being measured based on how customers value them. We've already mentioned Enso's Brand World Value Index and the Embankment Project. These approaches mark a pivotal shift to brand metrics – basing the calculations on people's perceptions of how much good each brand does in the world and going far beyond standard financial metrics.

Experts are also starting to track the performance of companies with big ideas. Check out Havas Group's "Meaningful Brands" for great global examples of companies that have drastically outperformed stock markets. Equally important, leaders are advising companies on purpose. Ernst & Young, for example, have created an Institute[*] to openly encourage shared learnings to navigate this new territory, and a global practice to support companies on purpose-led transformation.

This is hard. We get it. We've been there

Everything in this book comes from having been in the hot seat. We know what an identity crisis fueled by profit-as-purpose looks like for a company. We know what comes of uninspired decision-making. We can spot a model that incentivizes functional success over sustainable business success any day of the week. Most of all, we've seen how systems designed for the past create a lot more losers than winners.

---

[*] Beacon Institute was founded in 2014 by Valerie Keller, founding Global Leader of EY Beacon Institute and co-founder, Imagine LLC.

Our interest is in helping companies set their brands and businesses up in a way that the whole world will get behind. We've come at this from all angles. We've been in the functional leadership positions at a company coming out of a factory crisis and freshly reinspired by a mission statement reset. We've led the Nike Foundation, where we were asked to solve poverty within a corporate culture that expects people to solve the problems presented to them. Even ones as big as poverty.

We had opportunities to be inspired by big ideas and be guided by them. At the Nike Foundation, we stumbled our way through making new friends and getting **O**utsiders onside. This wasn't easy because we regularly found ourselves in the position of needing them more than they needed us. We lived through huge successes and monumental mistakes. We know what it felt like when no one wanted us to succeed because they did not trust people from a big company. We had to learn how to build trust, create shared purpose and lead with fierce authenticity.

After Nike we started working with companies looking to distinguish themselves and we discovered something else: We weren't alone. Most good business leaders know that their role and the expectations of them have changed dramatically. They're facing new and potent headwinds from the old ways of doing business and they're getting hammered from all sides.

And no one seems to know what to do about it.

This is where we felt like we had something unique to add. For all we know of what happens when the *crowd* doesn't trust you, we also know what it feels like when they do. From our experiences with Nike's large global business, Nike Foundation, and our current work with a host of other companies and leaders looking for better answers, we started to articulate the things that needed to be in place to create an *Inspired Company*.

This framework is only the start line

This framework is a starting place. It is not meant to fully define the next generation of *Inspired Companies*. That's your job – with the help of the *crowd*, of course. And we don't just want to know what good looks like. We want to know what *inspired* looks like. We want you to stress-test the ideas and poke holes where it's needed. We want to hear about entirely new and bold strategies that get the *crowd* onside. So tell us what we got right and where we need to keep pushing for better answers. Give us all even better ideas to navigate this new terrain. Take us somewhere new. Show the world you're at the forefront of understanding how to handle the new dynamics of today's marketplace and lead in new and totally surprising ways. The goal here was to give you a framework, building blocks and set of strategies to get started now, while there's still time to distinguish yourself.

If this story needs a hero, make it the next wave of companies that realign themselves to the power of the *crowd*. They will finalize the collapse of an outdated profit-as-purpose corporate system and create companies the world will get behind. As a new generation of leaders emerges that is pre-wired for a more connected, more collaborative, and inspired approach to business, we remain infinitely optimistic that a new legacy is in sight.

It's true that the *crowd* of *new C.E.O.s* has seized control, but there's one thing they cannot influence no matter how hard they may try: No one else can make your company an *Inspired Company*.

That is entirely up to you.

Acknowledgments

This work has benefited from an extraordinary group of thinkers, leaders, innovators, and pot-stirrers. We learned from these colleagues as we navigated the radical shift in power in favor of the *crowd* in our own careers and businesses; their experiences and imagination shaped the framework we offer to you. For this book, they have invested more time than we ever had any right to ask of them. They have done so graciously because they genuinely believe, as we do, that the corporate sector can deliver so much more:

Matthew Bishop (The Economist, The Rockefeller Foundation); **Alexis Bonte** (eRepublik Games, Spain); **Kathy Bushkin Calvin** (United Nations Foundation); **Gary Bowman** (Bond University, Australia); **Charlotte Cline** (Onemanband. studio, U.K.); **Niall Dunne** (Polymateria, U.K.); **Dr. Sonosuke Kadonaga** (Kao Corporation, Japan); **Valerie Keller** (Imagine, U.K.); **Julia Koppitz** (whitefox, U.K.); **Richard Marsh** (BT Group, U.K.); **Amanda McCluskey** (Stewart Investors, Singapore); **Jordan Millar** (ChekRite, Australia); **Emma Mcilroy** (Wildfang, U.S.); **James Parr** (Trillium, U.K.); **Dr. Kenichi Ohmae** (strategist & global economist, Japan); **Tim & Sam Shriver** (Special Olympics); **Donette Simmons** (Inspired Companies, Australia); **Mark Wilson** (NED Blackrock, U.S.); **Sian Winship** (Hershey Cause Communications, U.S.); **Peter Zandee** (Tony's Chocolonely, Netherlands); **Pat Zeedick** (Nike Global Young Athletes).

We are also very grateful for the organizations and artists behind the visuals in *Inspired INC.* Your contributions will make sure these ideas stick in the minds of leaders, so they can take us into a new era of *Inspired Companies*.

Finally, the crowd that matters the most gets the last word: thank you to Ryan, Joaque, Miel and Elle, whose support, love and patience inspire us every single day.

Endnotes

1   autolife.umd.umich.edu (2018). The Utilitarian
    Vision of Henry Ford. [online] Available at: www.
    autolife.umd.umich.edu/Design/Gartman/D_
    Casestudy/D_Casestudy2.htm [Accessed May 11,
    2018].

2   bloomberg.com (2018). Leaders with Lacqua:
    Aviva CEO Mark Wilson. [online] Available at:
    www.bloomberg.com/news/videos/2016-09-29/
    leaders-with-lacqua-aviva-ceo-mark-wilson
    [Accessed December 9, 2018].

3   Edelman Trust Barometer 2017 – UK Findings
    (2018). [online] Available at: www.edelman.
    co.uk/magazine/posts/edelman-trust-
    barometer-2017-uk-findings/ [Accessed May11,
    2018].

4   pac.org (2015). Can Big Companies Be
    Trusted? [online] Available at: https://pac.org/
    pulse/2015/can-big-companies-be-trusted
    [Accessed December 23, 2018].

5   2018 Edelman Trust Barometer (2018). [online]
    Available at: http://cms.edelman.com/sites/
    default/files/2018-01/2018_Edelman_Trust_
    Barometer_Global_Report_Jan.pdf [Accessed
    May 12, 2018].

6   2018 Edelman Trust Barometer (2018). [online]
    Available at: http://cms.edelman.com/sites/
    default/files/2018-01/2018_Edelman_Trust_
    Barometer_Global_Report_Jan.pdf [Accessed
    May 12, 2018].

7   Gallup, I. (2018). State of the Global Workplace.
    [online] gallup.com. Available at: http://news.
    gallup.com/reports/220313/state-global-
    workplace-2017.aspx#aspnetForm [Accessed
    May 11, 2018].

8   atkearney.co.uk (2018). Where are the Global
    Millennials. [online] Available at: www.atkearney.
    co.uk/paper/-/asset_publisher/dVxv4Hz2h8bS/
    content/id/8693136 [Accessed May 11, 2018].

9   atkearney.co.uk (2018). Where are the Global
    Millennials. [online] Available at: www.atkearney.
    co.uk/paper/-/asset_publisher/dVxv4Hz2h8bS/
    content/id/8693136 [Accessed May 11, 2018].

10 Williams, A. (2018). Move Over, Millennials,
    Here Comes Generation Z. [online] nytimes.com.
    Available at: www.nytimes.com/2015/09/20/
    fashion/move-over-millennials-here-comes-
    generation-z.html [Accessed May 11, 2018].

11 Beall, G. (2018). 5 Things Every Company Should
    Know About Gen Z. [online] HuffPost. Available
    at: www.huffingtonpost.com/george-beall/5-
    things-every-company-sh_b_12918636.html
    [Accessed May 11, 2018].

12 Bershidsky, M. (2018). Here Comes Generation
    Z. [online] bloomberg.com. Available at: www.
    bloomberg.com/view/articles/2014-06-18/
    nailing-generation-z [Accessed May 11, 2018].

13 slideshare.net (2018) . . . this is how Gen Z.
    [online] Available at: www.slideshare.net/
    sparksandhoney/generation-z-final-june-17/10-
    this_is_how_Gen_Z [Accessed May 11, 2018].

14 Jiang, J. (2018). Millennials stand out for their
    technology use. [online] Pew Research Center.
    Available at: www.pewresearch.org/fact-
    tank/2018/05/02/millennials-stand-out-for-
    their-technology-use-but-older-generations-also-
    embrace-digital-life/ [Accessed October 4, 2018].

15 Shrestha, K. and Shrestha, K. (2018). 50
    Important Online Reviews Stats You Need to
    Know [infographic]. [online] Vendasta Blog.
    Available at: www.vendasta.com/blog/50-
    stats-you-need-to-know-about-online-reviews/
    [Accessed May 11, 2018].

16 about.americanexpress.com (2018). Good Service
    is Good Business: American Consumers Willing
    to Spend More With Companies That Get
    Service Right, According to American Express

Survey. [online] Available at: http://about.
americanexpress.com/news/pr/2011/csbar.aspx
[Accessed May 11, 2018].

17 Schneider, M. (2018). 24 Statistics That Show
Social Media Is the Future of Customer Service.
[online] Social Media Today. Available at: www.
socialmediatoday.com/social-business/24-
statistics-show-social-media-future-customer-
service [Accessed May 11, 2018].

18 ipsos.com (2018). Consumers Share Positive and
Negative Experiences Equally. [online] Available
at: www.ipsos.com/en-us/consumers-share-
positive-and-negative-experiences-equally
[Accessed May 11, 2018].

19 apa.org (2018). Employee Distrust is Pervasive in
U.S. Workforce. [online] Available at: www.apa.
org/news/press/releases/2014/04/employee-
distrust.aspx [Accessed May 11, 2018].

20 Schwartz, T. and Porath, C. (2018). Why You
Hate Work. [online] nytimes.com. Available
at: www.nytimes.com/2014/06/01/opinion/
sunday/why-you-hate-work.html?_r=3
[Accessed May 11, 2018].

21 2018 Edelman Trust Barometer (2018). [online]
Available at: http://cms.edelman.com/sites/
default/files/2018-01/2018_Edelman_Trust_
Barometer_Global_Report_Jan.pdf [Accessed
May 12, 2018].

22 Grossman, K. (2018). The Part Where Candidate
Experience Buoys the Bottom Line. [online] Talent
Board. Available at: www.thetalentboard.org/
article/the-part-where-candidate-experience-
buoys-the-bottom-line/ [Accessed May 11, 2018].

23 Candidate Resentment Calculator (2018). [online]
Available at: www.hireright.com/calculator
[Accessed May 12, 2018].

24 Verhage, J. (2018). The 50 Best Places to Work,
According to Glassdoor. [online] bloomberg.
com. Available at: www.bloomberg.com/news/
articles/2016-12-07/the-50-best-places-to-work-
according-to-glassdoor [Accessed May 11, 2018].

25 Martin, C. (2016). The New Better Off:
Reinventing the American Dream (Berkeley, CA:
Seal Press).

26 Talent Board 2016 Candidate Experience
Research Report (2016). Talent Board.
Available at: http://3cmsd11vskgf1d8ir311irgt.
wpengine.netdna-cdn.com/wp-content/
uploads/2017/03/2016_Talent_Board_NAM_
CandE_Research_Report_FINAL_170202.pdf
[Accessed May 12, 2018].

27 Rubenfeld, G. (2018). Compliance Officer: Dream
Career? [online] Wall Street Journal. Available at:
www.wsj.com/articles/SB10001424052702303
33020457925072211453875o [Accessed May 11,
2018].

28 Mee, C. (2017). Greenpeace activists unfurl
anti-coal, anti-CommBank banner on Sydney's
Pyrmont Bridge. [online] Sydney Morning Herald.
Available at: https://www.smh.com.au/national/
nsw/greenpeace-activists-unfurl-anticoal-
anticommbank-banner-on-sydneys-pyrmont-
bridge-20170505-gvyynw.html [Accessed March
9, 2019].

29 Yeates, C. (2018). CBA facing potential class
action over disclosure of laundering allegations.
[online] Sydney Morning Herald. Available at:
www.smh.com.au/business/banking-and-
finance/cba-facing-potential-class-action-over-
disclosure-of-laundering-allegations-20170821-
gy196d.html [Accessed May 11, 2018].

30 Han, M. (2018). Court approves CBA's $700
million AUSTRAC settlement. [online] Australian
Financial Review. Available at: https://www.
afr.com/business/banking-and-finance/court-
approves-of-cbas-700m-austrac- settlement-
20180619-h11kr7 [Accessed March 9, 2019].

31 Kieler, A. (2018). Banks Turned Account
Overdraft Fees Into $11.16B In Revenue Last
Year. [online] Consumerist. Available at: https://
consumerist.com/2016/02/25/banks-turned-
account-overdraft-fees-into-11-16b-in-revenue-
last-year/ [Accessed May 11, 2018].

32 EurekAlert! (2018). Selling extended warranties
via independent companies lowers price but
hurts consumers: INFORMS. [online] Available
at: www.eurekalert.org/pub_releases/2015-01/
ifor-sew010515.php [Accessed May 11, 2018].

33 Airline ancillary revenue projected to be $59.2 billion worldwide in 2015 (2015). [online] IdeaWorks Company and CarTrawler. Available at: www.ideaworkscompany.com/wp-content/uploads/2016/04/Press-Release-103-Global-Estimate.pdf [Accessed December 9, 2018].

34 Browne, K. (2018). Credit card surcharge crackdown. [online] CHOICE. Available at: www.choice.com.au/money/credit-cards-and-loans/credit-cards/articles/credit-card-surcharge-crackdown [Accessed May 11, 2018].

35 Schwartz-Bloom, R. and Gross de Núñez, G. (2018). NOVA Online | Search for a Safe Cigarette | The Dope on Nicotine. [online] pbs.org. Available at: www.pbs.org/wgbh/nova/cigarette/nicotine_nfp.html [Accessed May 11, 2018].

36 Beaglehold & Yach, Globalization and the Prevention and control of non-communicable disease, the neglected chronic disease of adults, 2003, The Lancet, p.904.

37 CCC, ILRF, MSN and WRC (2016). Three Years After Rana Plaza, H&M Factories Still Not Safe. [online] Available at: https://laborrights.org/sites/default/files/publications/Memo_on_HM_CAPs_2May2016.pdf [Accessed December 9, 2018].

38 Albright, M. (2018). Business: Toysrus.com learned difficult Christmas lesson. St Petersburg Times.

39 Rothfeder, J. (2018). Toys "R" Us Battles Back. [online] strategy+business. Available at: www.strategy-business.com/article/16757?gko=1219e [Accessed May 12, 2018].

40 Isaac, M. (2018). Uber Investigating Sexual Harassment Claims by Ex-Employee. [online] nytimes.com. Available at: www.nytimes.com/2017/02/19/business/uber-sexual-harassment-investigation.html [Accessed May 11, 2018].

41 Strochlic, N. (2018). Uber: Disability Laws Don't Apply to Us. [online] The Daily Beast. Available at: www.thedailybeast.com/articles/2015/05/21/uber-disability-laws-don-t-apply-to-us.html [Accessed May 11, 2018].

42 Eidelson, M. (2018). Uber: The Company Cities Love to Hate. [online] bloomberg.com. Available at: www.bloomberg.com/news/articles/2014-07-03/uber-the-company-city-regulators-unions-love-to-hate [Accessed May 11, 2018].

43 Taylor, H. (2018). Uber and Lyft hate fingerprinting drivers, but new data show why they might be wrong. [online] CNBC. Available at: www.cnbc.com/2016/08/23/uber-and-lyft-hate-fingerprinting-drivers-but-new-data-shows-why-they-might-be-wrong.html [Accessed May 11, 2018].

44 Eidelson, M. (2018). Uber: The Company Cities Love to Hate. [online] bloomberg.com. Available at: www.bloomberg.com/news/articles/2014-07-03/uber-the-company-city-regulators-unions-love-to-hate [Accessed May 11, 2018].

45 Butler, S. and Topham, G. (2018). Uber stripped of London licence due to lack of corporate responsibility. [online] Guardian. Available at: www.theguardian.com/technology/2017/sep/22/uber-licence-transport-for-london-tfl [Accessed May 11, 2018].

46 Swisher, K. and Streiber, A. (2018). Uber C.E.O. Travis Kalanick's Warpath. [online] The Hive. Available at: www.vanityfair.com/news/2014/12/uber-travis-kalanick-controversy [Accessed May 11, 2018].

47 Edwards, J. (2018). Uber's leaked finances show the company might – just might – be able to turn a profit. [online] Business Insider Australia. Available at: www.businessinsider.com.au/uber-leaked-finances-accounts-revenues-profits-2017-2?r=UK&IR=T [Accessed May 11, 2018].

48 CR Magazine and Alexander Mann Solutions. The Cost of a Bad Reputation (2014). [online] Available at: http://insights.ethisphere.com/wp-content/uploads/The-Cost-of-a-Bad-Reputation_CR_Oct2014.pdf [Accessed December 9, 2018].

49 Turkcan, K. (2016). Are You Ready for Centennials. [online] www.slideshare.net/KateTurkcan/the-futures-company-are-you-ready-for-centennials. [Accessed December 9, 2018].

50 Harvard Business Review Analytic Services
Report, The Business Case for Purpose, 2015.
www.ey.com/Publication/vwLUAssets/
ey-the-business-case-for-purpose/$FILE/ey-
the-business-case-for-purpose.pdf [Accessed
December 10, 2018].

51 gallup.com (2018). The Damage Inflicted by Poor
Managers. [online] Available at: www.gallup.
com/businessjournal/200108/damage-inflicted-
poor-managers.aspx?g_source=EMPLOYEE_
ENGAGEMENT&g_medium=topic&g_
campaign=tiles [Accessed May 11, 2018].

52 Unilever global company website. (2018).
Unilever's Sustainable Living Plan continues to
fuel growth. [online] Available at: www.unilever.
com/news/press-releases/2018/unilevers-
sustainable-living-plan-continues-to-fuel-
growth.html [Accessed December 10, 2018].

53 Pleiter, S. (2018). Engaging Employees. [online]
smith.queensu.ca. Available at: https://smith.
queensu.ca/magazine/winter-2014/features/
engaging-employees [Accessed May 11, 2018].

54 gallup.com (2018). The Damage Inflicted by Poor
Managers. [online] Available at: www.gallup.
com/businessjournal/200108/damage-inflicted-
poor-managers.aspx?g_source=EMPLOYEE_
ENGAGEMENT&g_medium=topic&g_
campaign=tiles [Accessed May 11, 2018].

55 gallup.com (2018). The Damage Inflicted by Poor
Managers. [online] Available at: www.gallup.
com/businessjournal/200108/damage-inflicted-
poor-managers.aspx?g_source=EMPLOYEE_
ENGAGEMENT&g_medium=topic&g_
campaign=tiles [Accessed May 11, 2018].

56 Antioco, J. (2018). How I Did It: Blockbuster's
Former CEO on Sparring with an Activist
Shareholder. [online] Harvard Business Review.
Available at: https://hbr.org/2011/04/how-i-
did-it-blockbusters-former-ceo-on-sparring-
with-an-activist-shareholder [Accessed May 11,
2018].

57 Musk, E. (2018). The Mission of Tesla. [online]
tesla.com. Available at: www.tesla.com/blog/
mission-tesla [Accessed May 11, 2018].

58 tesla.com (2018). About Tesla. [online] Available
at: www.tesla.com/about [Accessed May 11, 2018].

59 Goel, V. and de la Merced, M. (2018). Yahoo's
Sale to Verizon Ends an Era for a Web Pioneer.
[online] nytimes.com. Available at: www.nytimes.
com/2016/07/25/business/yahoo-sale.html
[Accessed May 11, 2018].

60 Dunmore, M. (2002). Inside-out marketing. New
York, New York: Kogan Page, p.38.

61 slideshare.net (2018). Culture. [online]
Available at: www.slideshare.net/reed2001/
culture-1798664 [Accessed May 11, 2018].

62 Taft, D. (2018). Top 20 IBM Products/
Innovations. [online] eWEEK. Available at: www.
eweek.com/networking/top-20-ibm-products-
innovations [Accessed May 11, 2018].

63 remakinglawfirms.com (2018). Has the Juice
Been Squeezed from BigLaw's Business Model?
[online] Available at: www.remakinglawfirms.
com/biglaw-profitability-maister/ [Accessed May
11, 2018].

64 Krill, P., Johnson, R. and Albert, L. (2016). The
Prevalence of Substance Use and Other Mental
Health Concerns Among American Attorneys.
Journal of Addition Medicine, January/February
2016, Vol.1, Issue 1, pp.46–52.

65 McQueen, M. (2016). Here Come the Big Law
Millennials. The American Lawyer, [online] p.50.
Available at: https://www.smh.com.au/national/
nsw/greenpeace-activists-unfurl-anticoal-
anticommbank-banner-on-sydneys-pyrmont-
bridge-20170505-gvyynw.html [Accessed March
9, 2019].

66 performance.morningstar.com (2018). KAO Kao
Corp Stock Price History. [online] Available at:
http://performance.morningstar.com/stock/
performance-return.action?p=price_history_pa
ge&t=XDUS:KAO&region=deu&culture=en-US
[Accessed May 11, 2018].

67 worldsmostethicalcompanies.com (2018).
Companies – Ethisphere® Institute | Good.
Smart. Business. Profit.®. [online] Available
at: www.worldsmostethicalcompanies.com/
honorees/ [Accessed May 11, 2018].

68   Japan Association of Corporate Directors
     (2018). Japan Association of Corporate Directors
     Announces Its Corporate Governance of the Year
     2017 Prize Winners. [online] Available at: www.
     jacd.jp/en/conference/180219_japan-association-
     of-corporate-directors-announces-its-corporate-
     governance-of.html [Accessed May 11, 2018].

69   Baker, N. (2018). Surf clothing label Rip Curl
     using "slave labour" to manufacture clothes in
     North Korea. [online] Sydney Morning Herald.
     Available at: www.smh.com.au/business/surf-
     clothing-label-rip-curl-using-slave-labour-to-
     manufacture-clothes-in-north-korea-20160219-
     gmz375.html [Accessed May 11, 2018].

70   Rip Curl (2018). We Take Full Responsibility
     (Update). [online] Available at: www.ripcurl.com/
     us/blog/2016/03/01/we-take-full-responsibility-
     update/ [Accessed May 11, 2018].

71   Peacock, B. (2016). Rip Curl. When Cool Is Just
     Not Cool At All – B&T. [online] B&T. Available
     at: http://www.bandt.com.au/media/rip-curl-
     when-cool-is-just-not-cool-at-all [Accessed
     March 9, 2019].

72   Baker, N. (2018). Surf clothing label Rip Curl
     using "slave labour" to manufacture clothes in
     North Korea. [online] Sydney Morning Herald.
     Available at: www.smh.com.au/business/surf-
     clothing-label-rip-curl-using-slave-labour-to-
     manufacture-clothes-in-north-korea-20160219-
     gmz375.html [Accessed May 11, 2018].

73   Slavin, T. (2018). Four steps CEOs can take to
     increase their social impact – and valuations.
     [online] ethicalcorp.com. Available at: www.
     ethicalcorp.com/four-steps-ceos-can-take-
     increase-their-social-impact-and-valuations
     [Accessed May 11, 2018].

74   De Cremer, D. and Tao, T. (2018). Huawei's
     Culture Is the Key to Its Success. [online] Harvard
     Business Review. Available at: https://hbr.
     org/2015/06/huaweis-culture-is-the-key-to-its-
     success?referral=03759&cm_vc=rr_item_page.
     bottom [Accessed May 11, 2018].

75   Wang, Y. (2018). Forbes Welcome. [online]
     forbes.com. Available at: www.forbes.
     com/sites/ywang/2017/09/11/huaweis-

     smartphone-market-share-is-growing-fast-
     but-it-needs-to-break-the-u-s-market-and-
     soon/#cbd864a4333b [Accessed May 11, 2018].

76   globalreporting.org (2018). About GRI. [online]
     Available at: https://www.globalreporting.org/
     information/about-gri/Pages/default.aspx
     [Accessed 11 May 2018].

77   Madeleine, C. (2018). Huawei set to save 130,000
     tonnes of carbon thanks to pioneering contract
     with BT. [online] businessgreen.com. Available
     at: www.businessgreen.com/bg/news/3026760/
     huawei-set-to-save-130-000-tonnes-of-carbon-
     thanks-to-pioneering-contract-with-bt [Accessed
     December 10, 2018].

78   Tesla Motors (2015.) First Quarter 2015 Shareholder
     Letter. [online] Available at: http://files.shareholder.
     com/downloads/ABEA-4CW8X0/281255884x0x82
     7135/90332B15-F6AE-4F44-B634-624BE548291E/
     Tesla_Motors_Q1_15_Shareholder_Letter.pdf
     [Accessed December 10, 2018].

79   tesla.com (2018). Tesla Gigafactory. [online]
     Available at: www.tesla.com/gigafactory
     [Accessed October 4, 2018].

80   futurism.com (2018). Elon Musk: 100 Tesla
     Gigafactories Could Power the Entire World.
     [online] Available at: https://futurism.com/
     elon-musk-100-tesla-gigafactories-could-power-
     entire-world/ [Accessed May 11, 2018].

81   Tony's Chocolonely Annual Fair Report
     2015/2016, p.32.

82   EPIC: Embankment Project for Inclusive
     Capitalism. (2019). [ebook] Coalition for
     Inclusive Capitalism. Available at: https://
     www.epic-value.com/static/epic-report-web-
     df894ad112b70406d9896c39f853deec.pdf
     [Accessed March 9, 2019].

83   enso.co (2018). 2017 World Value Index. [online]
     Available at: http://enso.co/worldvalue/
     [Accessed May 11, 2018].

84   Kelly, E. (2018). The C-suite: Time for version
     3.0? [online] Deloitte Insights. Available at:
     http://dupress.com/articles/bus-trends-2014-c-
     suite-3-0/ [Accessed May 11, 2018].

85   Broggie, Michael, Walt Disney's Railroad Story
     (Walsworth Publishing, 1997).

86 Weber Shandwick and KRC Research (2014.) Employees Rising: Seizing the Opportunity in Employee Activism. [online] Available at: www.webershandwick.com/uploads/news/files/employees-rising-seizing-the-opportunity-in-employee-activism.pdf [Accessed December 10, 2018].

87 2018 Edelman Trust Barometer (2018). [online] Edelman. Available at: http://cms.edelman.com/sites/default/files/2018-01/2018_Edelman_Trust_Barometer_Global_Report_Jan.pdf [Accessed May 12, 2018].

88 Diamandis MD, P. (2018). Here's Why People Think Tesla Is the Most Innovative Company Today. [online] Singularity Hub. Available at: https://singularityhub.com/2017/04/27/heres-why-people-think-tesla-is-the-most-innovative-company-today/#.WUrSEmjyvIU [Accessed May 11, 2018].

89 www.nytimes.com/2018/09/29/business/tesla-musk-sec-settlement.html. [Accessed December 30, 2018].

90 Buck, S. (2018). Nike Spends Billions On Marketing, But Millennials Still Like Toms More. [online] Fast Company. Available at: www.fastcoexist.com/3061133/nike-spends-billions-on-marketing-but-millennials-still-like-toms-more [Accessed May 11, 2018].

91 Hackett, R. (2018). Read LinkedIn CEO Jeff Weiner's Letter to Employees. [online] Fortune. Available at: http://fortune.com/2016/06/13/linkedin-ceo-jeff-wiener-employee-letter/ [Accessed May 11, 2018].

92 Hempel, J. (2017). Now We Know Why Microsoft Bought LinkedIn. Wired. [online] Available at: https://www.wired.com/2017/03/now-we-know-why-microsoft-bought-linkedin/ [Accessed March 9, 2019].

93 CEO.com (2015.) 2015 Social CEO Report. [online] Available at: https://s3.amazonaws.com/www.ceo.com/wp-content/uploads/2018/03/09163404/CEOcom-Social-CEO-Report-2015.pdf [Accessed December 10, 2018].

94 Twitter (2018). John Zissimos on Twitter. [online] Available at: https://twitter.com/zissimos/status/642461771928748039 [Accessed May 11, 2018].

95 W3techs.com. (2018). Usage Statistics and Market Share of Drupal for Websites, May 2018. [online] Available at: https://w3techs.com/technologies/details/cm-drupal/all/all [Accessed May 11, 2018].

96 Gallo, C. (2018). Forbes Welcome. [online] forbes.com. Available at: www.forbes.com/sites/carminegallo/2013/10/04/7-social-media-tips-you-can-learn-from-richard-branson/#3cd732e05532 [Accessed May 11, 2018].

97 Bariso, J. (2018). Elon Musk Takes Customer Complaint on Twitter From Idea to Execution in 6 Days. [online] inc.com. Available at: www.inc.com/justin-bariso/elon-musk-takes-customer-complaint-on-twitter-from-idea-to-execution-in-6-days.html [Accessed May 11, 2018].

98 Wood, J. (2018). 15 Things You Might Not Know About Ben & Jerry's. [online] mentalfloss.com. Available at: http://mentalfloss.com/article/502418/15-things-you-might-not-know-about-ben-jerry's [Accessed May 11, 2018].

99 Everett, D. (2018). How Strava continues to change cycling. [online] CyclingTips. Available at: https://cyclingtips.com/2014/12/how-strava-continues-to-change-cycling/ [Accessed May 11, 2018].

100 www.drupal.org/about. [Accessed December 30, 2018].

101 Hallbjörnsson, K. (2019). Welcome to my blog. DrupalViking Blog | [online] Drupalviking.com. Available at: https://drupalviking.com/welcome-my-blog [Accessed March 6, 2019].

102 Exove. (2019). DrupalCon Munich. [online] Available at: https://www.exove.com/events/drupalcon-munich/ [Accessed March 7, 2019].

103 Vision Critical (2018). How NASCAR Increases Fan Engagement and Drives Business Decisions. [online] Available at: www.visioncritical.com/resources/nascar-fan-engagement/?thanks=1 [Accessed May 11, 2018].

104 Floyd County Times. January 5, 2017. Collins named to NASCAR Fan Council.

105 CNN interview published May 29, 2015 "Artist speaks about the making of famous Obama poster." www.cnn.com/videos/

politics/2015/05/29/shepard-fairey-obama-hope-poster-2009-bts.cnn [Accessed December 30, 2018].

106 zappos.com (2018). The Zappos Video Vault: Explore Zappos culture & the employee experience! [online] Available at: www.zappos.com/zappos-video [Accessed May 11, 2018].

107 Social Strategi LLC (2015.) The Social CMO Show – Interview with Martyn Etherington, former CMO Mitel. Available at: https://youtu.be/wYulPYJuMbE [Accessed December 10, 2018].

108 Social Strategi LLC (2015.) The Social CMO Show – Interview with Martyn Etherington, former CMO Mitel. Available at: https://youtu.be/wYulPYJuMbE [Accessed December 10, 2018].

109 Pafau, B. (2018). How an Accounting Firm Convinced Its Employees They Could Change the World. [online] Harvard Business Review. Available at: https://hbr.org/2015/10/how-an-accounting-firm-convinced-its-employees-they-could-change-the-world [Accessed May 11, 2018].

110 Parker-Pope, T. (2018). Writing Your Way to Happiness. [online] The New York Times. Available at: https://well.blogs.nytimes.com/2015/01/19/writing-your-way-to-happiness/ [Accessed May 11, 2018].

111 Neff, J. (2010). The Dirt On Laundry Trends Around The World. AdAge. [online] Available at: https://adage.com/article/global-news/global-marketing-dirt-laundry-trends-world/144398/ [Accessed March 9, 2019].

112 Edelman, R. (2016). Dirt Is Good: The Campaign For Play. Available at: www.edelman.co.uk/magazine/posts/dirt-is-good-the-campaign-for-play/ [Accessed December 10, 2018].

113 Mask Magazine (2018). Starbucks' #RaceTogether Campaign Gets the Response It Deserves. [online] Available at: www.maskmagazine.com/the-hustle-issue/work/starbucks-racetogether [Accessed May 11, 2018].

114 Carr, A. (2018). The Inside Story of Starbucks's Race Together Campaign, No Foam. [online] Fast Company. Available at: www.fastcompany.com/3046890/the-inside-story-of-starbuckss-race-together-campaign-no-foam [Accessed May 11, 2018].

115 McCord, P. (2018). Harvard Business Review: How Netflix Reinvented HR – Patty McCord. [online] Available at: https://hbr.org/2014/01/how-netflix-reinvented-hr [Accessed May 11, 2018].

116 Frolich, T. (2018). 7 companies with unlimited vacation. [online] USA Today. Available at: www.usatoday.com/story/money/business/2015/12/19/24-7-wall-st-companies-unlimited-vacation/77422898/ [Accessed May 11, 2018].

117 loxcel.com (2018). Loxcel Starbucks Store Locator FAQ. [online] Available at: www.loxcel.com/sbux-faq.html [Accessed May 11, 2018].

118 Starbucks Coffee Company (2018). Refugee Hiring. [online] Available at: www.starbucks.com/responsibility/community/refugee-hiring [Accessed May 11, 2018].

119 Fiske, W. (2018). Mark Warner says average holding time for stocks has fallen to four months. [online] @politifact. Available at: www.politifact.com/virginia/statements/2016/jul/06/mark-warner/mark-warner-says-average-holding-time-stocks-has-f/ [Accessed May 11, 2018].

120 Kozlowski, D. (2018). Top 10 Crooked CEOs. [online] TIME.com. Available at: http://content.time.com/time/specials/packages/article/0,28804,1903155_1903156_1903152,00.html [Accessed May 11, 2018].

121 Boynton, A. (2018). Forbes Welcome. [online] forbes.com. Available at: www.forbes.com/sites/andyboynton/2015/07/20/unilevers-paul-polman-ceos-cant-be-slaves-to-shareholders/2/#cfd13596f062 [Accessed May 11, 2018].

122 Tesla Motors (2015.) Third Quarter 2014 Shareholder Letter. [online] Available at: http://files.shareholder.com/downloads/ABEA-4CW8X0/3604469890x0x791902/d7b8cc04-9c3e-4216-9ce3-7fb4d7e0c00b/Q314 percent20SHL percent20Final.pdf [Accessed December 10, 2018].

123 Monica, P. (2018). Berkshire shareholders LOVE Warren Buffett. [online] CNNMoney. Available at: http://buzz.money.cnn.com/2014/05/03/berkshire-shareholders/ [Accessed May 11, 2018].

124 Edmans, A. (2015.) The social responsibility of business. TEDx Talks. [online] Available at: https://youtu.be/Z5KZhm19EO0 [Accessed December 10, 2018]

125 stewartinvestors.com (2018). Sustainable Funds Group. [online] Available at: www.stewartinvestors.com/en-US/our-funds/sustainable-funds-group [Accessed May 11, 2018].

126 McCarthy, J. (2018). LEGO builds a reputation as the UK's most trusted brand. [online] The Drum. Available at: www.thedrum.com/news/2016/09/29/lego-builds-reputation-the-uk-s-most-trusted-brand [Accessed May 11, 2018].

127 De Cremer, D. and Tao, T. (2018). Huawei's Culture Is the Key to Its Success. [online] Harvard Business Review. Available at: https://hbr.org/2015/06/huaweis-culture-is-the-key-to-its-success?referral=03759&cm_vc=rr_item_page.bottom [Accessed May 11, 2018].

128 Cendrowski, S. (2018). How China's Smartphone "Big Four" Are Fighting for Global Customers. [online] Fortune. Available at: http://fortune.com/2017/01/24/china-smartphones-oppo-vivo-huawei-xiaomi/ [Accessed May 11, 2018].

129 Bhuiyan, J. (2018). Tesla saw about 63,000 cancellations of Model 3 pre-orders. [online] CNBC. Available at: www.cnbc.com/2017/08/03/tesla-saw-about-63000-cancellations-of-model-3-pre-orders.html [Accessed May 11, 2018].

130 Chapman, L. (2018). Are you a robot? [online] bloomberg.com. Available at: www.bloomberg.com/news/articles/2017-04-27/domo-seeks-200-million-in-funding-as-ipo-plans-remain-on-hold [Accessed October 4, 2018].

131 "So Long Wall Street", Fortune (June 1, 2016).

132 Bergh, C. (2018). An Open Letter to Customers: Our Weapons Policy. [online] LinkedIn.com. Available at: www.linkedin.com/pulse/open-letter-customers-our-weapons-policy-chip-bergh [Accessed May 11, 2018].

133 Levi Strauss. Levi Strauss & Co. Announces First-Quarter 2017 Financial Results. [online press release] Available at: www.levistrauss.com/wp-content/uploads/2017/04/Exhibit-99.1-1Q-2017-Press-Release_final.pdf [Accessed December 10, 2018].

134 Gallo, C. (2018). Forbes Welcome. [online] forbes.com. Available at: www.forbes.com/sites/carminegallo/2016/12/02/how-starbucks-ceo-howard-schultz-inspired-us-to-dream-bigger/#42ce7c4246a8 [Accessed May 11, 2018].

135 Haag, M. (2018). Gilbert Baker, Gay Activist Who Created the Rainbow Flag, Dies at 65. [online] nytimes.com. Available at: www.nytimes.com/2017/03/31/us/obituary-gilbert-baker-rainbow-flag.html [Accessed May 11, 2018].

136 Kaufman, A. (2018). Here Are The 379 Companies Urging The Supreme Court To Support Same-Sex Marriage. [online] HuffPost UK. Available at: www.huffingtonpost.com/2015/03/05/marriage-equality-amicus_n_6808260.html [Accessed May 11, 2018].

137 Bender, A. (2018). Indiana's Religious Freedom Act Cost Indianapolis $60 Million In Lost Revenue. [online] forbes.com. Available at: www.forbes.com/sites/andrewbender/2016/01/31/indianas-religious-freedom-act-cost-indianapolis-60-million-in-lost-revenue/#624025852e2a [Accessed May 11, 2018].

138 Woodard, J. Twitter slams NC Gov. McCrory after NBA All-Star Game news. (July 21, 2016). The Island Packet. Available at: www.islandpacket.com/news/politics-government/article91098607.html [Accessed December 10, 2018].

139 Kurwa, N. (2018). "Black Lives Matter" Slogan Becomes A Bigger Movement. [online] NPR.org. Available at: www.npr.org/2014/12/04/368408247/black-lives-matter-slogan-becomes-a-bigger-movement [Accessed May 11, 2018].

140 Nunez, M. (2018). Mark Zuckerberg Asks Racist Facebook Employees to Stop Crossing Out Black Lives Matter Slogans. [online] gizmodo. com. Available at: http://gizmodo.com/mark-zuckerberg-asks-racist-facebook-employees-to-stop-1761272768 [Accessed May 11, 2018].

141 Brown, K. (2018). Facebook just put up a huge "Black Lives Matter" sign at its headquarters. [online] fusion.kinja.com. Available at: http://fusion.kinja.com/facebook-just-put-up-a-huge-black-lives-matter-sign-at-1793860154 [Accessed May 11, 2018].

142 McGirt, E. (2018). Read Nike CEO's Heartbreaking Letter to Employees About Race and Violence. [online] Fortune. Available at: http://fortune.com/2016/07/15/nike-ceo-letter-race-police/ [Accessed May 11, 2018].

143 Morrison, A. (2018). Here's the real deal on Ben & Jerry's support for Black Lives Matter. [online] mic.com. Available at: https://mic.com/articles/156163/ben-jerry-s-is-supporting-black-lives-matter-but-will-it-make-a-difference#.IoUrEK9Py [Accessed May 11, 2018].

144 Swerdlof, A. (2016.) Ben & Jerry's Agreed That Black Lives Matter and People Lost Their Shit. [online] vice.com. Available at: https://munchies.vice.com/en_us/article/bm3vkw/ben-jerrys-agrees-that-black-lives-matter-and-people-lost-their-shit [Accessed December 10, 2018].

145 YouTube (2018). Introducing Empower Mint. [online] Available at: https://www.youtube.com/watch?v=R8FrATXkNDA [Accessed May 11, 2018].

146 New York State Office of the Attorney General. (2012). A.G. Schneiderman Issues Best Practices For Breast Cancer "Pink Ribbon" Campaigns | New York State Attorney General. [online] Available at: https://ag.ny.gov/press-release/ag-schneiderman-issues-best-practices-breast-cancer-%E2%80%9Cpink-ribbon%E2%80%9D-campaigns [Accessed March 9, 2019].

147 Greenhouse, S. (2018). Nike Identifies Plants Abroad Making Goods For Universities. [online] nytimes.com. Available at: www.nytimes.com/1999/10/08/business/nike-identifies-plants-abroad-making-goods-for-universities.html [Accessed May 11, 2018].

148 Wells, G. (2018). Google Details Pay Methodology to Show It Has No Gender Gap. [online] Wall Street Journal. Available at: www.wsj.com/articles/google-details-pay-methodology-to-show-it-has-no-gender-gap-1491933510 [Accessed May 11, 2018].

149 Fiegerman, S. (2018). New Tesla Model 3 orders unlikely to ship before end of 2018. [online] CNNMoney. Available at: http://money.cnn.com/2017/06/06/technology/business/tesla-model-3-backlog/index.html [Accessed May 11, 2018].

150 Leaper, C. (2018). Donald Trump's directive that female staff should "dress like women" causes another social media backlash. [online] Daily Telegraph. Available at: http://www.telegraph.co.uk/fashion/people/donald-trumps-directive-female-staff-should-dress-like-women/ [Accessed May 11, 2018].

151 ey.com (2018). Shopping with a purpose: The new retail revolution. [online] Available at: www.ey.com/gl/en/issues/ey-beacon-institute-shopping-with-a-purpose [Accessed May 11, 2018].

152 Musk, E. (2018). All Our Patent Are Belong To You. [online] tesla.com. Available at: www.tesla.com/blog/all-our-patent-are-belong-you [Accessed May 11, 2018].

153 American Chemical Society (2018). Alexander Fleming Discovery and Development of Penicillin. [online] Available at: www.acs.org/content/acs/en/education/whatischemistry/landmarks/flemingpenicillin.html#increasing-penicillin-yield [Accessed May 11, 2018].

154 Gelles, D. (2018). Inside the Revolution at Etsy. [online] nytimes.com. Available at: www.nytimes.com/2017/11/25/business/etsy-josh-silverman.html [Accessed May 11, 2018].

155 Mitchell, N. (2018). Etsy made mistakes, but its commitment to social responsibility wasn't

one of them. [online] Quartz at Work. Available at: https://work.qz.com/1146365/etsy-made-mistakes-from-which-other-b-corps-can-learn/ [Accessed May 11, 2018].

156 Hays, C. (2000). Ben & Jerry's To Unilever, With Attitude. [online] The New York Times. Available at: www.nytimes.com/2000/04/13/business/ben-jerry-s-to-unilever-with-attitude.html [Accessed December 10, 2018].

157 Jones, G. (2005). Renewing Unilever (Oxford: Oxford University Press).

158 unilever.com (2018). Embedding Sustainability. [online] Available at: www.unilever.com/sustainable-living/our-strategy/embedding-sustainability/ [Accessed May 11, 2018].

159 Unilever. (2018). Unilever's Sustainable Living Plan continues to fuel growth. [online] Unilever global company website. Available at: https://www.unilever.com/news/Press-releases/2018/unilevers-sustainable-living-plan-continues-to-fuel-growth.html [Accessed March 9, 2019].

160 Bcorporation.net (2018). What are B Corps? [online] Available at: www.bcorporation.net/what-are-b-corps [Accessed May 11, 2018].

161 Business Chief (2015). Why do up to 90% of Mergers and Acquisitions Fail? [online] Available at: https://europe.businesschief.com/finance/390/Why-do-up-to-90-of-Mergers-and-Acquisitions-Fail [Accessed December 10, 2018].

162 Warren, T. (2018). Microsoft wasted at least $8 billion on its failed Nokia experiment. [online] The Verge. Available at: www.theverge.com/2016/5/25/11766540/microsoft-nokia-acquisition-costs [Accessed May 11, 2018].

163 Hempel, J. (2018). Now We Know Why Microsoft Bought LinkedIn. [online] WIRED. Available at: www.wired.com/2017/03/now-we-know-why-microsoft-bought-linkedin/ [Accessed May 11, 2018].

164 Sabbagh, D. (2018). Facebook to expand inquiry into Russian influence of Brexit. [online] Guardian. Available at: www.theguardian.com/technology/2018/jan/17/facebook-inquiry-russia-influence-brexit [Accessed May 11, 2018].

165 Thompson, N. and Vogelstein, F. (2018). Inside Facebook's Two Years of Hell. [online] WIRED. Available at: www.wired.com/story/inside-facebook-mark-zuckerberg-2-years-of-hell/ [Accessed May 11, 2018].

166 McCarthy, T. (2018). Facebook, Google and Twitter grilled by Congress over Russian meddling – as it happened. [online] Guardian. Available at: www.theguardian.com/technology/live/2017/oct/31/facebook-google-twitter-congress-russian-election-meddling-live [Accessed May 11, 2018].

167 Weller, C. (2018). Americans say Facebook is worse for society than Walmart or McDonald's. [online] Business Insider Australia. Available at: www.businessinsider.com.au/facebook-worse-for-society-than-walmart-or-mcdonalds-survey-2018-2 [Accessed May 11, 2018].

168 Haigh, P. (2018). What is the current situation with Uber in London? [online] metro.co.uk. Available at: http://metro.co.uk/2017/12/19/current-situation-uber-london-taxi-app-wont-stopped-time-soon-7171771/ [Accessed May 11, 2018].

169 Haigh, P. (2018). What is the current situation with Uber in London? [online] metro.co.uk. Available at: http://metro.co.uk/2017/12/19/current-situation-uber-london-taxi-app-wont-stopped-time-soon-7171771/ [Accessed May 11, 2018].

170 Rodenberg, R. (2018). Where is daily fantasy sports legal? A state-by-state look. [online] ESPN.com. Available at: www.espn.com/chalk/story/_/id/14799449/daily-fantasy-dfs-legal-your-state-state-state-look [Accessed May 11, 2018].

171 Airbnb blog. (2018). Belong Anywhere. [online] Available at: https://blog.atairbnb.com/belong-anywhere/ [Accessed May 11, 2018].

172 Dillon, L. (2018). California lawmakers can't figure out what to do with Airbnb. Here's why. [online] latimes.com. Available at: www.latimes.com/politics/la-pol-sac-airbnb-laws-california-legislature-20170203-story.html [Accessed May 11, 2018].

173 Ingram, M. (2018). The Regulators Are Finally Coming for Airbnb and Uber. [online] Fortune. Available at: http://fortune.com/2017/02/20/airbnb-uber-tech-regulations/ [Accessed May 11, 2018].

174 Levine, M. (2018). Airbnb's Public Fight to Stay Private Is Complicated. [online] bloomberg.com. Available at: www.bloomberg.com/view/articles/2018-02-09/airbnb-ipo-woes-brian-chesky-fights-to-stay-private [Accessed May 11, 2018].

175 Bort, J. (2018). Airbnb made $93 million in profit on $2.6 billion in revenue, but an internal clash sent the CFO out the door. [online] San Antonio Express-News. Available at: www.mysanantonio.com/technology/businessinsider/article/Airbnb-made-93-million-in-profit-on-2-6-billion-12556474.php [Accessed May 11, 2018].

176 Trieu K, Neal B, Hawkes C, Dunford E, Campbell N, Rodriguez-Fernandez R, et al. (2015) Salt Reduction Initiatives around the World – A Systematic Review of Progress towards the Global Target. PLoS ONE 10(7): e0130247. https://doi.org/10.1371/journal.pone.0130247

177 Sifferlin, A. (2018). 90% of Americans Eat Too Much Salt. [online] TIME.com. Available at: http://time.com/3944545/sodium-heart/ [Accessed May 11, 2018].

178 Collins, M., Mason, H., O'Flaherty, M., Guzman-Castillo, M., Critchley, J. and Capewell, S. (2014). An Economic Evaluation of Salt Reduction Policies to Reduce Coronary Heart Disease in England: A Policy Modeling Study. Value in Health, 17(5), pp.517–524.

179 nhs.uk (2018). High-salt diet linked to 1.6 million heart deaths. [online] Available at: www.nhs.uk/news/food-and-diet/high-salt-diet-linked-to-16-million-heart-deaths/ [Accessed May 11, 2018].

180 Head, B. (2018). Lower Sodium Deli Products-Meats-Cheeses. [online] Boar's Head. Available at: https://boarshead.com/nutrition-wellness/information/lower-sodium [Accessed May 11, 2018].

181 Layne, N. (2018). After bankruptcy and makeover, Japan Airlines returns. [online] Reuters. Available at: www.reuters.com/article/us-japanairlines-ipo/after-bankruptcy-and-makeover-japan-airlines-returns-idUSBRE88H1AP20120918 [Accessed May 11, 2018].

182 Layne, N. (2018). After bankruptcy and makeover, Japan Airlines returns. [online] Reuters. Available at: www.reuters.com/article/us-japanairlines-ipo/after-bankruptcy-and-makeover-japan-airlines-returns-idUSBRE88H1AP20120918 [Accessed May 11, 2018].

183 Layne, N. (2018). After bankruptcy and makeover, Japan Airlines returns. [online] Reuters. Available at: www.reuters.com/article/us-japanairlines-ipo/after-bankruptcy-and-makeover-japan-airlines-returns-idUSBRE88H1AP20120918 [Accessed May 11, 2018].

184 Reuters (2018). UPDATE 1-JAL lifts annual profit outlook on improved economy, lower . . . [online] Available at: www.reuters.com/article/japan-airlines-results/update-1-jal-lifts-annual-profit-outlook-on-improved-economy-lower-fuel-costs-idUSL4N1N62UY [Accessed May 11, 2018].

185 Schofield, A. (2018). Japan Airlines Considers Fleet-Plan Options. [online] aviationweek.com. Available at: http://aviationweek.com/commercial-aviation/japan-airlines-considers-fleet-plan-options [Accessed May 11, 2018].

186 www.nytimes.com/2018/04/28/business/nike-women.html [Accessed December 20, 2018].

187 Fletcher, N. (2018). BT loses almost £8bn in value as Italy accounting scandal deepens. [online] Guardian. Available at: www.theguardian.com/business/2017/jan/24/bt-loses-7bn-in-value-as-italian-accounting-scandal-deepens [Accessed May 11, 2018].

188 Fortune (2018). The greatest business decisions of all time. [online] Available at: http://fortune.com/2012/10/01/the-greatest-business-decisions-of-all-time/ [Accessed May 11, 2018].

189 www.bloomberg.com/news/articles/2018-12-21/j-j-s-tainted-talc-risk-expands-as-cancer-trials-triple-in-2019 [Accessed December 22, 2018].

190 Kottasova, I. (2018). United loses $250 million of its market value. [online] CNNMoney. Available

at: http://money.cnn.com/2017/04/11/
investing/united-airlines-stock-passenger-flight-
video/index.html [Accessed May 11, 2018].

191 J.D. Power (2018). 2016 North America Airline
Satisfaction Study. [online] Available at: www.
jdpower.com/press-releases/2016-north-america-
airline-satisfaction-study [Accessed May 11, 2018].

192 YouTube (2018). Aviva CEO Mark Wilson speaks
to Bloomberg's Leaders with Lacqua. [online]
Available at: www.youtube.com/watch?v=4INl-
kHtRj4 [Accessed May 11, 2018].

193 Jones, S. (2018). Wilson Disrupting U.K.
Insurance With Turnaround at Aviva. [online]
bloomberg.com. Available at: www.bloomberg.
com/news/articles/2015-01-09/wilson-
disrupting-u-k-insurance-with-turnaround-at-
aviva [Accessed May 11, 2018].

194 Jones, S. (2018). Aviva Turnaround Ahead
of Schedule as New Business Climbs.
[online] bloomberg.com. Available at: www.
bloomberg.com/news/articles/2015-05-07/
aviva-turnaround-ahead-of-schedule-as-new-
business-climbs-14- [Accessed May 11, 2018].

195 Harvard Business Review Analytic Services
Report, The Business Case for Purpose, 2015.
www.ey.com/Publication/vwLUAssets/
ey-the-business-case-for-purpose/$FILE/ey-
the-business-case-for-purpose.pdf [Accessed
December 10, 2018].

196 LinkedIn (2016.) Purpose at Work. [online]
Available at: https://cdn.imperative.com/
media/public/Global_Purpose_Index_2016.pdf
[Accessed December 10, 2018].

197 Walt, V. (2018). World Future Energy Summit.
[online] TIME.com. Available at: http://
content.time.com/time/specials/packages/
article/0,28804,1954176_1954175_1954172,00.
html [Accessed May 11, 2018].

198 Harvard Business Review Analytic Services
Report, The Business Case for Purpose, 2015.
www.ey.com/Publication/vwLUAssets/
ey-the-business-case-for-purpose/$FILE/ey-
the-business-case-for-purpose.pdf [Accessed
December 10, 2018].

199 glassdoor.com (2018). Working at Vivint Smart
Home. [online] Available at: www.glassdoor.
com/Overview/Working-at-Vivint-Smart-Home-
EI_IE403923.11,28.htm [Accessed May 11, 2018].

200 Spiegel, D. (2018). The most obvious reason
to doubt Uber's $66 billion valuation.
[online] CNBC. Available at: www.cnbc.
com/2016/06/08/ubers-66-billion-valuation-
may-ride-on-shaky-foundation.html [Accessed
May 11, 2018].

201 Pham, S. (2018). SoftBank deal would cut Uber
valuation by at least 20%. [online] CNNMoney.
Available at: http://money.cnn.com/2017/11/29/
technology/softbank-uber-investment-valuation-
discount/index.html [Accessed May 11, 2018].

202 Nink, M. and Robison, J. (2018). The Damage
Inflicted by Poor Managers. [online] gallup.
com. Available at: www.gallup.com/
businessjournal/200108/damage-inflicted-
poor-managers.aspx?g_source=EMPLOYEE_
ENGAGEMENT&g_medium=topic&g_
campaign=tiles [Accessed May 11, 2018].

203 Zak, P. (2018). The Neuroscience of Trust.
[online] Harvard Business Review. Available at:
https://hbr.org/2017/01/the-neuroscience-of-
trust [Accessed May 11, 2018].

204 Labich, K. and Carvell, T. (2018). Nike Vs.
Reebok A Battle For Hearts, Minds & Feet Agassi
And Sampras? Intense. Shaq And Jordan?
Spectacular. But For Murderous Rivalry, Few
Contests In Sports Can Match The War Of The
Sneaker Giants (September 18, 1995). [online]
archive.fortune.com. Available at: http://
archive.fortune.com/magazines/fortune/
fortune_archive/1995/09/18/206103/index.htm
[Accessed May 11, 2018].

205 Mullins, J. (2013). The new business road test
(Harlow, England: Pearson).

206 Malcolm, H. (2018). How Nike plans to turn
women's fitness into an $11 billion empire.
[online] USA Today. Available at: www.usatoday.
com/story/money/2015/11/08/nikes-11-
billion-dollar-plan-to-create-a-womens-fitness-
empire/74740318/ [Accessed May 11, 2018].

207 American College of Sports Medicine, International Council of Sport Science and Physical Education, and NIKE, Inc. (2012) Designed to Move: A Physical Activity Action Agenda. NIKE, Inc.

208 oceantomo.com (2018). 2011 Intangible Asset Market Value. [online] Available at: www.oceantomo.com/2011-intangible-market-value/ [Accessed May 11, 2018].

209 enso.co (2018). 2017 World Value Index. [online] Available at: http://enso.co/worldvalue/ [Accessed May 11, 2018].

210 Solomon, B. (2018). Forbes Welcome. [online] forbes.com. Available at: www.forbes.com/sites/briansolomon/2017/02/02/uber-ceo-quits-trump-advisory-council-after-deleteuber/#4bf386e52a4b [Accessed May 11, 2018].

211 Cuthbertson, A. (2018). Elon Musk hopes Donald Trump can help make humanity a multi-planetary species. [online] Newsweek. Available at: www.newsweek.com/elon-musk-trump-adviser-tesla-immigration-552113 [Accessed May 11, 2018].

212 Harvard Business Review Analytic Services Report, The Business Case for Purpose, 2015. www.ey.com/Publication/vwLUAssets/ey-the-business-case-for-purpose/$FILE/ey-the-business-case-for-purpose.pdf [Accessed December 10, 2018].

213 World Economic Forum. (2014). New Champions in Technology Innovation. [online] Available at: www.millwardbrown.com/docs/default-source/insight-documents/articles-and-reports/Millward-Brown_2014-Davos-Summer-EN.pdf [Accessed December 10, 2018].